The new treason of the intellectuals

Can the University survive?

Thomas Docherty

Manchester University Press

Published by Manchester University Press
Altrincham Street, Manchester M1 7JA

www.manchesteruniversitypress.co.uk

British Library Cataloguing-in-Publication Data
A catalogue record for this book is available from the British Library

ISBN   978 1 5261 3274 1   hardback

First published 2018

The publisher has no responsibility for the persistence or accuracy of URLs for any external or third-party internet websites referred to in this book, and does not guarantee that any content on such websites is, or will remain, accurate or appropriate.

Typeset in 10.5 on 12.5 pt Bembo Std Regular by
Servis Filmsetting Ltd, Stockport, Cheshire
Printed in Great Britain by
CPI Group (UK) Ltd, Croydon, CR0 4YY

For my teachers and my students, and for the University

Contents

Introduction

On 25 June 1945, a man named Emile Bercher visited Antony Babel, the Rector of the University of Geneva. Bercher, who was the director of a major advertising agency, had an idea that he wanted to explore. It was this meeting that would lead to the inaugural conference of what would become the Rencontres Internationales de Genève, an annual gathering of intellectuals, writers, artists, politicians, and scientists, convened around an issue of major public significance. The first 'Encounter', organized by the University (whose Senate had warmly embraced the idea), took place in September 1946. With the end of the Second World War, the organizing committee, partly prompted by Bercher himself, decided that Europeans and others should be brought together for debate and discussion about what constitutes 'the European Spirit'.[1]

Among the extremely distinguished list of speakers were Julien Benda, who opened the conference on 2 September, and Karl Jaspers, who gave the final presentation on 13 September.[2] Both Benda and Jaspers had published, that same year, 1946, new editions of works that they had initially written in the 1920s. Benda revisited his 1927 text (*The Treason of the Intellectuals* (*La trahison des clercs*), adding in the

---

[1] For the history of how this meeting came about, see Bruno Ackermann, 'Les Rencontres Internationales de Genève, 1946', *Schweizerische Zeitschrift für Geschichte*, 39 (1989), available at: https://www.e-periodica.ch/cntmng?pid=szg-006:1989:39::87 (accessed 23 November 2017).

[2] All the lectures given at the conference are available at: http://palimpsestes.fr/textes_philo/jaspers/rencontres.pdf (accessed 23 November 2017).

1946 edition a substantial new opening chapter. Jaspers re-published his 1923 text *The Idea of the University* (*Die Idee der Universität*). In its 1946 edition, this book became a key mechanism in the necessary and essential rehabilitation of the German University after its disastrous Nazification during the previous decade.

Two texts, then, each of them addressing the intellectual and the institutions given over to the functions of thought, constitute the frame through which the inaugural *Rencontre* considered the proper relation of the intellect to the polity. Both Benda and Jaspers – like the other participants – were profoundly aware that this was an extremely serious issue, of genuine international significance. At the root of the debates is a simple but potentially devastating question: what is the proper relation of the intellectual to a polity? How do we regulate the competing forces, values, and political claims of consciousness with those of material history? This was a key question for the participants in Geneva in 1946; and it remains a fundamental issue in our own time. It is at the centre of this book.

‿

Benda took the opportunity to refer to his own celebrated work during his Geneva presentation. He rehearsed his argument of 1927, that a certain 'intellectual nationalism' had 'contaminated' the best thinkers of the time, corrupting the purity of their thinking and leading them into a betrayal of their calling to the 'clerisy'. The intellectual, for Benda, should be devoted to abstract thought, explicit in its disavowal of practicality. 'Passions' or practical commitments were the enemy of such pure thinking. He visited shame upon those who, as intellectuals, had become compliant servants of the very passions that they should be contesting. 'Shame on the treason of the intellectuals', he said, publicizing the new edition of his work.[3] Such passions usually involved a political commitment.

The most significant and dangerous passion, as Benda saw it in 1927, was that of nationalism; and he took the view that subsequent events – the war of 1939–45 – were ample empirical evidence of what

---

[3] See Julien Benda's paper from *Rencontres Internationales de Genève*, 2–13 September 1946, 15, 26 (translation mine), available at: http://palimpsestes.fr/textes_philo/jaspers/rencontres.pdf (accessed 23 November 2017).

goes wrong when the intellectual is perverted from the duty towards reason by becoming complicit with a nationalist mentality. When he came to extend his argument in 1946, he retained the view that the intellectual must remain committed primarily to abstract reason. However, the significant modification that he made concerned the relation of the intellectual to democracy, in a move that seemed to re-open the door to political commitment by the intellectual. In the wake of the disaster of Nazism, Benda argued that 'the only political system that the intellectual can adopt while remaining faithful to herself or himself is democracy'. The reason for this concession is that democracy is opposed to the imposition of any kind of stable and fixed order, for it is committed to individual freedom. 'With its sovereign values of individual liberty, justice and truth', he wrote, democracy '*is not practical*'.[4]

What this signals is not any kind of attack upon the 'impracticality' or despair at an implied naïve lack of realism in the desire for democracy, but instead a realization that democracy is a political system that cannot be programmed in advance, and therefore cannot be imposed as a politically constraining form of order upon a people. The great new enemy in the 1946 text is 'order' as such. When 'order' becomes a political ideal, the threat of war (as an ultimate form of disorder) will be held always before the people, the better to invoke fear, to acquire and retain their obedience. The demand for social order is inevitably linked, therefore, to precisely the same war mentality that governed nationalist thinking and its perversion of the intellectual from her or his task. Democracy, by contrast and by its very definition, cannot share in the demand for this kind of order. Worst of all is the moment when politics becomes itself governed by the demand for 'organization', for this will inevitably entail an ideology of 'efficiency' that will disfigure any and all individual liberties. The intellectual who commits, therefore, to any political form – with the sole exception of messy and disorganized democracy – betrays her or his calling.

Benda's specific proposals to the 1946 Geneva conference – where

---

[4] Julien Benda, *La trahison des clercs* (Grasset, Paris, 1975), 81. Translations throughout are mine; and I have translated 'clerc' as 'intellectual' here as elsewhere. Benda's use of 'clerc' connotes the clerisy, those who have a calling or vocation in religious terms. I have retained the idea of such a 'call'; but have preferred 'intellectual', a term that (when Benda wrote in 1927) was of relatively recent date.

Jaspers sat in his audience – included the demand that education should be reformed, and that there should be a unifying European language (which he thought should be French, given that 'everyone' acknowledged its intrinsic rationality).[5] With respect to education reform, specifically, he insisted that science should assume an absolute priority over literature, on the grounds that science is universal (because it is abstract and not conditioned by particularized interests) whereas literature is merely local (because it is conditioned by the specifics of its occasion, and expressed in a particular national language). Literature is therefore, for Benda, much more prone to the passions, and thus much more likely to drive the intellectual astray, to perversely contaminate intellectual duty. The essence of intellectual duty, he argued, is to 'confer sovereignty on the universal'.[6] Anything that deviates from this is a betrayal of the proper function of the intellectual.

This is an argument that, at least in some respects, is eminently recognizable in our time in at least two important particulars. First, it has become almost a conventional truism that the laboratory sciences are eminently more worthwhile than the literary arts. In the contemporary moment, however, the reasoning for this is entirely different from that which governed Benda's thinking. Science is valued not for its abstractions, but rather because of its utilitarian practicality. It will contribute, it is thought, to economic growth; and this has become the central legitimizing argument for government or public support for its activities. While we will claim to value so-called 'blue skies' research, this remains much less 'legitimate' than science that leads immediately and directly to instrumentally useful outcomes; and the key outcome is always economic growth and profit somewhere in the general economy. Literature and the arts, by contrast, are seen as merely ephemeral, concerned with the life of the mind and emotions, and of little practical use. This remains the case even when artists point to the massive – if ostensibly peripheral – contributions that they make to economic activities. In other words, it is the very practicality of science that we are encouraged to validate today, whereas, for Benda, science was shaped precisely by its refusal to accommodate itself to the 'practical' lest it be hijacked from its pure pursuit of rational results.

[5] Jaspers presented his lecture in German and received several ovations.
[6] Benda, *Rencontres Internationales de Genève*, 31.

Yet more fundamental, however, is the second trait that is recognizably extant in our time from Benda's lecture. The contemporary moment bears witness to a sense that the intellectual should acknowledge the limitations of her or his calling. In attending to 'the universal' and 'the abstract' our contemporary intellectual should not meddle in the affairs of the world, but should operate only within the confines of the academy itself. Thinking should be constrained and conditioned by its institutionalization in the University, as the key proper – but isolated – domain for thinking. It is as if the very activity of thinking should be sequestered away from practical everyday life. Although we do not acknowledge it in explicit terms, our contemporary culture prefers to leave the intellectual in the fabled 'ivory tower'.

Today, intellectuals – who are 'distinguished' from the everyday precisely by the qualities of their thinking – allegedly represent only the particular vested interests, values, and norms of an 'elite', those who do not share in the commons. Thus, any meddling by the intellectuals in our everyday politics is intrinsically a betrayal of the wishes or interests of 'ordinary' people. For many, the intrusion of the intellectual into the public sphere, especially the political public sphere, is dangerous and a threat to the everyday norms that govern our polities. Some politicians encourage that belief, preferring to keep any critical intellectual thinking carefully secreted away from the realm in which they prefer to retain the privileges of their own control. Given the fact that, almost by definition, the intellectual devotes herself or himself to the life of the mind, he or she should have no substantive say in the everyday practical conditions of non-intellectual life. Perhaps needless to say, this view is contested.

Edward Said offers a series of descriptions of the intellectual today that are relevant to these arguments. The intellectual, he argues, can be distinguished from the bureaucrat precisely because the intellectual is, in fact, personally committed to and engaged in everyday practical activity: intellectuals really believe in the arguments they make, and commit their very existential being to those beliefs. 'They cannot be mistaken for an anonymous functionary or careful bureaucrat' who has no actual personal commitment to their statements or actions. This makes intellectuals dangerous to those who will try to retain their own existing privileges by formalizing those privileges into a bland and abstract 'official' or bureaucratic inevitable norm.

The intellectual breaks with regulation (if not 'order' as in Benda) in this account. A particular characteristic of the intellectual is that he or she represents views that official culture – the polity – tends to elide, for whatever reasons. The intellectual has a specific talent: she or he 'is an individual endowed with a faculty for representing, embodying, articulating a message, a view, an attitude, philosophy or opinion to, as well as for a public'. The talent by definition must be made public. Intellectuals must engage the polity, in this respect. The effect, however, is never itself reassuringly ordered. On the contrary, the intellectual is someone 'whose place it is publically to raise embarrassing questions, to confront orthodoxy and dogma (rather than to produce them)'. Insofar as the intellectual refuses – as in Benda – to be co-opted for order, 'the whole point is to be embarrassing, contrary, even unpleasant'.[7]

Such a stance is one that is increasingly at odds with the governance and presiding ideologies that shape our contemporary University institutions. The more such institutions are converted into commercial enterprises, with consumers instead of students, the less acceptable is it for academic staff to be 'embarrassing, contrary, even unpleasant'. Such a stance will not play well in the demand that we 'provide' a pleasant and comfortable 'student experience', and will not play out well – at least *prima facie* – in the National Student Survey, which assesses essentially how 'agreeable' a degree programme is for its purchasers/students. This official survey 'gathers opinions from students about their experience of their courses', from which it proceeds, without any logical explanation, to derive claims regarding 'the quality of higher education in the UK'.[8] Doubtless the provision of luxury accommodation, say, makes it agreeable to return to one's room after a lecture; but it says nothing about what has gone on, intellectually, at any moment in the preparation of the student or teacher for that lecture, nor anything about the quality of education that occurs in relation to the lecture. The real question that the intellectual would ask here is about the relation between that luxury accommodation and, say, the increasing number of homeless people sleeping in the streets around the institu-

---

[7] Edward Said, *Representations of the Intellectual* (Vintage, London, 1994), 10.
[8] See the website of the National Student Survey at: www.thestudentsurvey.com/about.php (accessed 23 November 2017).

tion. The National Student Survey, in fact, is part of the marketization of the sector, determinedly committing institutions to the ideology of market-fundamentalist commerce and co-opting students to that end. As the managers of our institutions become increasingly focused on the 'delivery' of a 'product' that will yield consumer satisfaction, they also increasingly require that academic staff conform to the University's brand. By no stretch of the imagination can this be called an intellectual commitment to anything other than to an ideology of market fundamentalism. It is an evisceration of the intellectual, and one that *requires* the betrayal of the calling. The institution no longer welcomes the kind of intellectual who is 'embarrassing, contrary, even unpleasant', preferring instead the individual who will subsume the requirements of thinking to the demands of monetization. We have entered a new state in the betrayal of the intellectuals.

What does this mean in everyday practice in a University? Put simply, a degree programme now increasingly has to justify its existence not through the importance of the field or the intellectual values it embraces, but rather in terms of how much financial profit it will make. It must be 'popular' enough to bring in fees and research grants. As we have seen, for an obvious example, if a French literature department does not bring in whatever a finance director has determined as the 'appropriate' or satisfactory number of students and income, then we should simply close it down. This is not just crude; it is utterly simplistic, and based on utterly false presuppositions.

Why does an individual 'choose' to study French, say – or law, or medicine, or Chinese, or ancient archaeology, or physics, and so on? Individuals are not born with a predisposition to choose these fields. Instead, really existing material and historical circumstances predetermine and circumscribe the choices we make. People 'make their own history', Marx rightly argued, urging us non-controversially (and without anything specifically 'Marxist') towards a responsibility for our actions; 'but', he goes on, 'they do not make it just as they please; they do not make it under circumstances chosen by themselves, but under given conditions directly encountered and inherited from the past'.[9] The degree programmes that we have exist because the

---

[9] Karl Marx, *The Eighteenth Brumaire of Louis Bonaparte* (Foreign Languages Press, Peking, 1978), 9.

polity in general has decided that these are worthwhile fields of study, thereby legitimizing them and rendering them available on our menu. It is when the general polity makes the decision to degrade French language and literature, say, that we diminish the attractiveness and popularity, and thus also the availability, of that particular field.

When senior management in a University 'manage' the institution's intellectual activity by falling back on ostensibly rational economic determinations like this, they are fundamentally avoiding their intellectual responsibilities towards history and towards their societies. The political culture in general – of which the University's managers constitute a 'leading' element – is largely responsible for predetermining, circumscribing, and even limiting the kinds of degree programmes that are deemed to be valid, valuable, and worth including in a University's activities. It is simplistic to the point of falsification to claim that there is a 'free market' in disciplines, where completely autonomous and atomized discrete individuals make 'rational free choices'. When it is put like this, it becomes clear that this entire approach is based in the logic and ideology of 'rational choice market fundamentalism'. Whatever one's view of this political ideology, it cannot be denied that it is a fundamentalist ideology. To adopt it – or to hide behind it, as our institutions increasingly do – is a further betrayal of the intellectual. The choice and value of intellectual pursuits is being determined by money. It is as if one becomes a lawyer or doctor, say, primarily in order to become rich, instead of pursuing justice or saving lives, or as if such wealth is what determines these vocations as worthwhile. What makes this awful is that this is precisely the reasoning that our contemporary political culture – and our institution – encourages our next generation of students to take towards their studies.

↜

I noted that the inaugural Geneva *Rencontre* was the idea of Emile Bercher.

If an Emile Bercher today were to approach a University with an idea for an annual extremely prestigious and high-profile international conference, we can rest assured that – completely unlike Geneva in 1946 – the resulting event would be one that was covered in advertising and in boastful sponsorship. We can be equally sure that our contemporary institution would see the event as a business opportunity, or as something that would add to the prestige of the University's brand, thus attracting more 'custom'. The intellectual content of the event would have a much lower priority than in the 1946 Geneva case.

Certainly, Bercher in 1946, himself an advertising executive, saw the commercial possibilities that the *Rencontres* would provide. He had seen how Lucerne had benefited enormously by hosting an annual 'International Music Week', which attracted the world's best orchestras and conductors, with the attendant commercial stimulus that that gave to the city.[10] At the same time, he was also taken explicitly by the fact that the event in Lucerne contributed to the general everyday life of the city, quite beyond any particular commercial interest. As Bruno Ackermann explains, Bercher's initiative had a double aim: 'to re-stimulate in Geneva a cultural and artistic life of the highest order, and to spread the renown of the city and its University far and wide'.[11]

In our time, 'renown' is measured in financial terms. This, in fact, is one of the key ways in which we can understand our new treason of the intellectuals. There is less a perversion of the intellect by nation (though, as we will see, that certainly exists), and more a perversion of thought through its institutional financialization. To put this in crude and raw terms, thought counts for little in our institutions unless and until it is monetized. As Nigel Thrift, former Vice Chancellor (VC) of Warwick, puts it, 'Whether people like it or not, Universities are now economies, and to try and make out that they are something else I think just will not work.' He goes on to argue that 'simply because of their size and the turnover they become economic entities in their own right'. Thrift then asserts what he calls the inevitable logical corollary: 'Governments look for growth and Universities become framed as major export industries, susceptible to government and corporate influence'.[12] Benda would feel thoroughly vindicated; Said would be appalled. It is one thing to be 'susceptible' to influence; it is a betrayal to comply, and to insist that this is simply a matter of real fact ('whether people like it or not'), beyond dispute.

---

[10] A useful chronology is provided on the website of the Lucerne Festival: https://www.lucernefestival.ch/fr/le-festival/historique (accessed 23 November 2017).

[11] Ackermann, 'Les Rencontres Internationales', 65 (translation mine).

[12] See Nigel Thrift's lecture 'The University of Life', available at: https://www2.warwick.ac.uk/newsandevents/events/distinguishedlecture/nigelthrift/ (accessed 23 November 2017). The passage cited comes at 11'30".

Such an attitude was far removed from the consciousness of Jaspers when he spoke in Geneva. Jaspers, too, had a book to publicize, although – unlike Benda – he made no reference to the new edition of *The Idea of the University* at all in his presentation. Jaspers listened attentively to Benda, and in his response to the presentation he pointed out that you cannot found an idea, identity, or spirit of Europe on the rationality of science (and thus on its absolute priority over literature, say), on the simple logical grounds that scientific reason is not specific to Europe. In fact, he argues, there is a danger in 'wanting to give oneself an idea of a Europe' that would see Europe as 'separate' and distinguished from the rest of the world. In short, he is indicating to Benda that, in the critique of a nationalistic passion that perverts the intellectual from her or his task, Benda is simply substituting 'Europe' for the individual nation state. Such an attitude is apparent – although Jaspers is diplomatically politic enough not to draw explicit attention to it – in Benda's ostensibly 'reasonable' suggestion that the language of Europe should be French. As he put it in a letter to his former student Hannah Arendt, a few days after the conference, 'some of the speakers [he clearly had Benda in mind] developed something resembling a European nationalism'.[13]

Notwithstanding what might have been an irritation at Benda's valorization of the French language as a supposedly obvious choice for a trans-European language, Jaspers argued that 'communication' is absolutely crucial to the intellectual in her or his activities. In 1946 Geneva, Jaspers himself was – as also in his re-issued *Idea of the University* – 'communicating' to the world for the first time since 1938, when the Nazi authorities in Germany had banned him from publishing his work or thoughts. The political background is important here. In January 1937, the Nazis passed the 'German Civil Servants' Law', requiring 'that not only civil servants but also their spouses were required to be "citizens" (Reichsbürgers [sic]), as opposed to "subjects" (Staatsbürger)'.[14] Gertrud Jaspers was Jewish, and was thus barred from being a 'citizen'. The Rector of Heidelberg University, Ernst Krieck, obeyed the law

---

[13] Karl Jaspers, letter of 18 September 1946, in *Hannah Arendt – Karl Jaspers Correspondence 1926–1969*, ed. Lotte Kohler and Hans Saner, trans. Robert and Rita Kimber (Harcourt Brace, New York, 1992), 57.

[14] Steven P. Remy, *The Heidelberg Myth: The Nazification and Denazification of a German University* (Harvard University Press, Cambridge, MA, 2002), 80.

of the land and, accordingly, fired Jaspers. Because his fame made such an act controversial, the dismissal was subsequently changed formally to 'retirement', conveniently enough 'on health grounds' (Jaspers did indeed have life-long health problems).

A year later, the Nazis effectively isolated Jaspers completely with the publication ban. He was thus deprived of communication with his peers, and he found himself excluded from official intellectual activity – especially, of course, from the life of the University. The couple managed to survive the war years, though Gertrud only narrowly escaped with her life, for she was scheduled to be deported from Heidelberg in April 1945. She was saved by the arrival of the US army in Heidelberg right at the start of that month.

When the Americans arrived in Heidelberg, they compiled a 'White List' comprising individuals 'whose character, professional standing, experience and political reliability' made them suited to leadership positions, especially in higher education.[15] Jaspers was on this list; and it was under the aegis of the dismantling of Nazi ideology that he re-published his *Idea of the University*. Now, in 1946, that idea was one that had to clarify that the Nazi politicization of the institution was utterly incompatible with intellectual activity, that it had been a fundamental betrayal of the intellectuals.

For Jaspers, as for Benda, a specific explicit politicization of the institutions of the intellectual raises serious issues. Jaspers had the example of Heidegger, whose Rectorship in Freiburg showed his complicity with those who engendered a betrayal of some fundamentals of academic and of University life. Heidegger stated in his Rector's Address in 1933 that 'the much-lauded "academic freedom" will be expelled from the German university'.[16] Jaspers felt the effect of this fully.

However, it did not follow, for Jaspers, that the intellectual – and by extension the University – should divorce itself entirely from the

---

[15] 27 October 1944, Appendix A to Directive No. 8 in *Dokumente der Deutschlandpolitik 3 September 1939 bis 8 Mai 1945*, ed. Herbert Elzer (R. Oldenbourg Verlag, Munich, 2003), 883. See also Henric L. Wuermeling, *The White List and Zero Hour in Germany 1945* (Herbig, Munich, 2015).

[16] Martin Heidegger, 'The self-assertion of the German university', 1933 (German title 'Die Selbstbehauptung der deutschen Universität'), available at: http://la.utexas.edu/users/hcleaver/330T/350kPEEHeideggerSelf-Assertion.pdf (accessed 23 November 2017).

practical in the kind of extremist position of Benda. He made it clear, in
Geneva as in his re-issued book – that the intellect was fully immersed
in the world of practice. Indeed, in that same letter to Arendt of 18
September 1946, he noted that in Geneva 'all the reasonable people
had the world in mind'. This engagement with the world formed the
cornerstone of a philosophy in which Jaspers noted that there is no
intrinsic logic that dictates that reason will serve only that which is
good. Reason can equally be deployed in the service of evil and bad
ends. Something else is needed if the intellectual, engaged in the world,
is to find a role that will essentially lead to her or his legislating for the
good.

In a straightforward way, that is the question governing this entire
book. The fundamental gambit is that, in principle, participants in a
polity are involved in the search for the good society. Views as to what
constitutes the goodness of such a society will differ; and so we have
it as axiomatic that we must explore different hypotheses regarding
the good society. This will, of necessity, involve us in the kind of
communication that was so important for Jaspers. In our institutions,
this entails the full development and extension as far as is possible of
academic freedom. The point of academic freedom, however, is that
it cannot remain 'merely' academic: if the intellectual is in and of
the world, academic freedom must be the cornerstone of all human
freedoms. By this, I do not mean to privilege the thinking that goes on
in Universities, but rather simply to render to thinking – wherever it
is carried out – its due.

Freedom of thought is thus yet more fundamental than freedom of
speech.[17] If we are to pursue whatever it is that we can agree to call
'the good', then thought must be completely unconstrained to make
possible that search or research. Further, if we are to 'agree' to identify
some state of affairs as the good, then two things follow, again axiomatically. First, this 'agreement' requires that communication among
participants be central to a good society: agreement can be founded
only on the possibility and even the desirable necessity of disagreement.
Secondly, 'the good' cannot be fixed or eternal and unchanging: if
it is subject to agreement through discussion, then such agreements

---

[17] For a detailed argument relevant to this, see Timothy Garton Ash, *Free Speech*
(Atlantic Books, London, 2016), 283ff.

must be forever provisional, and open to change and new discussion from both new and existing participants. 'The good' in this sense is historical: it is not always and everywhere the same. To subscribe to an idea of the good (or 'the true') as being identifiable and definitive is to be a fundamentalist of some kind; and fundamentalism means the end of discussion and of communication. The claim of any one party to an absolute truth is a claim that defies any possibility of further dialogue, much less egalitarian dialogue. It bans argument and demands obedience, servitude, and compliance. In this respect, it is inimical to freedom in every fundamental, academic and otherwise.

A University and its intellectuals should welcome this state of affairs, for it ensures that the University is utterly enmeshed in the public sphere while, at the same time, indicating that that sphere resists hierarchization of its compositional elements. People will be free if and only if they are equally free. As Jaspers then puts it, 'Given that a person is free if and only if other individuals are also equally free, it follows that we should reject any freedom that isolates the individual and avoids the need for communication'. He adds that 'real freedom believes only in holding life in common, as when a man evolves along with the surrounding world'.[18]

It follows from this that any thinking that determinedly hierarchizes the social world, that denies the search for freedoms, that avoids the principles of egalitarian communication while preferring 'instruction', constitutes a betrayal of (and sometimes by) the intellectual. This suggests that, among the most basic of the requirements for honouring the human capacity for thinking itself is a democratic impulse. The intellectual, thus, has a responsibility towards government, but does not have the right to govern others. There can be no 'philosopher-king' because, in a genuine democratic polity, there is no king.

Are the hypotheses advanced here 'true'? This is another major concern for the intellectual, especially in an age in which formulations such as the 'post-truth' or 'post-fact' world have gained currency. The problem here is that truth, like freedom and like 'the good', is subject to history. I do not mean to suggest that truth is relativistic in any sense; rather, what constitutes 'the true' depends to a great extent on

---

[18] Karl Jaspers's paper from *Rencontres Internationales de Genève*, 2–13 September 1946, 376, 377 (translation mine), available at: http://palimpsestes.fr/textes_philo/jaspers/rencontres.pdf (accessed 23 November 2017).

the condition of our knowledge, and that condition is one that must always be changing. It must always be changing because of the primacy of communication, which determines that the truth can never be finalized. Truth is inimical to such fundamentalism; and, indeed, any fundamentalism must be based on the irrationality of unfounded faith. It has nothing to do with the thinking individual. When someone tells us that 'there is no alternative', that 'this is the reality of the world', we should realize that this individual is trying to arrest the possibility of thinking. They are betraying the intellectual and, in doing so, are also trying to arrest history. Given that our current historical condition is one of massive world inequalities, they are simply protecting their own interested privileges and trying to silence any criticism of them.

～

Democracies and silence do not sit easily together, and are in fact deeply antithetical to each other. Benda called on Montesquieu to support this claim. According to Montesquieu's 1734 text *Considérations sur les causes de la grandeur des Romains et de leur décadence*, when you cannot hear the noise of dispute in a polity, then you can be sure that liberty is absent from that State. Governments that are concerned for the extension of freedoms are noisy, 'always agitated', and such a government 'could not sustain itself unless it is capable of being corrected under its own laws'.[19]

Benda alludes approvingly to this in his 1946 edition of *The Treason of the Intellectuals*, where he is at pains to stress that his interests are in democracy and justice. After the historical disasters of the years between 1927 and 1946, he now clearly sees that nationalism was but a symptom of a deeper betrayal of the intellectual: the betrayal of justice and the disavowal of democracy. Part of the impetus behind Benda's thought, even in 1927, derived from his attitude to the Dreyfus Affair, that utter travesty of justice whose motivation lay in a combination

---

[19] See Benda, *La trahison des clercs*, 42. Benda misquotes Montesquieu. The original text says that 'as a general rule, any time you see everyone tranquil in a state that calls itself a republic, you can rest assured that there is no liberty there'. Benda has, instead, what looks like a made-up misremembered phrase, 'When in a State you don't perceive the sound of any conflict you can be sure that there is no liberty there.' See Montesquieu, *Considérations sur les causes de la grandeur des Romains et de leur décadence*, new edn (Copenhagen, 1761), 79, 84 (translation mine).

of prejudicial racism (in its established form as anti-Semitism) and the desire to protect the privileges of specific officers as well as the privileges of 'office' itself. The protecting of official privilege, or 'rule by the offices', is, as Arendt points out, the proper and literal definition of bureaucracy. It is also, as Arendt describes it, a dreadful mode of governance. In her account, bureaucracy is 'unhappily the rule of nobody and for this very reason perhaps the least human and most cruel form of rulership'.[20] It was precisely this form of cruelty from which Jaspers, her teacher, suffered under the prejudices of Nazism.

Running through all of the story thus far is a fundamental aspect of the betrayal of the intellectual: prejudice, pre-judging. Prejudice – with its attendant conformity – is at the root of all conventional behaviour. It is anathema to the intellectual. Said advances the character of Bazarov, from Turgenev's *Fathers and Sons*, as a model of the intellectual, a character seemingly constitutionally unable to conform to the norms of his society. Bazarov is a figure characterized by 'the sheer unremitting force of his questioning and deeply confrontational intellect'.[21] He is unconventional – in the strict sense that he refuses to be bound by convention, by what makes an existing community cohere. The values and norms that make his society are insistently called into question; and it is this that Said sees as the first kind of intellectual.

The intellectual, then, can be 'unpleasant', in Said's terms. However, is it any more 'pleasant' to live and think in conformity with a social order that is racist, prejudicial, shaped by the demand that thinking and thinkers should be sequestered away from everyday living? The topic of this book is certainly discomforting, even discomfiting. The questions that I raise, however, are fundamental, and they call for an active response.

In his letter to Arendt after the Geneva conference, Jaspers argued that philosophy – and, by extension, thinking itself – 'has to be concrete

---

[20] Hannah Arendt, *Responsibility and Judgment*, ed. Jerome Kohn (Schocken Books, New York, 2003), 31; and cf. Arendt, *The Human Condition*, 2nd edn, introduced by Margaret Canovan (University of Chicago Press, Chicago, 1998), 40, where Arendt relates it directly to tyranny. See also her extended and detailed observations regarding the relation between bureaucracy and totalitarian government in *The Origins of Totalitarianism* (1951; Penguin, London, 2017), 319–40.

[21] Said, *Representations of the Intellectual*, 12.

and practical'. Even though he claimed that his 'intellectual possibilities are so limited', he stated definitively that 'it's always better to do what you can than to do nothing at all'.[22] By way of a sustained and detailed response to what had gone on in Geneva, Arendt dedicated her *Sechs Essays*, published in Germany in 1948, to Jaspers. In her dedicatory note, she paid tribute to her teacher, and revealed a good deal of what had come out of their conversations together.

The first key observation that she makes indicates the worldliness of her philosophy. As an intellectual, she is immersed in the world and history. 'None of the following essays was … written without awareness of the facts of our time.' She has also learned to be resistant to accepting the seeming inevitability of contemporary conditions: 'I have not accepted the world created by those facts as necessary and indestructible.' For Arendt, thinking has a responsibility to realize that the world, and our polity within it, need not be as it currently is. The way that she puts this is extremely telling, in this present context. She has learned explicitly from Jaspers, she says, 'to find my way around in reality without selling my soul to it'. That is to say, notwithstanding the discomfort that comes from being an intellectual, it is indeed possible to sustain the dignity and value of intellectual activity without falling into supine complicity with contemporary norms. The Faustian metaphor hints, at least surreptitiously and perhaps even without Arendt herself noting it, at the fact that compliance with those norms is too often embraced for financial profit, or the commercialization of intellect itself. Finally, she notes that, given these first principles, 'one has to live and think in the open and not in one's own little shell, no matter how comfortably furnished it is'.[23]

The real point of intellectual work is to contest necessity, but to do so in a manner that acknowledges failure, and acknowledges equally that the work is never finalized. We face the demand, as Jaspers had it, to 'try again' in the face of what he called his intellectual inadequacy. Beckett would extend this, famously, in *Worstward Ho*, whose narrator tells himself to 'Try again. Fail again. Better again. Or better worse. Fail

---

[22] Jaspers, letter to Hannah Arendt, 18 September 1946, in *Hannah Arendt – Karl Jaspers Correspondence*, 58.
[23] Hannah Arendt, 'Dedication to Karl Jaspers', repr. in Arendt, *Essays in Understanding 1930–1954*, ed. Jerome Kohn (Schocken Books, New York, 1994), 213.

worse again.'[24] There must be a certain humility if the intellectual is to respect the dignity of thought, for the individual intellectual is not and never can be the only thinker in any given situation. Perhaps the greatest lesson that Arendt learns from Jaspers – and this will be key to all that follows in this book – is 'the realization of the fact that all human beings are rational but that no human being's rationality is infallible'.[25]

These observations yield us a good place from which to explore the conditions that have led to the new treason of the intellectuals in our time; and also, through the exploration of that betrayal and its consequence in crisis, how we can recover from such betrayals and bear witness to the survival not just of the intellectual but also of her or his worldly social and political environment.

[24] Samuel Beckett, *Worstward Ho* (John Calder, London, 1983), 8.
[25] Arendt, *Essays in Understanding*, 213–14.

Part I
Betrayal

1

Private study

It is by now something of a cliché to suggest that the UK's University system is excellent, outstanding, and even world-leading. Virtually every University-related marketing site will tell you so. It is also something of a cliché to argue that the UK University in our time is in a crisis, and that government must do something to get the sector to catch up with other, world-leading sectors in different jurisdictions. Thinking these two contrary things at once is confusing. When both propositions are proposed as true, it is probably safe to say that either we are in the realms of ideological mystification or, less grandly, we are listening to the mind-numbing power of cliché. We can begin here by offering a way of trying to think behind these clichés, to seek a clearer sense of the actual condition of the University in our time.

The University is an institution that has been systematically betrayed, both in the UK and elsewhere, over the last forty years or so. It has been betrayed primarily by governments and by the political class; but these have been amply and enthusiastically supported in that betrayal by a rising managerial class that has assumed leadership and control of the institution. This managerial class – in the University as in other institutions – is committed to a discourse designed as a celebration of 'world-leading excellence'. That language is also governed by the idea of continuous improvement: we were not always excellent, and became so only through careful direction at the hands of a managerial class whose primary function is the identification, description, and evaluative measurement of 'the excellent'. We have 'changed' to become excellent; and we will continue to change in order to maintain that excellence. The institutionalization of 'management', further, thereby embeds the function of 'change-management' at the centre of our practice.

Yet here lies our fundamental self-contradiction: if we are already intrinsically world-leading, why must we change? The resolution proposed to this conundrum is that we are excellent precisely because of change and because of the very principle of change-management; and it is this that sustains the myth of continuous improvement, governed by a demand that we can never be 'complacent'. The logic of this programme now starts to become clear: we are excellent and world-leading not because of what we do as academic staff and students, but thanks to the supervisory diligence of our management. If the academy wants to sustain its position and to survive in a harsh competitive global climate (to borrow further contemporary clichés), then it must learn to work in the service of management.

The managerial class is also responsible, therefore, for the endless management-led and administration-led 'reforms' and structural reorganizations of the University. Indeed, these are what constitute the very business of management, its basic *raison d'être*. Such reforms have led the sector – and above all its academic staff and students – into a contemporary crisis of confidence, in which the academy is no longer either certain of its purposes or secure in its standing. The combination of this insecurity with the demands of a rather spurious 'competition' in the educational 'marketplace' produces the hyperbolical discourse of global excellence.

On one hand, therefore, the University – and especially its senior management – has a determined stake in validating the institution as being not just in fine fettle, but also in a perpetually improving condition of excellence, if not perfection. At the same time, the managerial leadership of the University has a vested interest in generating a sense of continuous crisis in order to fulfil what management and leadership see in our day as their own role. That role is one in which senior management justifies its own existence and standing by very visibly 'doing its job', primarily by instigating change, labelled as 'reform'; and the argument is that such reform is needed in order to generate that excellence in the first place. In short, there is a clear trajectory here, in which the ostensibly standard idea of an administration serving the academy (or staff and students) is reversed, such that, increasingly, the academy is there to serve the needs and demands of the managerial class. Further still, the academy's own identity is increasingly merged with the identity of the culture (and cult) of management itself.[1]

The danger of such a logic is that this becomes a somewhat desperate spiral of destruction: if the University is in crisis, then – the convenient and ready-to-hand cliché says – it needs 'reform'; but the reform is what has caused the crisis in the first place. The implementation of this reform generates further crises of confidence, leading to yet further and deeper reform; and so on and on until eventually nothing recognizable as a University will be left. The reformers, at this point, can claim that they have 'modernized' the institution, and have brought it into conformity with the demands of our new times, with its banal clichés about 'a fast-changing environment' full of 'challenges' that must be miraculously translated as 'opportunities'.

The truth, however, is markedly different; and that truth is occluded by the refusal of the speakers of cliché to engage properly and fundamentally with the key issues of what a University is, or even to subject the language in which the endless clichés are expressed to proper scrutiny. In short: they do not know what they are saying. Neither our contemporary politicians nor our sector managers know what they are talking about when they talk of the institution of the University; and that explains why they turn insistently to the substantially mindless 'proverbial wisdom' of 'common sense' or, more often, simple cliché.

Some key questions increasingly demand answers in our time. What does a University do? Why do we have such an institution as a University at all? If we decide that we must have such an institution of 'higher' education, then how does it regulate or calibrate the demands of 'exceptional' and higher thinking or intellectual work with the more routine demands of 'ordinary' life? How does it deal 'justly' with differing and even contradictory claims among not only its own faculties, but also among the citizens who depend upon the University and its faculties for a 'higher' or better knowledge regarding the existing conditions of life? How does it help the people in a society – both

---

[1] On this, see Liz Morrish, 'Institutional discourse and the cult(ure) of managerialism', *Discover Society*, 6 May 2014, available at: http://discoversociety.org/2014/05/06/institutional-discourse-and-the-culture-of-managerialism/ (accessed 23 November 2017).

'exceptional' and 'ordinary' – to judge things adequately or properly, such that they might live better lives; and thus how might it serve to understand the values that govern social norms? How genuinely open to new ideas and to new constituencies is it? Does it aid or contest democracy, or is it intrinsically given over to elitism and hierarchies of various kinds? Is it committed to extending the range of human possibilities and freedoms, or does it prefer to ensure that it serves the already existing commercial world and national economy?

These and other fundamental issues are never properly addressed, partly because they are complex. Perhaps more importantly, further, they are not properly addressed because answers to them might actually threaten to change the way things stand not just in our institutions of education but also in the society that subtends them. Those with an interest in maintaining things as they are – that is to say, those who have been privileged or who have personally advanced under our existing social conditions and norms – thus have a vested interest in collapsing debate into cliché. This is visible in the UK government's 2016 White Paper *Success as a Knowledge Economy*. There, we find that we are 'excellent'; we promise 'success as a knowledge economy'; we 'rank among our most valuable national assets'; we are 'powerhouses of intellectual and social capital'; we 'drive competitiveness'; we 'nurture values'; we are 'life-changing'; and so on.[2] However, the more such clichés are extended, the more suspicious we become that all is not well and needs further 'reform'; and this is why those phrases can be used as the foreword to a governmental White Paper that advocates precisely such further reform, and that claims that substantial reform is urgently needed.

How can the institution survive in these circumstances, circumstances that determine its condition as being 'critical' such that it requires governmental intervention like this? The first thing to say, I believe, is that cliché is the single most fundamental and menacing enemy of the University; and that those who resort to cliché in their arguments – like the UK's Minister of State for Universities, Jo Johnson

2 The phrases here are lifted from the foreword to the UK government's 2016 White Paper *Success as a Knowledge Economy*, written by Jo Johnson, MP, Minister of State for Universities, Science, Research and Innovation, available at: https://www.gov.uk/government/uploads/system/uploads/attachment_data/file/523396/bis-16-265-success-as-a-knowledge-economy.pdf (accessed 23 November 2017).

in the foreword from which I quote him above – are endangering the survival of the institution and standing in its way as a fundamental obstacle to proper understanding of the purposes of a University.

In passing, although I have here singled out a politician, Jo Johnson, my observation is not directed at an individual. Indeed, cliché works only because many other people do not call the clichéd statement into question, and they thereby implicitly endorse its banality. Jo Johnson's words have currency and authority not just because of his established political position as a government minister, but also because no one in the sector's leadership seems capable of challenging what he says. Bullshit passes for thought because those in authority in our institutions allow it to pass – and, too often, repeat it.

Thus, when some thinkers do challenge cliché or simplistic intellectual banality and suggest that things might be different, we are often met dismissively with the claim that we are being too idealistic, or not realistic in our grasp of the current climate and its economic conditions. When cliché gains traction by not being challenged, it starts to stand as a statement of fact, adequate to empirical reality. The world-weary demand, made by the cliché-mongers, that we should 'be realistic' is itself yet another – but absolutely foundational – energy-sapping cliché. All it means is that we should accept reality as it currently is, and not as something that can be made, remade, reconstituted differently from our current conditions.

This demand for a very specific and identifiable 'realism' goes hand-in-glove in our time with the political demand that requires us to observe the absolute primacy of economic considerations in all circumstances. Translated, all that this does is to say that our society lacks the political will to make different decisions about what constitutes 'success' or 'knowledge' and its relation to an 'economy'. In short, it strives to arrest and circumscribe debate about the survival of the University and to keep it safely within the existing framework of a particular economic structure, dominant in our times, which is tacitly proposed as being not just of our times but rather as being a natural and unchangeable economic condition.

Cliché is a formidable rhetorical weapon. When deployed in any argument, it serves the very specific function of arresting – or at the very least suspending – the possibility of extending or simply continuing the argument. It operates in the same way as a proverb; and, like the proverb, it stakes a claim upon some allegedly eternal truth, 'a truth universally acknowledged'.[3] It is thus ideologically committed to dogma, and to a requirement for conformist orthodoxy regarding truth claims. Its function is to pretend that there must be consensual agreement on both sides of the debate around this one basic accepted truth, the truth as implicitly evinced in the cliché. Thereby, it seems to quell the immediacy of the conflict around which an argument is ranged. However, one does not need to be a Freudian to see that a repression of conflict simply defers the moment when the conflict returns, quite possibly in more direct modes of engagement and even in violence of one kind or another.

An illustrative literary example of how cliché produces quietism and resignation is found in Beckett's *Waiting for Godot*. On no fewer than eight occasions in the play, Didi or Gogo proposes to do something decisive, but the two immediately fall back into paralysis or stasis. Why can't they carry out any action? 'We're waiting for Godot', says one; to which the other invariably replies with a weary 'Ah'. It is in that 'Ah' that we find the proverbial nature of cliché, and an acknowledgment of its power to stifle the hope that things might be made differently from how they are. Once the 'Ah' is accepted, draining any possible energy into paralysis, it operates as a period at the close of a sentence, it closes a thought, and it leads to the refrain 'Nothing to be done.'

Cliché afflicts, and stands as an insult to, the very fundamental principles of the University as an institution. Its rhetorical purpose is to drive participants in debate into the demoralizing and debilitating attitude whereby all that we can do is to echo the tramps' dispiriting refrain of 'Nothing to be done.' Yet if the University has any broadly accepted definition, it is that institution whose most fundamental purpose is that of 'hosting thought' itself. Cliché is a rhetorical device designed to arrest thinking, and to ensure that banal truisms, merely conventional beliefs, or ideological claims regarding 'reality' can continue without being subjected to thoughtful scrutiny or critique.

---

[3] Jane Austen, *Pride and Prejudice* (1813; repr. Penguin, London, 1972), 51. This famous opening brings economics into intimacy with truth itself. Further, although this may be 'universally acknowledged', Austen does not say that it is acknowledged 'as true'. Indeed, the rest of the novel subjects the opening sentence to profound examination, and finds it wanting. For more on this and related arguments, see my *Literature and Capital* (Bloomsbury, London, forthcoming).

I have already drawn brief attention above to some clichés that permeate the UK government's 2016 White Paper. However, the operations of cliché are utterly pervasive in our contemporary institutions. We recognize it most immediately in the managerialist jargon that structures and dominates every aspect of our work. For the most basic example, the formidable energy that can be released through any teaching and learning situation is dampened and subdued by managerial demand and process. As every University teacher now knows, officially, the seminar or laboratory must be organized around the managed and controlled 'delivery' of a specific 'learning outcome' that is to be securely guaranteed by the deployment of a particular 'teaching strategy' whose mechanical operation by the teacher will ensure that 'by the end of this module, the student will be able to ...' – and here, in this final gap, just fill in some selections from a list of acknowledged 'transferable skills'. This same primacy of process over substance is not specific to the descriptors that we must provide for every module (and sometimes every seminar); it actually pervades every aspect of the University's work in our time.

We should recall that, in Orwell's *Nineteen Eighty-Four*, the purpose of Newspeak was to narrow the range of human thought, and eventually to strictly delimit its possibilities, such that individuals would no longer think, but simply conform to the demands of a totalitarian government. 'Thinking' was supplanted by the mindless repetition of popular songs and tunes, as if it might properly be included under the heading of 'entertainment'.[4] The individual would become fully a 'human resource', a simple function in an operation. Managerialist discourse in the University – and arguably in other institutions as well – is our Newspeak; and it aims to serve a function similar to that of Newspeak in Orwell's dystopian novel. Managers do not 'fire' anyone

---

[4] George Orwell, *Nineteen Eighty-Four* (1949; repr. Penguin, London, 1982), 175–6. Orwell, however, does not demean the proletarian woman who sings under the window of Winston and Julia. Her song is set alongside birdsong, and then the real difference arises: 'The birds sang, the proles sang, the Party did not sing' (p. 176). In this respect, Orwell's attitude to popular culture differs completely from that of Adorno. In the present context, the point is that the bureaucratic and financial importance of the National Student Survey – in which we measure how much students 'enjoy' their courses – drives academic staff towards a prioritization of fun and entertainment, instead of the complexities and difficulties of study.

these days, for instance; rather, they 'restructure' a department in a way that eliminates a specific function – oh, and also, incidentally, a specific person – in the name of efficiency gains. Given that I am but a functionary, it follows logically that if the function disappears, so too do I. As a mere functionary and operative within a system, moreover, I cannot dispute this effect; indeed, I no longer even have the vocabulary with which to contemplate a resistance to the logic.

The same thing happens at all levels. The 'efficient management of information flows' replaces what we once called 'knowing things'. The adept use of the web and similar technology replaces 'research'. Above all, 'argument' cannot be permitted, because it reeks of conflict, which produces uncertainty and the possibility that minds might be changed with regard to any specific topic. Accordingly, argument – once the very lifeblood of the University – is suppressed under a process called 'managing difficult conversations'. This whole process of linguistic subterfuge is something that has been imported into the University from the world of private enterprise and business. As I will show, it is part of a concerted drive in which the distinction between a private sphere on one hand and public activities and duties on the other is insistently elided; and such an elision has massive institutional – and political – consequences for all intellectual work.

〜

Everyone knows that, with respect to the University, while the government must obviously intervene to prod us towards reform in the name of excellence, there is 'nothing to be done' in the way of additional financial investment from the public funds that are managed by government. 'Why?' we might ask. Inevitably, the reply is that 'We are in a period of austerity.' Too often, the response to that is that defeatist trampish 'Ah'. In such a time of austerity, public resources must be rationed as much as possible, as we restructure our economy while knowing that, as Liam Byrne MP put it when he left the Treasury in 2010, 'There's no money left'. In short: 'Nothing to be done.'[5]

---

[5] See Paul Owen, 'Ex-Treasury secretary Liam Byrne's note to his successor: there's no money left', *Guardian*, 17 May 2010, available at: https://www.theguardian. com/politics/2010/may/17/liam-byrne-note-successor (accessed 23 November 2017). Interestingly, Liam Byrne also revealed that he felt near-suicidal when the note was used by the Conservatives during the next general election campaign; but

One moment's pause to consider this will reveal a very different reality. Austerity is not at all general: austerity today is itself austerely rationed and not at all equally distributed among the population, either in the UK locally or, more adequately considered, in an international context either. Like globalization, austerity is experienced very differently depending on where you stand in the world or in a local society. We might equally be 'all in it together' (in the repeated cliché of the former Chancellor of the Exchequer George Osborne), but some (as Orwell might have said) are more equally 'in it' than others. Further, this period of austerity, since 2008, is itself hardly new. In fact, austerity has been with us for some time, although under different names; and the political recourse to the rhetoric of austerity drives a very specific purpose for the government of our society, and also for the governance of our University institutions.

The first major period of austerity that is relevant here and that predates our contemporary predicaments is that which followed in the aftermath of the 1939–45 war.[6] This was a time when resources were indeed extremely scarce and depleted. Indeed, food rationing that had started during the war years continued until 1954. However, the post-war Attlee government dealt with this not by starving institutions of funds, but rather by a systematic expansion of the public sphere. This took the political form of the nationalization of key resources and industries. David Kynaston writes that 'The Bank of England was followed in fairly quick succession by Cable and Wireless, civil aviation, electricity, the coal mines, transport (including the railways and road haulage) and gas.' Although some of this would be reversed by Churchill in the early 1950s, as Dominic Sandbrook notes, the general impetus remained, and became the cornerstone of a 'mixed economy' that left most business in private hands while taking key resources into

he also revealed that what saved him was his uncle's citation of Samuel Beckett, from *Worstword Ho!*: 'Ever tried. Ever failed. No matter. Try again. Fail again. Fail better.' See Lydia Wilgress, 'Liam Byrne says he considered throwing himself off a cliff after leaving Treasury "no money" note', *Telegraph*, 12 October 2016, available at: www. telegraph.co.uk/news/2016/10/12/liam-byrne-says-he-considered-throwing-him- self-off-a-cliff-after/ (accessed 23 November 2017).
[6] For a useful account of this, covering many social, political, and cultural institutions, and detailing the effects of austerity on everyday life, see Michael Sissons and Philip French, eds, *Age of Austerity 1945–51* (Penguin, London, 1963).

public ownership.[7] In 1948, in the Attlee administration, Nye Bevan launched the National Health Service as a public service designed – without private investment – to ensure that the population as a whole (at that time, some fifty million people) would be guaranteed proper treatment for their physical and mental wellbeing throughout their lives.

During this same period, we also saw the first stirrings of what would become a powerful and seemingly unstoppable drive towards University expansion. It began with an increase in student numbers; and it is above all the rate of increase that is remarkable. Between 1945 and 1951, there was an increase of almost 70%, with numbers rising from 50,000 in 1945 to some 84,000 by 1951.[8] That bears repeating: in six years, a 70% rise, and a continuing increase afterwards. More recent efforts, under our contemporary agendas, such as 'widening partici-pation', 'social mobility', and 'access', start to look exactly as they are in comparison: pretty feeble. One might even go so far as to suggest that these are slogans whose repetition is intended to cover the fact of a profound failure to increase and broaden the substantial positives of a higher education system. In the immediate post-war years, there was also a demand for new types of institution and for the elevation in status of some existing colleges. This was the start of a process that would eventuate in the celebrated Robbins Report in 1963. By the time that Robbins reported, a significant number of additional Universities had already opened; and the report recommended not just consolidation of those but also a further rapid expansion. The recommendations were accepted and funded by government.

Throughout this period of post-war growth, there was an abiding concern to extend the appeal of University to less privileged students or students from less financially secure backgrounds. As a consequence, it was understood that not only would tuition be free for the student, but also that the student would receive a maintenance allowance. The justification for this expenditure lay in hard economic calculation, with the knowledge that the cost incurred for each graduate would

---

[7] David Kynaston, *Austerity Britain 1945–51* (Bloomsbury, London, 2007), 139. See also Dominic Sandbrook, *Never Had It So Good* (2005; repr. Abacus, London, 2008), 61.

[8] Kynaston, *Austerity*, 462, and Sandbrook, *Never Had It So Good*, 426.

be outweighed more than ten-fold in terms of future and sustained economic benefit to the society as a whole. Even recent research, in our very different contemporary environment, shows such benefit. In its 2015 report *The Economic Role of UK Universities*, Universities UK called upon research by Price Waterhouse Cooper showing that 'For every £1 spent on research by the Arts and Humanities Research Council, the UK may derive as much as £10 of immediate benefit and another £15–£20 of long-term benefit.'[9] This yields a financial return that is inconceivable in any other systematic form of governmental investment. We need to understand how it has come about that, notwithstanding such figures, our governments refuse to make a similar investment today. It seems a no-brainer; but that phrase itself only serves to highlight the current attack on workers-by-brain.

The logic – a logic that persisted at least until the 1980s – was that of an investment in the student, combined with the social contract of an intergenerational bond. Each generation would tie itself and its interests not just to each other, but also to the future, by subsidizing the cost of University; and each graduate knew that he or she, in turn, would contribute again to the continuation of this through general but progressive taxation. Knowledge would be oriented not just to the past (knowing what has happened, knowing the things that science has shown to work) but also to the future (realizing possibilities not yet dreamt of in our contemporary philosophies). The University's present would stand in a tension between these drives, a tension heightened in intensity by the sheer excitement of learning.

It is important to note that, in this first post-war period, it was eminently 'realistic' to see things in terms of this logic. First, knowing things was thought to be a good thing, and better than celebrating ignorance in the name of anti-elitism; but that knowledge was to be a knowledge shared by the public and serving the public good and not primarily oriented instrumentally towards private and particular benefit. General taxation was regarded as a signal of one's commitment to the maintenance of the public sphere, and thus as a sign of our commitment to a shared identity and common interests. The proviso

---

[9] Universities UK, *The Economic Role of UK Universities* (2015), 40, available at: www.universitiesuk.ac.uk/policy-and-analysis/reports/Documents/2015/the-economic-role-of-uk-universities.pdf (accessed 23 November 2017).

was that such taxation must be progressive, to ensure that the less well-off were not subsidizing the better-off through their taxes, but rather vice versa; and this was especially so if the rich attended a University while the poor did not. The combination of progressive tax based on the ability to contribute, a social bond or contract, and a determination to increase the numbers of financially underprivileged attending a University provided the basis for a progressive and engaged public sphere built around common interest.

Something happened to this realism, however. The transition began in the 1980s and, today, we have witnessed a complete reversal of these ideas, with the concomitant existential threat to the survival of a functioning public sphere. We may well continue to advocate further growth in the Universities, further engagement of individuals from underprivileged circumstances, and lots of 'new providers' as they are referred to in the 2016 White Paper. At the same time, however, we seem to be intent on accepting the new version of 'realism', in which the entire project is regarded as something that will serve what we can call the ideology of acquisitive individualism. Acquisitive individualism – for short, let us call it greed – works on some clearly visible, though usually unstated, principles. They are usually unstated – or rendered as cliché – because when they stand naked in the light of day, they are neither attractive nor appealing.

First, acquisitive individualism yields the principle that governs my very motivation for attendance at a University: I do this primarily for my own individual benefit. Second, there is the atomization of the social world, for I sense no compelling argument whatsoever that might persuade me to use my higher education primarily for the benefit of others or for a general public good. Hard reality tells me that I must be 'in it to win it', with my 'eyes on the prize'. Third, a University education grants me not a 'degree' of quality in my thinking, not a degree marked ethically 'with honours', but primarily a degree of distinctiveness in the job-market, giving me a personal advantage over others in that competitive search for sustenance called work. Fourth, that distinctiveness is made clear and is fully articulated in my salary, being marked there as a wealth differential or a 'graduate dividend' that will extend inequality among the atomized individuals in our society. Fifth, it follows logically that a contribution to the public good through progressive taxation is a hindrance to these fundamental principles, and so tax is a 'burden' and can be neither a commitment to my neighbours nor a contribution to a general and shared public interest or public sphere. As a final codicil to this, we claim that this is all meritocratic, and that there are no barriers restricting access to a higher education; and so, if there are individuals who do not attend, it is either their own choice, or their own fault: they 'lack aspiration'.[10]

In an attempt to find a balance – or, more seriously, to manage the potential conflict – between establishment and meritocracy, Peter Hennessy has argued that we need meritocracy 'as both a balancer to Establishment and as a bringer of a more efficient and productive society in which the capable and the meritorious receive their rewards'. This is the private gain that meritocracy usually celebrates. He goes on to add, 'But we don't want meritocracy at the price of creating a detached and self-regarding elite insensitive towards those who have not soared up meritocratic ladders of their own.'[11] This is the check, to try to haul the meritocrat back to the public sphere and to responsibility. One question for us is whether such a balance can be sustained, politically and as a matter of empirical fact. A further question pertains to what the intellectual and her or his institution, the University, might have to say about such a potential conflict of interests between private and public benefits.

'In or about December 1910 human character changed', argued Virginia Woolf, in a celebrated 1924 talk and essay, given for the first time to the Heretics Society in London on 18 May that year.[12] The essay creates a Mrs Brown, a character used by Woolf to indicate how difficult it is to make a compelling fiction. We can re-write this for our own moment, by noting the effect that a certain Mr Browne (whom Hennessy notes as a friend, both men sitting in the House of Lords) had on the condition of the University exactly one century later. 'In

---

[10] The Browne Report, *Securing a Sustainable Future for Higher Education*, is explicit in making this disingenuous statement that there are 'no barriers to access' (p. 9). See: https://www.gov.uk/government/uploads/system/uploads/attachment_data/file/422565/bis-10-1208-securing-sustainable-higher-education-browne-report.pdf (accessed 23 November 2017).

[11] Peter Hennessy, *Establishment and Meritocracy* (Haus, London, 2014), 60.

[12] Virginia Woolf, *Selected Essays*, ed. David Bradshaw (Oxford University Press, Oxford, 2008), 38. In this edition, the essay appears under the title 'Character in fiction'.

or about December 2010, the character of the University changed', we might say. The Browne Review, *Securing a Sustainable Future for Higher Education*, published two months previously (12 October 2010), established the conditions of what has become accepted as the new 'realism'. On 9 December 2010, the Coalition government firmed up that new reality by voting through a tripling of the then standard £3,000 p.a. University tuition fees in England.[13] This would replace funding from central government, thus ensuring that the tuition costs of a higher education would be transferred almost entirely to private individuals. The founding principle underpinning this is Browne's insistence that a University education is 'primarily a private benefit'.

This is a symptom of what might more generally be called 'the enclosure of the intellectual commons'.[14] Essentially, it reverses completely the earlier post-war settlement that had stressed the existence of the public sphere. It turns any principle of nationalization on its head, and completes a process of privatization of all interests that had begun during the 1980s.

The 1980s were also a period of austerity, in fact. It was in this decade that a neoliberal economic agenda, encapsulated under the name of 'Reaganomics' but fundamentally indebted to the Chicago School of Economics and to the writings of F. A. Hayek, was embraced enthusiastically by the UK's Thatcher administrations. In the UK, the agenda took the form of a policy of explicit 'privatization', in and through which the public sector would be systematically starved of funding, as the process began of transferring public and shared wealth into a concentrated form in the hands of a small number of individuals. The very idea of 'the public' would be placed in jeopardy, as all things public found their sustenance and very legitimacy questioned.[15] Needless to say, the process was never described in these terms; rather,

---

[13] It is important to note that other UK jurisdictions, especially Scotland, found different solutions to the question of funding higher education.

[14] This phrase was shared by Tamson Pietsch, M. M. McCabe, Martin McQuillan, and myself when we constituted the Executive of the Council for the Defence of British Universities in 2012.

[15] See Claire Westall and Michael Gardiner, *The Public on the Public* (Palgrave, London, 2016) for a full account of the status of 'the public' in political discourse.

Thatcherism laid a relentless emphasis instead on the idea and language of securing 'value for money' in all public sector activities. In doing this – ostensibly a reasonable enough thing – she installed a culture of surveillance, measurement, and the quantification of all qualities at the heart of intellectual work.

In reality, it was never 'value' for money that was being sought; rather it was simply 'more money' for the initial investment that Thatcher and her like-minded right-wing politicians demanded. Profit and profitability became the presiding principle; and thus public sector institutions were instructed to behave 'like a business' and orient themselves towards making a financial profit. For those who were not successful in this, there was the threat of reductions in state funding, threats that would be realized when the government persuaded Universities to jeopardize their own position through the peer-evaluation process of the 'Research Assessment Exercise'. University leaders during this decade, keen to curry favour with a curmudgeonly and Scrooge-like government and hoping for preferment for their own institution, eagerly complied.

It would have been controversial for the government explicitly to divest from University research; so the tactic of 'peer-review' – itself a fundamental guarantee of scholarly authority – would be used. The result was that University academics became responsible for their own cutbacks. The Research Assessment Exercise (RAE), subsequently re-labelled as the Research Excellence Framework (REF), began its life under a 1982 pilot scheme with a different acronym: RSE, which stood for 'Research Selectivity Exercise'; and the idea behind this was to find an acceptable way to reduce state funding for University research by limiting the provision of state funds to a small number of selected institutions. When it became a 'Research Assessment Exercise' instead, in 1986, the academy acted on what seemed to be an assumption that the government would be using the exercise not as a means of reducing its interest in research through 'selection', but as a vehicle for increasing it or at least justifying an ongoing steady commitment to it. All that would change would be the distribution of funding.

The consequence, however, was the start of the corruption – and betrayal of the sector's fundamental ethical principles – that we cover up under the terms of 'gaming the system'. In the earliest full formal exercise, for example, the panel judging the Unit of Assessment for the discipline of English was austere in its ratings, while other disciplines seemed happy to dole out top ratings for all departments nationwide. The result of this was a substantial cut nationally in research funding for the discipline of English, and a massive increase in other fields. English – and any other discipline whose panels had acted with complete integrity – thus savaged itself, and government escaped the blame.

The University became complicit with the establishment of the new 'realism' of hierarchical selectivity and of private interest as the key driver and motivational force and rationale for any activity. Behind this lies the work of Milton Friedman and the Chicago School of Economics. In a television interview with Phil Donahue in 1979, Friedman was asked whether he felt any qualms about a capitalist system that operates on greed. He replied, 'Is there some society that you know that *doesn't* run on greed?' This is a classic example of the 'be realistic' manoeuvre at work: it involves no argument, and calls on no evidence, but suggests that any suggestion of a society that has a higher ideal than this is simply non-existent, unreal. Friedman rehearses his claim that greed is the key motivational force for any good, and for any social or individual progress. This has the benefit of being simple, endlessly repeatable – rather like a cliché.

Notwithstanding the fact that it is pronounced by a Nobel Laureate in economics, it is not in fact simple at all; rather, it is crudely simplistic, and should therefore be resisted by an institution whose basic activity is to avoid such spuriously simplistic final or determinate solutions to any and all human predicaments. What makes it simplistic is that Friedman circumvents all the complexity of a problem by pretending that its entirety can be encapsulated in a banal phrase. Yet more simplistic is his action of perverting an economic principle into a political one and then confounding the two, suggesting that politics is nothing but economics and is governed by a specific economic dogma in which greed – more recently known as profit-seeking or rent-seeking – becomes the sole description of human motivation.[16] In short, his claim is a clear and even paradigmatic example of the inappropriate intrusion of money (finance economics) into government (politics);

[16] For a good analysis of *rentier* society, see Thomas Picketty, *Capital in the Twenty-First Century* (2013), trans. Arthur Goldhammer (Harvard University Press, Cambridge, MA, 2014).

and the consequence of that is a tacit acceptance of the financialization of political government itself.[17] The claim about greed is acceptable if and only if one has already accepted that it is a good idea to consider politics in purely financial cost-benefit terms as those terms apply to an individual. In short, the claim is a tautology; and it falls apart as soon as one questions that first underlying assumption.

This makes Friedman's a simplistic claim; yet it is also a claim that is made plausible precisely and purely by the refusal to scrutinize the fundamental principle on which it rests. As soon as one suggests that the financialization of government is a corruption of politics, then it becomes equally clear that, despite being simple and plausible, Friedman's position is misleading. Nevertheless, the University sector has gone along with the 'realism' of the Friedman hypothesis, a hypothesis that lies behind the normalization of a Thatcherite agenda of the privatization of what were once common interests – including knowledge – and the consequent demise of the public sphere. Following this, the University has systematically betrayed its principles, and has preferred to become tacitly politicized as an arm of governments that also wanted such simplistic clichés – 'let's be honest; greed motivates us all' – to become the source of our values and norms.[18]

The Friedman position is one that Oliver Stone satirized in the character of Gordon Gekko in *Wall Street*, with Gekko's famous lecture on how 'greed is good'. The satire, however, did nothing to arrest the dissemination of the basic claim. On the contrary: it helped to normalize the claim, coming as it did through the hugely popular medium of cinema and in the voice of Michael Douglas, son of an actor – Kirk Douglas – most famous for his role as leader of popular insurrection against the power of the State in *Spartacus*. Reaganomics

---

[17] The ultimate completion of this logic would be the election of a businessman as President, say.

[18] An example – admittedly anecdotal but historically true – illustrates this at work. When he arrived as VC of Warwick in 2006, Nigel Thrift led a drive to boost research income from sources other than government. His rationale for this, stated explicitly at his first meeting with all Heads of Department, was that 'money means freedom'. Among the shocking things about this is the fact that, coming from an allegedly left-wing geographer, it echoes exactly the words of Margaret Thatcher, in her 1968 speech 'What's wrong with politics': 'Money ... enables one to live the kind of life of one's own choosing.' See: www.margaretthatcher.org/document/101632 (accessed 23 November 2017).

and Thatcherism both bought into this ideology of private acquisitive individualism, based as it is on the atomization of the whole social order, and they sought political capital from it. Because it had been stated openly, if satirically, by the character of Gekko/Friedman, they no longer needed to state it openly themselves; but it lay behind their economic principles. It might be salutary here to recall Peter Cook's reminder about the political force of satire. Opening his 'Establishment Club' in 1961, he said it would be a venue for satire, just like 'those wonderful Berlin cabarets which did so much to stop the rise of Hitler and prevent the outbreak of the Second World War'.[19]

'Human character' changed indeed during the period between the 1980s and our contemporary moment. Indeed, we can go so far as to say that 'human character' itself started to become privatized under the guiding principle of greed, self-help (à la Samuel Smiles), 'self-improvement', 'self-enhancement', or acquisitive individualism. And if a government can fully instate a condition whereby it says that resources are scarce, then a certain logic of such acquisitive individualism becomes indeed normative: it becomes a means of individual survival. As I will argue in detail later in this book, it heralds a return to the world that Hobbes advises us against, a state of nature in which there is a war of all against all.

By the time of the Browne Review in 2010, privatization has become a key cornerstone of neoliberal and general right-wing economics; but it has also contaminated all other forms of economic thinking, such that alternatives to acquisitive individualist philosophy started to appear to be unthinkable. It has also become a fundamental but unstated normative ideology around which all University policy is formed. The logic of privatization transforms the University into an empty shell whose central purpose is simply to be a vehicle through which we produce ever higher degrees of inequality of wealth and of resources. In many ways, the actual content of what we do in the sector does not really matter at all; our fundamental *raison d'être* is economic: our purpose is simply to keep money circulating, while ensuring that

---

[19] See John Bird, 'Obituary: Peter Cook', *Independent*, 10 January 1995, available at: www.independent.co.uk/news/people/obituary-peter-cook-1567341.html (accessed 23 November 2017). The precise wording varies a little depending on the source; but the joke is always the same.

whatever we do makes no opposition to the foundational goal and purpose of transferring public wealth – and above all the resources of knowledge – into private hands.

In October 2017, Jo Johnson decided to extend his acronyms. The REF is established; and the Teaching Excellence Framework (TEF) is also now under way. Caught up in the banal rhymes of REF with TEF, he decided to add a KEF or Knowledge Exchange Framework to the roster. The point of this new KEF is to measure how much University research yields for the commercial and business sector. That is to say, University research will increasingly be funded according to how much it serves the interests of private business concerns by providing them with the know-how required to extract more profit from the general public's engagement with technology and other commercial products and services. This is, straightforwardly, even brazenly, a demand that University research be directed towards serving the demands of the private sector; and those demands are for private sector profit. Indeed, government will provide funding – public funding – on the basis of how well each individual University does this. The KEF is an example of an increasingly brazen privatization of commonly shared wealth – and the knowledge that should be at its base. Johnson is 'keen to explore what more we can do to evaluate the extent of knowledge exchange, engagement, collaboration and commercialisation – the impact that universities are having on the economy – and to recognise which of our universities are leading the way'.[20] He does not say explicitly where this route leads to; but this is what I will address in what follows here.

We should explore more fully the intimacy of the relation between the politics of neoliberal economics and the diminished status of the University. To do this is, I think, not in the least controversial. However, its implications will be seen to be significant and substantial. In this book, I will make it clear that the University is not at all innocent with regard to those international political conditions in which we

[20] See 'In full: Jo Johnson speech to the Hefce annual conference 2017', *Times Higher Education*, available at: https://www.timeshighereducation.com/blog/full-jo-john son-speech-hefce-annual-conference-2017 (accessed 23 November 2017).

witness the rise of the populist and often neo-fascist right wing. Indeed, I will go so far as to claim that, by giving up on the primacy of its role in the public sphere and in accepting the logic of the privatization of all interests, the leadership of the University sector is partly responsible for this disturbing political situation. The key to understanding this claim is found in the University leadership's complicity with the privatization of knowledge, and the reduction of its activities to commercial transactions among discrete individuals seeking social distinction from others through the medium of their individual wealth.

More locally, my argument will cover the claim that the University is partly responsible for some major political shocks of 2016: the UK's Brexit vote of 23 June and the election in the USA of Trump on 8 November. To be sure, those and similar political events do have other sources, of course; yet at their centre are questions about what constitutes knowledge, good judgement, truth – and these are subjects that should be at the heart of the University as a series of presiding issues or concerns. However, through its complicity with a neoliberal agenda that entails the privatization of knowledge, good judgement, and truth, the University has subjected – and, indeed subjugated – these issues and concepts to crude financialization. It is less a pragmatism of 'what works', and more an opportunism of 'what pays, and how much' that now governs the sector's primary concerns. This is damaging to what should instead be our more ethical primary interests and functions.

To bring this state of affairs about, knowledge itself must be degraded. Here is how that happens. We can start by differentiating three categories: data, information, and knowledge. 'Data' is what we are given, the empirical facts of whatever case we are examining or, simply, 'what happens'; 'information' is what we get when we try to put that data into a meaningful sentence; 'knowledge' is what we get when we realize that the same data yields different versions of information, and therefore we have to discuss, debate, and find a way of legitimizing one account over others. In other words, knowledge is conditioned by scepticism and doubt, by dialogue and debate, and not by certainty. It is not a product but a process, an activity of coming to know things while also being aware that all knowledge is provisional in that it is subject to new information.

Lest there be doubt, I should make it clear that my validation of provisional knowledge is not at all an accession to the claim that all knowledge is relative to a specific point of view. The position I outline here is, in fact, the antithesis of relativism. The relativist submerges the demand for truth under opinion, claiming that the world is as it appears, given a specific location or identity of its subject. Relativism, in its crudest forms, subscribes to truths that are gendered, raced, classed, and so on. It is akin to a belief that there exists, say, Marxist science and bourgeois science. In thus multiplying truths that are in contest with each other, truth as an absolute category disappears, to be replaced – as Plato once feared – by mere opinion.

A claim that truth is provisional, by contrast, asserts absolutely that there are things that are true, entirely regardless of the point of view from which they are viewed. At the same time, it also accepts that research provides new information; and that, in the contest of accounts that this new information enters into, new truths are discovered. For example, it is not the case that the pre-Copernican world thought that the earth was at the centre of the universe just from a particular point of view. There was no other point of view; and, for the pre-Copernican, it was absolutely and utterly true that the earth sat at the centre of the universe. Copernicus simply provided new information and, once that information is factored into debates about what is the relative position of the earth, the sun, and the other planets, the truth now is that the sun is at the centre of the universe. This, too, has become subject to new knowledge, of course, in astrophysics; and it will become incumbent on us – if we have any interest in truth at all – to factor in the new information that we continue to produce. The fact that truth changes when the known information or facts change – that is to say, that the future is different from today or that research and continued thinking might actually matter – is no reason whatsoever to assume a complete relativism of all truths and the abandonment of truth as a meaningful category.

Doubt, however, is a hard sell precisely because, by definition, it lacks clarity and certainty. If you buy something, you want to know what it is, surely and definitively. It follows from this, of course, that knowledge – again by definition – cannot be bought: conditioned by doubt, it is unstable and subject to modifications through further debate or consideration of the data and the varying interpretations that constitute 'information'. By contrast, information itself has all the appearance of certainty. It comes in statements that have the look of being absolutely definitive and determining. If the University is going to operate as a business, it has to ensure that its 'offer' lies in good commodities, commodities that a buyer will want and that he or she is willing to pay for. The easiest way to do this is to ignore the category of knowledge completely, and to substitute information and the skills of information management in its place. Even better, it is a good commercial idea to ensure that this information is the kind that will please a buyer, rather than the kind that might disturb her or him or provoke doubts in their existing world-view.

In fact, of course, Universities do not ignore the category of knowledge; rather, they view it as the troublesome fly in the ointment, an ointment that otherwise guarantees the slick and smooth operation of its business; and that business is itself now reduced to the management of information flows whose purpose is to appease and satisfy. The public sphere, governed increasingly by market fundamentalism, is transformed into a marketplace where individuals choose their information; and, if we have to pay for it, we want the solace of information that confirms our own prejudices. This way, the commodity of information assures me that I am always in the right, and that I do not need to learn anything that might change my mind or disturb the ideological prejudices that give my life its current 'real' meaning and identity. In short, I can say with Michael Gove MP that I've 'had enough of experts' with their elitist claims to a knowledge that requires debate and dialogue to find.[21] I'll settle for gut instinct, or uninformed prejudice. After all, this is me 'being realistic' and attending to the real me.

The most obvious new 'realism' with which we are dealing in the case of the Trump presidency, for example, relates to the massive disconnection between what we know to be factually the case (data) and what Trump and his acolytes assert to be the case (information). There is the deployment of a 'shock doctrine' that works through a massive information overload, with the President issuing a series of executive orders, many of them deeply controversial, in quick

---

[21] Michael Gove made this statement, infamously, in an interview with Faisal Islam during the Brexit campaign. See: www.youtube.com/watch?v=GGgiGtJk7MA (accessed 23 November 2017).

succession.[22] Opponents of such orders are left wondering where to begin amid the plethora of controversial and often fallacious claims that are advanced to justify and explain the supposed 'necessity' of the orders. These are supplemented then by a steady stream of tweets, many of which are inconsistent with facts and all of which serve to distract attention from serious issues. In the midst of this extraordinary 'wealth of information', this excessive economy, this new 'realism', is missing one key element: reality itself. In such circumstances, it must surely become more difficult for the conservative voice to endorse 'being realistic' and to go on resisting any challenge to what passes for 'realism'.

The political purpose of the 'alternative facts' agenda in the Trump administration is to not to sow doubt about the truth, but to sow confusion about what the data is in any circumstance. Doubt about the truth can in fact be helpful in the extension of democratic argument, for it is concerned with knowledge. Confusion about the data, however, amounts to the denial of reality. A politics with this latter predisposition is akin to the 'historian' who denies the fact of the Holocaust. It is not here a question of interpretation of facts that lead to different accounts of the data; it is the destruction of the data itself, and the coercive expectation that the data will not be discovered, uncovered.

The declaration that the media are 'the enemy' is designed to destroy the authority of newspapers such as the *Washington Post* or the *New York Times* and of television companies such as CNN. Trump's explicit designation of the authoritative media as 'the enemy' is a phrase that has a particular poignancy also in the UK Brexit vote context, a context that was shaped by an 'alternative facts' agenda every bit as much as the pathological lying that constitutes the 'politics' of Trump or, closer to home, of Boris Johnson. There, when an appeal is made to the authority of the judiciary to decide on the constitutional particulars of government, the Brexit-backing *Daily Mail* describes the judges as 'enemies of the people'.[23]

22 This is an information version of the material shocks described by Naomi Klein in *The Shock Doctrine* (Penguin, London, 2008): shocks that are designed to destabilize other governments. In the case of Trump's administration, the assault is not on a government, but on the truth claims of certain media, and even the truth claims of empirical reality itself.

23 See James Slack, 'Enemies of the people: fury over "out of touch" judges who have "declared war on democracy" by defying 17.4m Brexit voters and who could trigger

Such an appeal to 'the people' and the designation of some institutions as an enemy has clear roots in the populist tendencies of both
Thatcher and Reagan during the 1980s. In the UK's case especially,
Thatcherism worked systematically to denigrate the authority and
standing of any and all institutions that might contest the views of
Thatcher's own government. There were concerted attacks on the
teaching profession (allegedly intrinsically 'left-leaning' and doc-
trinaire), on the judiciary (elderly men out of touch with the real
world), and the medical profession (playing God with transplanta-
tion technology and genetics). Thatcher's background in an austere
Methodism preferred robust self-reliance and the 'self-help' practice
of the Victorian Samuel Smiles over the possibility that we might give
credence to such institutional authorities. The ethic of such muscular
Christianity sat very comfortably alongside a specific reading of one
part of Adam Smith's liberal economics which was based on individuals
seeking their own advantage in all circumstances.[24] The culmination of
this aspect of Thatcherism came with the miners' strike in 1984. This
was the attack on the institution of the trade union as such, and it was
especially significant for the Thatcher government because the trade
union signalled the authority of collectivism in place of individualism.

At the same time as this was happening, the draconian reductions in
public spending in the first three budgets of Geoffrey Howe, between
1979 and 1981, had affected the funding for Universities, leading to
an effective freeze on all recruitment at this time.[25] The University,

constitutional crisis', *Daily Mail*, 3 November 2016, available at: www.dailymail.
co.uk/news/article-3903436/Enemies-people-Fury-touch-judges-defied-17–4m-
Brexit-voters-trigger-constitutional-crisis.html (accessed 23 November 2017). It is
unclear whether the journalists at the *Daily Mail* were aware of Ibsen's 1882 play *An
Enemy of the People*, concerning an ethically upright individual, Dr Stockmann, and
his struggle against a corrupt newspaper and government. The label 'enemy of the
people' also has a long history in political revolution worldwide, and is used to justify
violence.

[24] See Samuel Smiles, *Self-Help* (1859; repr. John Murray, London, 1958); and Adam
Smith, *The Wealth of Nations* (1776; repr. Penguin, London, 1982). In both these
thinkers, individual self-interest is, in fact, fundamentally modified by a sense of
common and public duties.

[25] For details on these budgets, see the official website of the Margaret Thatcher
Foundation: www.margaretthatcher.org/archive/1981_budget.asp (accessed 23
November 2017). For a detailed examination of the politics of the miners' strike, see
Seumas Milne, *The Enemy Within*, updated edn (Verso, London, 2004).

too, was increasingly seen as a difficult institution for the government, precisely because its constitution – with both academic freedom and tenure – meant that its members could act with integrity to question any and all social norms. Kenneth Baker's Education Reform Act of 1988 dealt with these by the formal abolition of tenure.[26] This is an act of real significance, for it attacks what has been a cornerstone of academic freedom, which includes the freedom to question received opinion and social norms without fear of jeopardizing one's position. When tenure is abolished, the academic profession immediately becomes more precarious. This matters not because academics are some kind of exception to the general rule of work conditions; rather, it matters because it jeopardizes the normal exercise of academic freedom. Academic freedom thrives upon – and cannot survive without – dissent. However, dissent, after 1988, is less attractive if it may lead to the academic being declared redundant, and thus fired.

This government Act of 1988 had a further significant effect. It started a process that is still ongoing and becoming more and more normative every day. Traditionally, when one had tenure as a guarantee of academic freedom, the academic could pledge a primary allegiance to the demands of her or his discipline and its rigours and protocols. That is not just a professional position, but also an ethical one, for it pledges allegiance to the discovery and dissemination of knowledge, no matter how edifying or unpalatable that knowledge may be and, indeed, no matter how much it impinges on conditions that are strictly beyond the disciplinary framework in which the academic works. It thus protects the academic when, for example, as a result of her or his research (into literature, for a random example) he or she is able to aver that a government is operating a discriminatory practice based on intrinsic sexism. Equally, it protects the academic in any criticism of the governance of her or his own institution.

With tenure abolished, however, that primary allegiance covertly and coercively shifts, especially if one is guarding against the precariousness of employment in an age of cutbacks and austerity. Now, there is a pressure on the academic to maintain allegiance to the presiding norms that govern the University itself. This produces a tacit demand

---

[26] Notwithstanding this Act, Kenneth Baker has been awarded honorary degrees by the Universities of Warwick, Wolverhampton, and Plymouth.

for conformity to whatever the University sees as its identity.[27] In many if not all cases, that identity is the identity claimed by senior managers and articulated in a brand or 'reputation'. At this stage, any statement or activity that a senior manager dislikes, or with which he or she simply wants to disagree, can be re-cast as a damage to the institution's reputation, and as grounds for dismissal.

Through this shift, the academic now becomes an ambassador for the brand. Even worse, the University itself feels the pressure to conform to the beliefs and desired norms of its funder, the government of the day. Political ideology trumps knowledge. The institution itself has to protect the reputation of the government and has not to be seen to be doing anything that might undermine the government's claims to authority − even to authority over what might constitute knowledge. The academic, finally in this chain, thereby becomes re-designated essentially as a civil servant, whose primary allegiance has to be to the government itself and to its presiding ideology.[28] This − if we strip it back to essentials − is the pledge of allegiance to the demands of money itself and to a specific understanding of economics on which that ideology − of the financialization of knowledge and the enclosure of the intellectual commons − rests.

In economic terms, the dominant policies of Thatcherism and Reaganomics in the 1980s were determined by the logic of market fundamentalism. In this, all value could be monetized, every value could be quantified and measured; and the standard determination of value became, quite simply, financial profit for individuals. The value

[27] In the case of the Russell Group, that identity is precisely the identity of the VC. It is not enough noted that, formally and constitutionally, there is no such thing as a 'Russell Group institution'. The group is a membership organization, with (currently) twenty-four *individuals* − the VCs − as its membership. When one of those VCs identifies herself or himself with the institution, we have reverted to the age of feudalism, in which individuals are identified as baronial holdings, such as 'Warwick', 'York', 'Exeter', and so on.

[28] In a letter of 9 July 1946 to Karl Jaspers, regarding his *Idea of the University*, Hannah Arendt notes that a key problem entailed by State funding of Universities is the State's expectation that professors become civil servants, thereby betraying their intellectual duties in deference to State interests. But 'a dictatorial regime will "bring the universities into line" anyhow, whether they are financed by the state or not'. See *Hannah Arendt − Karl Jaspers Correspondence 1926–1969*, ed. Lotte Kohler and Hans Saner, trans. Robert and Rita Kimber (Harcourt Brace, New York, 1992), 49.

of something is translated into the price that it can command in an allegedly 'free' market whose shape is determined by supposedly free individuals making rational choices that are configured according to their judgement as to what will profit them.

Resources – including natural resources – are re-conceptualized as commodities. In this way, the shared natural resources of the planet can be sold off to individuals for them to control. It begins with tele-communications in the UK, with the sell-off of British Telecom. This is followed rapidly by gas, electricity, and water. At this point, the pri-vatizing zeal of the government starts to encroach upon the necessities of life itself. Water is fundamental to human survival; but if the source of the water is 'owned' by a private individual or corporate company, there is a massive transference of power. This is important, for it signals a further stage in the economic structure of our politics. Within it, further, there is the appeal to 'the people', in that the privatizations allegedly give individual people shares – or a private interest – in these and other businesses and resources.

⌐〜

The populism that supported the normalization of privatization takes its determining form in the sell-off of council housing, where it is called the establishment of a 'property-owning democracy'. It is surely surprising that there is no objection to this, given that the phrase recalls an earlier historical moment, when there was no universal suffrage and when voting was restricted by a property-owning requirement. Instead, the position that gains traction is not at all the democratic one, but its populist perversion: when I see my council house neighbours buying their property, I realize that 'it could be me'. If they can do it, so can I; and I start to support the idea, even if it never becomes – or even never could become – a reality. The phenomenon of fantasy politics starts here.

This is the fantastical populism that we see entrenched, for example, in all national lotteries: 'the winner could be you'. Such lotteries are essentially a form of 'poverty tax': the poor (who are disproportion-ately the biggest group participating) pay for their tickets, hoping for and believing in the instant transformation of a private life. It is also the populism of the extraordinarily successful television talent show, which likewise promises the instant gratification achieved through the

transformation of an ordinary life. Simultaneously with the establishment in the UK and Europe of the national lottery and the seemingly
irresistible rise of various formats of television talent show worldwide
(from singing to dancing to baking to cooking to drawing to pottery
and so on and on, in a seemingly inexorable drive to render every
activity and hobby into a 'competition'), two parallel things happen in
the University sector. First, the expansion of numbers says, especially to
the disenfranchised, 'it could be you'; and second, it promises, as with
success in the talent competition, to be a 'life-changing opportunity'.

The substantive and fundamental corollary of these – which promise
instant gratification for minimum effort – is the increased demand for
'efficiency' in all and every human activity; and so we see the start
of a process in which, for example, the length of a degree comes
under pressure, and the first UK private University, the University of
Buckingham, advertises itself on the basis of the economic efficiency
and advantage of a two-year degree programme. Next, we have the
installation everywhere of time-management evaluations, in which
academics must account for every hour of their work. In response to
our 'consumers', we become obsessed also with the counting of, and
quantitative evaluation of, contact-hours between individual students
and individuated academics.

As in the adage, when you cannot count what is actually important,
you start to decide that the important stuff is what you can count. This
becomes the perverse dogma of managerialist accountancy, counting
everything except the things that really matter, and thereby degrad-
ing the actual intellectual work of the institution and its activities.
Thinking, we might say, now counts for nothing, and even counts as
nothing.

Initially, then, Thatcherism says that there must be no rival authority
to that of the Conservative government. This is a constituent element in Thatcher's own class-warfare, targeting the assumed privilege
and unearned authority of the aristocratic class, which was her initial
bugbear (and whose supremacy in the Conservative Party she temporarily overthrew). Thatcherism constitutes a thoroughly 'bourgeois'
revolution. However, it is never really a revolution at all, despite what
its admirers often suggest, because it falls short of completing its own
intrinsic logic. Indeed, what follows from Thatcherism is not that the
Prime Minister assumes full control of realities. That, after all, would

be akin to totalitarianism, or elected dictatorship. Likewise, and by the same token, power is not given over to the people either. After all, most of those shares that were purchased through the privatization processes are now owned by large corporates, who moved in when individuals began to realize their stock-market profits.

The actual outcome of Thatcherism is that authority and social power are now vested in money and wealth: it's the premise of the 'Good Samaritan', who, according to Thatcher, could help the less fortunate only because he had money in the first place.[29] Money and wealth become signifiers of value; and since the individuals who hold the most wealth are the financial services, it turns out that they will eventually assume all the power and authority within the new 'realism' that governs our social norms. The ground is fully laid here for the financial disaster of 2007–08, and for all that follows from that.

These conditions affect the University directly. It is not that the primacy of the banks takes over from our intellectual authority. Rather, it is that we became complicit with the commercialization of knowledge and with the monetization of intellectual activity. This is also governed by a revitalized logic of austerity, a logic that – as should by now be clear – is a political choice and not a necessity. The Coalition government in the UK of 2010–15 made precisely that choice. A central plank of the policy is the transfer of funding for a University degree into private hands, with the concomitant responsibility for such funding being the private debt of individual students, whose futures are now being fully mortgaged. The final stage in this transition comes with the proposed sale – privatization – of the loan book itself, through which corporates will be able to profit directly from that private debt.

Privatization, in this way, becomes revealed as a state-sponsored subsidy for the rich. In failing to mount a defence of public interest, the University sector became complicit with this process. Worse, Steve Smith, then VC of Exeter and President of Universities UK, stated publicly that the Universities 'welcome Lord Browne's recommendations'.[30] This is not just craven complicity, through which individual

---

[29] See Margaret Thatcher, speech entitled 'What's wrong with politics', delivered on 11 October 1968, available at: http://www.margaretthatcher.org/document/101632 (accessed 23 November 2017). See also Ha-Joon Chang, *Bad Samaritans* (Random House, London and New York, 2007) for a more nuanced examination of the issues.

[30] See Hannah Richardson, 'Browne reforms "mark end of publicly funded degrees"',

VCs might seek individual preferment for their institutions from a miserly government. Wendy Piatt, the Director-General of the Russell Group of VCs at the time, went even further, stating, 'We support the urgent and necessary reforms outlined by the Browne Review.' This constituted a fundamental betrayal of the sector by those who were its leading spokespeople and representatives. The views of these 'elites' were not at all uniformly shared across the sector; but their views prevailed and became normative, effectively silencing any dissenting position.[31]

A further shift, however, is required to complete the transformation of the University; and, as in the finance sector, it depends upon technology and on how technological advance changes the very idea of efficiency. Efficiency itself now becomes a performance measure of all activity: output must exceed input; minima must engage 'leverage' to produce maxima; the processes by which this works are more important than any actual product or outcome; and all must be done instantaneously, with the utmost speed and no spare moment at all in our operations. As in high-frequency trading in the affairs of the finance sector in the City, there must also be no single moment that is left vacant or 'unaccounted for' in the activity of the University. Everything is counted; everything is inserted into the financial accounts; and only that which individually and discretely shows profit in the accounts can be sustained.

Once this is all achieved, we can finally reach the state of affairs in which knowledge and thinking can be reduced fully to bits of information that can be clearly identified and quantified; and so the University discovers its business product and its unique selling point. It trades not in knowledge or study, but in information as its own specific commodity in a market where information has become the newest and most fundamental resource of all. This goes all the way from

BBC, 12 October 2010, available at: www.bbc.co.uk/news/education-11519545 (accessed 23 November 2017).

[31] See 'Standard note SN/SP/5739' (House of Commons Library), 29 October 2010, available at: http://dera.ioe.ac.uk/22796/1/SN05739.pdf (accessed 23 November 2017). Wendy Piatt's comment is on p. 15. It is interesting to note that the self-proclaimed 'top' institutions were gushing in their support of Browne, while the Million+ group, the National Union of Students, and the University and College Union all found it harmful.

the government-inspired demand for information about graduate out-comes and salaries, as they are related to specific degrees in particular institutions, up to and including the reduction of teaching and learning to the efficient management of information.

These, covered now – astonishingly, surely – by the legislation of the Competition and Markets Authority, not only get rid entirely of the very category of 'the student', who is now replaced by 'the consumer', but also seek to provide fodder for an economic system that subscribes to the mechanical cause-and-effect falsehoods around which 'rational choice free-market' economics is based. The information shows that, for example, a degree in engineering from Sudbury leads to £50k per annum; and therefore, as a rational choice free-market consumer, I will choose to do that rather than a degree in French from Anglesey, which yields £23k per annum.

Two questions follow: (1) who in their right mind does this? and (2) who in their right mind believes that this is how individuals operate? In the above example, what if I am pretty outstanding at French, but cannot possibly do engineering because I am innumerate? Only an institution that has so lost its way as a University that it can accept gov-ernance by regulation from the Competition and Markets Authority could possibly ignore the data – the empirical facts of the case – here. It would do so under the shadow of complicity with its own politici-zation as an arm of the neoliberal state.

This is what must change if the University is to survive as a University at all. The argument in this book will analyse the betrayal in more detail in order to work through the crisis to the survival of the University in our time.

Part II

Crisis

2

Titles and entitlements: why 'University'?

Imagine having the power, freedom, and responsibility to organize an entire people into some kind of social, political, ethical, and cultural arrangement. Where might you begin? Almost certainly, you would not begin by suggesting that the first thing we would need is an institution like our contemporary University. Plato, in *Republic*, for example, starts his consideration of civic and social life with a different question, the question of justice. Fairly quickly, however, he comes to explore how justice itself seeks legitimation. The question is how justice itself can be justified, how the people of his ideal society will experience justice, and how they will know it to be just. Through exploring this issue, he comes, as early as Books II and III of *Republic*, to consider education as something that can provide such legitimation, and thus as something that might yield a fundamental institutional framework for a good society. Book II closes with the question of how to adjudicate or discriminate between good and bad; and Plato then extends this to ask whether the issue of education as such 'will help us at all in our main enquiry into the origin of justice and injustice'.[1]

Although one might not begin with a consideration of the University, then, this early thought-experiment suggests that some form of education would be envisaged fairly early as a necessity and even as an absolute priority for the making of a good society. Before thinking about your design and framework for the good society, you would presumably want to have some knowledge or even foreknowledge

---

[1] Plato, *Republic*, trans. Desmond Lee (Penguin, London, 1974), 129.

of possible outcomes and consequences of what you plan to do. You would hypothesize some general idea of a social arrangement regarding, for example, a system of laws, and then try to envisage how the particularities of that system might fit an overall scheme of things, including (as in Plato) physical health and wellbeing.[2] In a word, you would be doing some *research* as the very foundation of your work.

You would also find yourself, thereby, centrally impelled to engage with whatever passes in your time as the prevailing conditions of knowledge. Insofar as your thinking impinged upon material realities at all, you would surely have to begin from a conviction that some conceptual ideas fit the material facts of the world, while other ideas constitute falsehoods or lies; and you would have to test and therefore come to know which is which. Plato's model for this is the watchdog who can discriminate or judge between who is friend and who is foe whenever someone approaches the camp.[3] In this case, a judgement is based on empirical evidence found in the historical material conditions (the visceral evidence of smell); but what the dog is helping us to judge is a conceptual, philosophical, or theoretical matter: the question of what constitutes friendship, solidarity, neighbourliness, love – and the opposites, such as menace or danger.

Three possible outcomes follow from this, which we might ourselves adopt as a basic procedure. First, if your initial hypothesis regarding the good society turns out to be ideal, then you might claim to know something and, more importantly, to be able to prove your knowledge by legitimizing the idea against the material facts of the case (this is how the world wags, as it were). Second, if your initial hypothesis turns out to be wanting in some respect, then you are engaged in that process called learning: you now know more than you did before, and (more importantly) you know differently from what passed as the state of your knowledge in the first place (this is how the world might wag, so the question is 'should we try it?'). Third, you have to realize that either or both of these two previous outcomes must also be subject to further possible change, for it is certainly the case that, whether your society is ideal or not, you will continue to think about it and to reflect upon it further, even if only to persuade yourself, in a spirit of

---

[2] Ibid., 126.
[3] Ibid., 127–8.

optimism, that all now is for the best in the best of all possible worlds.[4] If you do not share such optimism, of course, you may want to reflect on things in order determinedly to change them. This entire process exemplifies the basic relations that exist between consciousness and history, between the operations of thought and the historical facts of material realities. In short, it asks us the question: what is the relation between the University (as the home of thinking as such) and history (the world of material action)?

No matter what the outcome of these initial propositions, you would return by necessity to Plato's first principle, which concerns the search for what we can call a 'just judgement'. While Plato calls that a principle of proper 'discrimination' between the good and the bad, the word that we usually use for it, in our contemporary moment, is 'criticism', which is itself intimately related, etymologically and in other ways, with Platonic 'discrimination'. To judge justly is to implement a mode of critical thinking. Yet this criticism presupposes also the desire to persuade someone other than yourself of the validity or otherwise of your own proposals for the ideal society. Logically, therefore, your plan must be subject to engagement and cross–fertilization with other rival proposals, which presupposes that there is dialogue among multiple voices and persons, sharing generally in the desire to make a good society. Further, in the act of attempting to persuade others about the preferred validity of one proposal over another, you are engaged in *teaching*.

Now, in the wake of all of this, it can be seen that the processes of research, learning, and teaching are all, indeed, fundamental to any sentient construction and arrangement of a social order. Moreover, these key elements of education are all directed towards the general social good. Insofar as we are conscious at all, our consciousness is formed according to some guiding and motivating drivers. The very condition of our consciousness is structured by education, and there are three basic elements that we can discern here. Firstly, our education is grounded in a search for principles of judgement, and thus also for the grounds of *justice*. Secondly, this education necessarily produces

---

[4] This, of course, is a simplistic parody of philosophical Optimism, as envisaged in Leibniz and satirized in Voltaire. See Voltaire, *Candide (suivi du poème sur le désastre de Lisbonne)*, ed. J. H. Brumfitt (Oxford University Press, Oxford, 1968).

the conditions of respectful debate or dialogue over rival contentious points of view or accounts of justice; and this yields the discovery that we are engaged in a search for *democratic* interpersonal relations, which are aimed towards a general egalitarianism. Thirdly, we have here an education whose purposeful motivation lies in the quest by all to realize as much of our human possibilities as possible; and we might usefully characterize this as an ongoing search for greater and greater human *freedoms*.

In all cases, the processes of education (research, teaching, learning) lead us to discover that things need not be as they currently are. Placing this in a broader philosophical frame, we might say that the search to extend justice is always ongoing, that we can always seek to extend the scope and ambit of democracy, and that freedoms are, by definition, infinite. Education does not provide justice, democracy and freedom, because these are concepts that are always to be sought, and always to be expanded and extended. The world is not just part-nature and part-construct, but is also subject to change, by intrinsic historical necessity. Although we may as humans be a part of nature, we are also, as conscious and sentient beings, set at an angle to nature and able to engage meaningfully with it.[5] That engagement is what we call the processes of civilization itself. Yet civilization is also not one eternal state of affairs, but rather a condition that is never definitive but always to be sought: as Gandhi apocryphally said of Western civilization, 'it might be a good idea'. Civilization is always to be desired, always itself to be further civilized. This means that education must be edifying in that it must always open up further new imaginations of yet greater democracy, justice, and freedom to extend the range of human possibilities.

In short, education seems to be fundamental to thinking itself, especially when we consider thinking as itself concerned with material and historical realities. Thinking and education are linked as in an intimate

[5] Behind this lies a distinction made by Hannah Arendt, in *The Human Condition*, 2nd edn, introduced by Margaret Canovan (University of Chicago Press, Chicago, 1998), between basic biological existence and the political existence given to us by speech and action. It is a distinction deployed extensively by Giorgio Agamben, especially in *Homo sacer*, trans. Daniel Heller-Roazen (Stanford University Press, Stanford, 1998) and in *Remnants of Auschwitz*, trans. Daniel Heller-Roazen (Zone Books, New York, 2005).

and even umbilical relation: one is in the womb of the other, and they promise the continuation of life – our ecological survival – itself. In at least this fundamental sense, then, thinking relates inevitably to education; and education leads, equally inevitably, to a realization that it is fundamental to history and to historical change in some basic fashion.

All of this places an extremely heavy responsibility on an institution that identifies itself as a house of thinking. Responsibility brings certain freedoms – for it must always be open to new reasoning – but it also raises questions about the entitlement to such freedoms. With this in mind, we can begin to examine the contemporary condition of our University institutions. We can ask why we have such institutions in our time and in our societies, and we can explore how they are titled and 'entitled' as 'Universities'.

↩

2010 saw the publication of the Browne Review *Securing a Sustainable Future for Higher Education*. The Browne reviewers had been set the task of focusing on the question of how to finance higher education in the future. It was for this reason that the abiding concern of the review itself, as also of the many responses to the review (both approving and hostile), would be primarily with money. The relatively small panel for the review (six members, under Browne's chairing) included three colleagues whose primary interests are financial (the economist and former Treasury adviser Diane Coyle; the banker Peter Sands; and Rajay Naik, who was at the time a board member of the 'Big Lottery Fund'). Browne himself was an engineer, as was one of the two VCs on the panel, Julia King. The two remaining members were Michael Barber, an educationalist with special interests in secondary-level education and a senior adviser on primary and secondary education to the Blair administration; and David Eastwood, Vice Chancellor at Birmingham and former Chief Executive of the Higher Education Funding Council for England (HEFCE).

Funding for higher education is undoubtedly difficult, and it is a *canard* to suggest, as some do, that academic staff and students prefer to ignore the costs and to expect that we are entitled to a free lunch at someone else's expense. Such an idea is a lingering relic of an age of deference to class privilege, an age when a highly privileged social class or elite assumed and then consolidated their minority right to a

University education that was to be paid for by the generality of the people through taxation alone. That age of deference, when such an arrangement was to be treated without complaint or resentment – when it was expected that I would 'know my place' – can no longer prevail. 'My place' is itself historically contingent on how I occupy it, and how others seek to control our shared place, be it the shared space of our nation, our community, or even our world.

This said, the political class has lacked the will necessary to find ways of funding a University sector that is now, at least in principle, dedicated to a mass system. It is accurate to state that, historically, the political class of all persuasions has completely and unquestionably respected the importance of higher education while, at the same time, it has consistently tried to find ever more ingenious ways of avoiding the responsibility of paying for it as a social good and the concomitant logic of accepting the costs of a University as the responsibility of government. Above, I have indicated that, ideally, the University is conditioned by a responsibility to the public good, to the search for a good society. That is jeopardized by a political structure that yields governments directed by the interests of the contemporary political class.

What, though, is this 'political class'? Not every politician is a member; but there is a relatively recent phenomenon that allows us to identify some specific class characteristics among our political leaders. In recent years, especially in the UK, we have witnessed the growth of the 'professionalization' of parliamentary politics. This is characterized by a specific professional career, in which some individuals follow what is now a well-trodden path from a degree in PPE (Politics, Philosophy, Economics), usually taken in a prestigious University, onwards to a position as researcher for an established political party, through to a post as an adviser to an already elected MP, which culminates in selection as a candidate for a 'safe seat'. Once in that seat, the new MP looks for an adviser in turn, taken from the cohort following that same route.

Elsewhere in the world, such political classes are shaped by different modes of corruption. In the USA, financial interests play the key role; and this is a model for many emerging economies in which essentially votes can be bought. As Joseph Stiglitz succinctly puts it, the USA is governed by a specific kind of democracy: 'one dollar, one vote', which is itself shaped by the massive corporates who now have most of the dollars.[6] The US political class consists of those who are 'incorporated' and kept in Congress by the interests of money, and this is given legitimacy by the activities of lobbying, a legitimized form of 'corporate welfare'. Outside the advanced economies, such practices are labelled more accurately and straightforwardly as 'corruption'; but they are all governed by the establishment of a political class governed primarily by its own interests and its own advancement.

Why is it important to note this? Well, it leads to a narrowing of the interests of establishment politicians – who thus become identifiable as a specific political class. They are no longer organically linked to a constituency in a society, and find instead their allegiances to parties and individuals. In short, the culture of this class is introspective, and not one that directs the primacy of government through the motivation of responsibility to a society. It is the inverse of what I have described above as the responsibility of the University.

We thus have a situation in which government becomes introspective and turns its back on its responsibilities to the public good, preferring the advancement of private careers. That stance contaminates the University system, driving it along exactly this same path. Internally, institutional governance is increasingly a matter of establishing its own version of the political class, which I have identified above as the managerial class. The problem with all of this – and the reason why it is important to note it – is that both the government and the University should be attending to their responsibilities outwards, directing energies towards the establishment of a good society and social order, but both have become introspective and governed primarily by the primacy of private interests. This whole phenomenon raises issues to do with a sense of 'entitlement' deriving from perceived advantages associated with membership of the political class – and, by extension, of the University that mimics the same mode of so-called professionalization.

The result of this introspection, through which government resists the responsibility to fund the University, is twofold. First, resentment is now inbuilt into the system, for the University is mediated as that type of institution – a public institution – that threatens to drain the public purse of resources. This is the view that constructs the figure of the 'taxpayer'

---

[6] See Joseph Stiglitz, *The Price of Inequality* (Penguin, London, 2013), 166; and see Stiglitz, *The Great Divide* (Norton, New York, 2015), *passim*, for the analysis of this.

as a curmudgeonly 'ordinary' individual, but one rather like Tolkien's Gollum, hoarding 'my precious' and becoming deformed through the obsession with the Ring as a hoard or resource.[7] Consequently, the sector finds itself in the unenviable position of having constantly to justify its own present existence or presence within a society, never mind future survival or sustainability. Secondly, the very idea of higher education as a mass system serving the public good is re-channelled into an account of the University that sees it primarily – and even purely – as a private good. That position, as I showed in Chapter 1 above, is the fundamental ideological driver that shaped Browne, from whose legacy the institution – and our society in general – now suffers.

Browne notes the growth in student numbers over the past fifty years or so, but then makes the first of a series of fundamental yet false assertions: 'The system was funded through general taxation, though those who benefited were generally from higher income back-grounds.'[8] This associates benefit solely with participation, and assumes that participation leads to private financial gain. To claim this is already to consider the University in a very narrowed and impoverished way, for it sees it only as a mechanism for individuals to seek private wealth. Yet it is simply a fact that the whole of society shares fully and fundamentally in the benefits of higher education. Higher education has helped us to engineer new and better roads for all, to establish better health care for all, to make more satisfying consumer products, and many things besides. Yet, for Browne, these public benefits are far outweighed by the private benefit of greater individual wealth (p. 21). This account of why we might have such a thing as a University at all has led to a new set of norms in which the sector has to be considered as a mechanism through which individuals seek private profit. In fact, this becomes, for Browne, the legitimizing force that underpins the very existence of the University.

---

[7] See Stefan Collini, *What are Universities For?* (Penguin, London, 2012), 96 on 'the taxpayer' as a 'mythical creature ... morose, prickly ... intensely suspicious of all contact with others ...'.

[8] The Browne Report, *Securing a Sustainable Future for Higher Education*, available at: https://www.gov.uk/government/uploads/system/uploads/attachment_data/fi le/422565/bis-10-1208-securing-sustainable-higher-education-browne-report.pdf (accessed 23 November 2017), 18 (subsequent references will be by page number in the text).

Further, Browne justifies the privatization of funding for the University by pointing out that attendance is a matter of choice and not compulsion: 'Unlike primary and secondary education which are paid for out of general taxation, higher education is neither compulsory nor universal' (p. 21). While this is true, it is true if and only if we view the matter purely and simply from the point of view of the individual student; and to do this is already to pre-judge matters and to convert the student into a consumer of a product. From the point of view of society as a whole, by contrast, the University as an institution is an absolute necessity: it is de facto compulsory that 'we' have the University as a core social institution, even if it is not compulsory that 'I', as a specific individual, should attend it. It is compulsory, as it were, for any society that believes in those fundamentals that we saw in Plato's *Republic*: the necessity of seeking justice and the desirability of such justice serving a shared public good. It is fundamental to any society that considers knowledge as itself intrinsically a good, and thus as something that is best shared and widely distributed. It is even more important if the use of the knowledge in question is directed not at enlarging the wallet of some fortunate individuals, but rather towards enhancing those basic and axiomatically good principles and conditions of an ever greater justice, democracy, and freedom.

Browne's review stands upon and yields unquestioningly what we recognize as the neoliberal University, an institution that has too easily accepted its misrepresentation as a mechanism for the privatization of knowledge in a society dedicated to the service of increasing the wealth of a specific class of individuals. The class in question may now be wider than the 6% privileged elite of the 1930s, say, yet it is still a class that is encouraged to see itself as divorced from the social and public good, at least in terms of its motivations for seeking and deploying knowledge. Within the now enlarged class of people who attend a University, there are, of course, sub-classes offering finer granularity to our class structure: the so-called elite Russell Group, usually set over Million+, ancient over redbrick, redbrick over former polytechnic, glass-plate, and so on. Thanks to the hierarchical stratification that structures this, we can in fact safely suggest that the 6% elite of the 1930s actually does still persist, even if it does so under the cover of a supposed classless widened participation.

The mass, while admitted, don't gain admittance to the inner sanctum, as it were, while those in that hierarchical centre of power and authority retain their social, political, and cultural standing. To put it crudely, while England used to have two elite institutions and half a dozen or so 'ordinary' Universities, now it has twenty-four elite institutions (the 'Russell Group') and around 130 others. Expressed as a percentage, this appears to be a disturbing worsening of class distinctions. The obvious question arises once we see this: has the prevailing class condition of 'entitlement' persisted, despite the ostensible growth in those who become 'entitled' (as BA, BSc, PhD, Professor, etc.) by our University system?

⤺

We started above in my initial thought-experiment from a position that considered the University as part of a society. Now, however, the norm that governs our institutions is one that more or less endorses the privatization of knowledge. In doing so, it essentially excludes the generality of people from knowledge – a position that might be loosely translated as 'keeping the masses entertained and ignorant', keeping us alive and amused with the distractions of Juvenalian 'bread and circuses'. In this sequestration of knowledge and its shared benefits, the neoliberal University provides a structure that has a familiar political history. Throughout the eighteenth century, what was once common land, commonly shared and tended, was serially 'enclosed'. Ostensibly, this was to improve agriculture; but its fundamental effect was to drive a wedge between increasingly wealthy landowners and rural individuals who lost their livelihoods. The legal 'title' to land established a class- and wealth-based social structure of 'entitlement' through the ownership of land. The equivalent now, in our supposed knowledge economy, is what we can most appropriately describe as the enclosure of the intellectual commons.

The contemporary University, insofar as it is governed by the demands of money-making for private gain, is one that is entirely complicit with, and even indeed largely responsible for, this enclosure of the intellectual commons. In its fundamental privatization and sequestration of knowledge (that is, of thinking and of criticism as such), this structure is one that drives a wedge between the University and its general public. Further, this University seeks to atomize the general public and also those who work within the University, thanks to its intrinsic logic of individualist competitiveness. Against all our prevailing contemporary pieties (especially those extolling our importance under the name of 'impact', which is simply the respectable name given to 'profit' or GDP growth), this has placed the University, surreptitiously and in an unacknowledged fashion, back into its mythic place as an 'ivory tower'. Browne succeeds in reducing the massive scope, ambit, and potential of the institution of the University – as an institution serving freedom, democracy, and justice – to the merest engine or machine for individual self-advancement in purely financial terms. He makes it an engine of greed, and reduces its ethos to one of acquisitive individualism.

Since 2010, when Browne gave legitimizing cover for this perverse ideological programme, there has been an acceleration of the process of privatization in the University sector. A good deal of that acceleration depends not just upon the drastic reduction of the University's 'mission', but also upon the narrowing of the lexicon about education, so that any talk of the University becomes talk about money. Stefan Collini summed it up succinctly when he wrote that 'it is scarcely an exaggeration to say that the greater part of public discourse about universities at present reduces to the following dispiriting proposition: universities need to justify getting more money and the way to do this is by showing that they help to make more money'.[9] In short, the single greatest indicator of 'success' in the University now is an increase in annual turnover. The institution has become a shell for the circulation of money, and thus a mechanism for boosting GDP, which is itself, of course, simply a somewhat superficial index of economic activity, shifting money around.[10]

Those nobler ideas of justice, democracy, and freedom have been increasingly ignored in the rush for private profit and for the privatization of all profits in all spheres. In the resulting drive towards the enclosure of the intellectual commons and the privatization of all knowledge, the contemporary University has forgotten not just its public duty and responsibility, but the very existence of the public sphere itself as anything other than a marketplace of commodities,

---

[9] Collini, *What are Universities For?*, x.
[10] For an excellent lay-person's guide to GDP and the 'multiplier' effect, see John Lanchester, 'Let's call it failure', *London Review of Books*, 31:1 (3 January 2013), 3–6.

among which we now trade our own product. In so doing – and especially because knowledge is not and can never be a product or a commodity at all – the University enters into a crisis of sustainability. That crisis is bigger than a problem for the University solely: it is a crisis that encompasses the whole of society. At stake is the profound ecological question of how the University might relate to an environment that includes the world of nature as well as that of civilization.

When our great and exciting initial promise – how to imagine a social order – is reduced in this way to an obsession with financial input and output, then we have much diminished not just the idea of the University, but the material fact of it. The neoliberal University – the University that exists simply as a particular instance of business turnover in a nation's GDP – has had the effect not just of shrinking the idea of the University in this way: it has also had the effect of shrinking the range of human possibilities and freedoms, including the freedom to sustain ourselves ecologically on the planet.

This trajectory must be resisted, self-evidently, if we assume that there is some desire to sustain our own existence and that of both our social and natural environments. Thus, we must re-think the question 'Why "University"?' We can begin this, in some detail, and with one of the most recent – and revealing – documents that indicate how a government typically considers the University in 2016. The UK government here stands as typical of the current dispensation more or less through all the advanced economies.

⮑

In September 2015, the UK government issued a document called *Guidance for Higher Education Providers: Criteria and Process for Applying for University and University College Title*. The first thing we see, on opening this document, is not discursive prose, but instead a visual diagram. This is the 'process flowchart', outlining the various stages of managerial and administrative procedures leading to the conferring of the title of 'University'. It is laid out like a family tree diagram, starting at the top with the first thing to be done, which is to 'contact HEFCE', followed immediately by instructions to 'select a name' and set up an audit to validate student numbers and governance. At this point, you submit the application.

HEFCE then assesses the application, and the next stage is for

HEFCE to make its recommendations to what was then the relevant government department, the Department for Business, Innovation and Skills. At this point, the chart diverges, depending on whether the Secretary of State decides against (in which case you get a letter saying why) or approves for further action. If your hypothetical institution is to be HEFCE-funded, the process then goes through the usual Privy Council approval stages; but if it is not to be HEFCE-funded, then, essentially, that's it: you are now a University (subject to approval at Companies House, essentially a business procedure).

One might imagine that there would be, somewhere, some stringent criteria regarding the constitution of a University institution, on which the Secretary of State might base a decision. After all, when the document turns away from visuals and to discursive prose, the first thing it does is to make a fundamental and serious statement: 'University title is prestigious, desirable, and valuable.'[11] Yet the criteria for entitling oneself as 'University' – with all the other potential entitlements and responsibilities that such a title entails – appear to relate almost entirely to the observance of procedural protocols.

There is no doubting the high seriousness of these processes. They show the extremely rigorous and complex mechanics of an exacting challenge for any institution that seeks the title. The process has to be rigorous, certainly, for it is a process that is intended 'to protect the interests of students and the wider public by regulating access to university title and university college title and protecting its integrity' (Introduction, paragraph 1). As in a market for commodities or resources, value is related in proportion to scarcity: not everyone who applies will succeed, and success depends upon overcoming the challenges posed by the processes. The door to an obvious paradox opens here, as in any market-driven construction of prestige and value, for the more institutions there are bearing the title, the less valuable will

---

[11] See 'University title and university college title', available at: https://www.gov.uk/government/uploads/system/uploads/attachment_data/file/459763/BIS-15-523-university-title-and-university-college-title.pdf (accessed 5 January 2018). Subsequent references will be to paragraph numbers and located in the text. The language is consistently odd in the document, in that every reference to the 'university title' comes with neither indefinite nor definite article. It is never 'a university title' nor 'the title', with the peculiar effect that it sounds like a literal translation from a language that makes no use of such articles, like Russian or Mandarin, say.

the title become according to the economics of supply and demand. At the same time, the document exists in the first place precisely in order to encourage 'new providers' to secure the title. The more the document succeeds in that aim, therefore, the less prestigious will the title become according to its own underlying commercial ideology or structure for determining 'value'.

Casting this intrinsic problem concerning marketization aside for the moment, we must acknowledge that the process will be governed by an exacting rigour. Standards must be met. Everything depends on how successful you are in describing how your administrative and managerial procedures conform to the standards set by government. The 'prestige' of the title derives from the fact that those who secure it have proved themselves as being of the required standard to join an elite – even if this elite is now ever widening and thus designed to be less elitist. However, it is very important to note that all the relevant standards in question here relate only to *procedural and bureaucratic* practices. There is no substantive criterion that describes what the title describes: that is, no description as yet of what a University is or might actually be. It starts to look, although this is unstated, as if the prestige is really the prestige of the management of the institution rather than that of its academic practices.

Alongside the troubling commercial logic here – according to which scarcity raises prices – there is another logic at work: a logic of seduction or 'desirability', in the document's own term. In tantalizingly proffering something as available only if you follow its exacting demands, you make it seem (literally) attractive and thus desirable. To grasp it is to promise the satisfaction of that desire; and satisfaction is not and cannot be guaranteed for all, else it would not be desirable but only commonplace. The logic of desire promises also disappointment and, very importantly, exclusion or exclusivity. The downside of this is a culture of inbuilt resentment, a *ressentiment* that Pankaj Mishra, for example, traces as the root of what he describes as today's 'age of anger'.[12]

We can therefore be in no doubt about the value, desirability, and prestige of the title: this title will be highly valued precisely because of its rarity, and measured by the difficulty of achieving success in

---

[12] Pankaj Mishra, *Age of Anger* (Allen Lane, London, 2017), 14 and *passim*.

acquiring the title. We can, however, be in some doubt regarding the fundamental commercial logic that underlies the thinking in the document. In considering the University in market terms, logic dictates that it is a reduction in the number of Universities that will ensure prestige, value, and desirability. This is at odds, of course, with the driving principle, which is to bring more and more institutions into being. To square that circle, the thinking is that with an increase in the number of Universities, 'competition' for differentiation and distinction among them will be the driver of value. In the banal cliché that persists even today in the thinking of Browne, competition will 'drive up standards'.[13]

Title and – more importantly if also more surreptitiously – entitlement have completely supplanted any concern whatsoever for the actual substance of what a University does, or what it might be for. What is at stake in the government's document, and what explains the seeming self-contradictions, is not really the question of the title at all; rather, what is at stake is the 'entitlement' that derives from the name of the University. This is one reason, of course, why the document starts the entire process by choosing an appropriate name for your institution, as if having a name were the most important and fundamental aspect of the exercise. There must be no possible confusion between your organization and any other organization that might have a similar name. It would be inappropriate for 'Private Study' to claim the salary of 'General Knowledge', for example.

However, we see this at work in the private sector. The big data organization Cambridge Analytica is not a part of Cambridge University, but surreptitiously trades on its name; and combine 'Cambridge' with 'Analytica', and you claim the prestige of learning from ancient times, hinting in that Latinate name also at the intellectual standing of A. N. Whitehead and Bertrand Russell's *Principia Mathematica*. Titles are not really about value, prestige, and desire at all, in fact. Really and more honestly, titles are about the value of a name and of a reputation. In short, the document's tacit message is about the

[13] John Browne, 'Driving force: the rationale for the reforms', *Times Higher*, 16–23 February 2017, available at: https://www.timeshighereducation.com/features/he-bill-why-universities-are-not-supermarkets?utm_source=the_editorial_newsletter&utm_medium=email&utm_content=other_stories&utm_campaign=the_editorial_newsletter (accessed 23 November 2017).

status of an unquestioned entitlement, an entitlement that depends not on the substance of what one actually does but upon the tradability and commercial value of a name. Often, this kind of entitlement is an entitlement to money; almost always, it is an entitlement to status and comparative power, the power that comes with unearned social standing – just as with class.

What is most striking, then, about the government's document is that it never once indicates any definition of the substantive essence of what constitutes a University. It is almost as if the entitlement is not related to anything substantial, other than an ability to go through certain procedures and motions with the required rigour. There is something oddly disconcerting – even fraudulent – about this: it is like the more or less fraudulent acquisition of an academic title – 'professor', say – without having done any properly academic work, but having only conformed to certain protocols or bureaucratic practices. The same might apply to senior positions, where a VC might not have demonstrated anything other than an ability to secure administrative-led promotions, the 'ability' in question being conditioned by conformist 'playing the managerial game'.[14]

We have seen instances of such 'entitlement' historically; and they relate to the idea and functions of an aristocracy. Individuals in this kind of social class sedimentation become 'entitled' not by virtue of anything substantial that they may do, but rather purely by dint of who they are through the merest accident of birth or genetics.[15] To subscribe to the political view that some individuals can be differentiated from others as being 'aristocrats' is to endorse an idea of the innate and inborn value of all individuals. It yields an 'elite' in its older theologically transcendental form as a group who are 'elect' or chosen by a transcendental power through a form of essentialist predestination. The

---

[14] In wider society, we know of some recent scandalous entitlements: Jimmy Savile was knighted in 1990 'for charitable services', and was given a 'Papal Knighthood' that same year. It appears that he used the standing given by these 'entitlements' to engage in sexual abuse. Another example might be Fred Goodwin, who was knighted 'for services to banking' in 2004. There was a controversy over the annulment of that knighthood in 2012, and a further controversy over Goodwin's 'entitlement' to an extraordinarily generous pension.

[15] See Pierre Bourdieu on the 'aristocracy of culture' in *Distinction* (1979), trans. Richard Nice (Routledge, London, 1986), 24.

class distinctions that follow from this are to be taken as self-validating; and there can be no such thing as serious agency for any individual. Your place in the order of things is given, fully and essentially: it is precisely the *Brave New World* of Huxley's 1932 dystopia.

Yet, if the contemporary University institution is anything, it must surely be an institution that seeks to *legitimize* titles and entitlements in terms of actual material and historical research, teaching, learning, and working for the benefit of the society that sustains and benefits from these activities. The very fact that the University is an institution that deals in consciousness as such means that it is diametrically opposed to any idea of an essential or somehow pre-ordained identity or selfhood for any individual historical being. It subscribes to the belief that actions must be accounted for, and that they should be legitimized according to agreed norms and legislations.

The reason why the typical University structures itself around examinations, qualifications, and accreditations is precisely that it does not accept 'prestige' or distinction as something inbuilt: prestige, in this context, has to be attained and worked for. In 'entitling' individuals, a University lends them credibility and authority; but such authority has always to be earned. When individuals claim an unearned authority, the authority itself is illegitimate, and it deviates into an assertion of power instead. The danger in any society that is organized around such power is that it can easily lapse into force and violence as a means of expressing an argument or a predisposition or preference. It is precisely the earning of authority – through the free exploration of justice and knowledge – that can alleviate that tendency to resolve conflict or difference through brute physical or martial power.[16] Indeed, one might go so far as to claim that the proper practising of politics is precisely the positive transformation of violence into dialogue, with a view to establishing a solution of conflicting interests that can be legitimized by an appeal to a common ground to be found via just debate.

Against all this, the governmental guidance document seems tacitly to presuppose that the procedural criteria for securing the title

---

[16] For a fuller exploration of the key issues here – concerning power, force, violence, and strength – see Hannah Arendt, *On Violence* (Harcourt Inc., New York and London, 1970). On prestige, see Stephen Shapiro's excellent account in his 'Intellectual labor power, cultural capital, and the value of prestige', *South Atlantic Quarterly*, 108 (2009), 249–64.

will simply and straightforwardly reveal what a University is in fact. Those procedural criteria are fully and boldly stated. To gain the title, you must have degree awarding powers; you must have a cohort of students (which can be relatively small); you must show that you are well governed; your management arrangements must conform to good corporate practice and guidance; and you must show that your finances and financial planning and forecasting indicate that you can sustain yourself (without specifying for how long).

When it comes to what we might expect as the core activities of teaching, learning, and research, we find this: 'We need to be assured as to the current and future *management* of your standards, the quality of your learning and teaching and your academic performance' (paragraph 5; stress added). The priority throughout, as in this paradigmatic example, is always focused not on matters of substance, but rather on the management of and assurance of the 'quality' of a generalized 'performance'. This, then, is of little actual help in letting us know what a University actually is or might be.

The criteria are bland, and at times vacuously tautological. If you award degrees, you are a University; and if you are a University, you are that institution that awards degrees. If you have students, you are a University; and if you are a University, you must have some students. It starts to look here as if the government believes that what makes a University a University is determined entirely by the internal processes that keep its engine ticking over on a daily basis, and by the determined preference of some institutions to claim their entitlements. There seems to be scant interest in what are the nature and purpose of the engine that is actually ticking. What 'defines' a University, in this document, is procedure and protocol. When we arrive at what might look to be core substantive issues – the substance of teaching and learning (there is no mention of research) – the document falls in to the nebulous rhetoric of a generalized notion of an 'assured quality', and of the processes by which such quality is 'assured'. There is, of course, a difference between establishing the substantive and material quality of something and merely assuring us of its existence.

We can turn now to some considerations of that substance, and of the conditions that govern the structures and ethos of the contemporary University, in these times when we work under the assumed entitlements that are ingrained within neoliberal economics.

3
The exceptional and the ordinary

The contemporary University, shaped by the prevailing norms of market fundamentalism and the commercialization of all human interests, does not spring up like a rabbit from a magician's hat. Like all institutions it develops historically and according to specific conditions that make its emergence seem not only possible but also reasonable or even inevitable. As an institution that tacitly embodies conventionally agreed values, it passes as entirely ordinary, uncontroversial – and merely 'realistic' – when its specific configuration at each moment appears to be coherent with its wider social environment and all its tensions. This may be one reason why the neoliberal University has no explicit code or defined rationale: its intrinsic essence appears to be so comfortable with its moment that it becomes self-evident that the University must adopt the values that it does at the present time.

Historically, we have had to provide a specific and dedicated rationale for the University only at moments of significant change, or when the institution has irrupted into an existing network of social relations, usually because of some degree of social unrest, conflict, or dissenting social movements. Some historical examples will help clarify this. At the turn of the eighteenth century, Giambattista Vico outlined the form and function of the University of Naples through his Rectorial Addresses at the start of each academic year between 1699 and 1707. This was a period when Naples was itself at the centre of the War of Spanish Succession, and Vico's construction of the University is largely concerned with a specific mode of 'cosmopolitanism' appropriate to these conditions.[1] In 1810, Wilhelm von Humboldt saw the University of Berlin as the mechanism for the expression of a national culture, national character, and identity, all suitable for the emerging identity of a new German state.[2] John Henry Newman delivered the lectures that became his *Idea of the University* in 1858, specifically to establish a Catholic University in Ireland in a period when it was becoming increasingly contentious to believe that only a Protestant intelligence could adopt a position of social authority and power. Jaspers also wrote an 'idea of the University', initially in 1923 and during the tumult of Weimar; and he then re-wrote it, advancing a very different account in 1946, when his presiding idea was the de-Nazification of the institution.

Closer to and more relevant to our current predicaments, the student revolts and 'events' of May 1968 that spread across Europe had received an impetus from the USA in campus protests against the Vietnam War. For at least a brief historical period, the University became associated not just with a renewed interest in imperialism and its consequences, but also and yet more fundamentally with dissent.[3] The events gathered a momentum behind the demands that we should hear the voices of the politically dispossessed and the silenced; and this gave a determining force to the promotion of free speech and, with that, the absolute value of dissent as a foundational principle governing any free or democratic society. It is, in fact, the end of this period that we are currently witnessing; and it coincides with a systematic clamping down on freedom of speech, especially through the restrictions that are increasingly placed on academic freedom worldwide.

What is it that lies behind the current situation, then? It is helpful if we see this in terms of the ethical and political demand that we attend to the voices of 'ordinary' people; and part of doing that

---

[1] See Barbara Ann Naddeo, *Vico and Naples: The Urban Origins of Modern Social Theory* (Cornell University Press, New York, 2011), esp. 50–88. See also John Robertson, *The Case for the Enlightenment: Scotland and Naples 1680–1760* (Cambridge University Press, Cambridge, 2005).

[2] See Bill Readings, *The University in Ruins* (Harvard University Press, Cambridge, MA, 1996), 46, 65ff.

[3] At the same time, it should also be noted that some of this is governed by the self-interest of middle-class students, who were now being drafted in large numbers, after the State had already drafted the poor and largely black community for the war effort.

involves silencing those 'exceptional' people – the intellectuals among them – who have enjoyed an authority to speak out and to be heard heretofore. My contention here is that this attitude offers an extremely perverse account of 'democracy', an account in which a socially privileged class – those who have entitled themselves – patronize people precisely by describing them as 'ordinary', and then seek to control and to mobilize 'ordinariness' as an instrument of politics, with many concomitant appeals to 'the people'.

The few examples of the historical construction of 'ideas of the University' above demonstrate that whenever we feel impelled explicitly to construe a version of what a University is, much depends on the particular historical circumstances in which we pose the question. Further, it becomes imperative to question the configurations of what constitutes legitimate 'knowledge' and its institutional forms precisely at moments when both the society and the existing forms of the University are entering into some critical moment, a moment of disjunction that shows in any form of social unrest. We are now, again, at just such a moment, a moment when knowledge itself is becoming increasingly characterized as illegitimate because it is 'exceptional' and not on the side of 'the people'.

Our contemporary predicament is one that constitutes a moment that – after the 2008 financial crisis, collapse and depression – has brought about a failure of trust in many of our existing social institutions. Those institutions – governmental, educational, religious, political – no longer command the respect that they might once have enjoyed. The University, now – and especially in times that are described as 'post-truth', and when knowledge itself is demeaned as 'elitist' – sits precisely in the centre of this critical moment.

One small example will suffice here to show what this means. Interviewed by Chuck Todd on NBC news, Kellyanne Conway, senior adviser to the US President Donald Trump, famously came up with the concept of 'alternative facts'. At one point in the interview, she said that 'there's no way to really quantify crowd numbers', referring to the lies advanced by Trump and his press secretary Sean Spicer about attendance at the inauguration. On the tape, you hear Todd's bemused response to this, and Conway immediately adopted the position of the wronged victim, wronged by one who has superior knowledge: 'You can laugh at me all you want.' The key here is the insertion of 'at me', which serves two functions: it immediately personalizes the argument instead of focusing on its substantive value; and it displaces the issue of the value of an argument onto the valuation of an individual.

As Conway shrugs her shoulders, she is also shrugging off the factual correction of her case and argument, and showing that she – as a representative of the entire political establishment that she serves, that new US 'political class' that is governed by a corrupting intimacy with corporate business – cares nothing for those who 'evaluate' her at anything less than her own self-evaluation.[4] Knowledge of facts cedes place entirely here to a trashing of knowledge as such, and its replacement with 'alternative facts' that are no facts at all, but rather just what an individual prefers to say. It is not even that Conway 'believes' her alternative facts; it is enough simply to present them and state them to be facts.

To 'correct' this with empirical proof is taken here as an attack upon those who identify not just as 'ordinary' people, but also, in the extreme, as 'ignorant'. The correction is no longer understood properly for what it is: an attack upon ignorance itself.

This political complex is played out also in the very institutions that should centre their identity on the assault upon ignorance: the University and associated educational institutions. The problem that is arising now, however, is that any suggestion that ignorance and prejudice (pre-judging issues) might be 'corrected' by teaching and by research institutes an explicit but unintended split between the 'ordinary' and the 'exceptional', with the exceptional being re-cast as elitist, its advocates allegedly pursuing their own privileged elite interests at the expense of ordinary people. In this state of affairs, we are coming dangerously close to an identification of thinking itself as intrinsically elitist and self-interested – and therefore never to be trusted. This is in turn tantamount to a validation and legitimization of prejudice.

There exist at least two cultural precedents that will shed light on this state of affairs. The first is in Shakespeare's *Othello*. In the long and

[4] For the recording of the interview, see: www.realclearpolitics.com/video/2017/01/22/chuck_todd_to_kellyanne_conway_alternative_facts_are_not_facts.html (accessed 23 November 2017).

troubling middle scene of this play, Act 3 scene 3, Iago taunts Othello with the false information that Desdemona has been unfaithful to him by sleeping with Cassio. Othello hovers uncertainly throughout this, desperate to believe that Desdemona is faithful, but now troubled by thinking of her with Cassio. He cannot bear the condition of doubt, and demands certainty instead; in his mind, 'to be once in doubt / Is once to be resolved'. His determination to have absolutely clear and distinct knowledge leads him to the extraordinary position where he demands of Iago, 'Villain, be sure thou prove my love a whore / Be sure of it; give me the ocular proof'. Iago responds by giving Othello what he now wants: a picture that will confirm what is simply a pre-judgement, a prejudice: 'Would you, the supervisor, grossly gape on – / Behold her topp'd?' Othello, now having a pre-judgement confirmed by a pure act of imagination, replies, 'Death and damnation'.

This is instructive as an example whereby the search for knowledge can easily veer into the confirmation of prejudice, without regard for the truth. It is, of course, a prejudice from which Othello himself has suffered, a prejudice against himself as a Moor that he has internalized. Genuine knowledge depends, ostensibly paradoxically, upon the entertainment of doubt, and not upon the determination to validate what one currently thinks, suspects, or wishes to be the case. As this case shows, survival itself depends upon the sustaining of doubt and the avoidance of succumbing to final solutions.

In terms of titles and entitlement, *Othello* is again very much to the point. Virtually all the central characters are concerned for their name. In Act 2 scene 3, Iago forces Michael Cassio to drink alcohol. Cassio then gets into a drunken brawl that disturbs Othello, rousing him from the bed he shares with Desdemona. Cassio is publicly disgraced, at which point he falls into lamentation: 'Reputation, reputation, reputation! O! I have lost / My reputation! I have lost th'immortal part of / myself, and what remains is bestial.' At this point in the play, Iago is utterly dismissive of the value of reputation, saying that 'Reputation is an idle and most false / imposition: oft got without merit, and lost without / deserving: you have lost no reputation at all, / unless you repute yourself such a loser.'

Yet Iago learns from this, and indeed learns to use the power of reputation to advance an evil falsehood. Playing on Othello's growing suspicious mind, he makes an insinuation (in Act 3 scene 3) about the possibility of Othello being damaged precisely by the loss of a good name: 'Good name in man and woman, dear my lord, / Is the immediate jewel of their souls: / Who steals my purse steals trash; 'tis something, nothing; / 'Twas mine, 'tis his, and has been slave to thousands: / But he that filches from me my good name / Robs me of that which not enriches him / And makes me poor indeed.' What Iago has learned here is precisely that reputation can be more powerful than money, and he uses this fact to gain in power over Othello's mind and emotional wellbeing.

What these competing views of reputation demonstrate is that it need not have any bearing on reality at all. It is indeed 'oft got without merit' (Act 2 scene 2); yet, once it is indeed gained, it can become 'the immediate jewel' (Act 3 scene 3) of a human soul, worth more than anything that can be designated by mere money. It is this construction of reputation – in the form of the name, title, entitlement, and brand of a University – that is now so important. The same is observable in politics, which has now largely become a matter not of governing but of the making and trashing of reputations and of the political status – and authoritative entitlements – that such reputations give.

The second cultural example, from a much more recent date, lets us see that reputation – or the clear identification of someone or some institution through the recognition of a name – is indeed utterly independent of empirical realities. The situation in which we thus find ourselves has itself already been satirized. In 1933, the year in which Hitler assumed the Chancellorship of Germany, the Marx Brothers released their movie *Duck Soup*, directed by Leo McCarey. Like almost all the comedies of the Marx Brothers, this one depends on a series of quite serious situations that are dealt with in the manner of farce.

The political corruption that underlines the installation of Rufus T. Firefly (Groucho Marx) as Ambassador of Freedonia (under threat internationally from Sylvania) by Mrs Gloria Teasdale (Margaret Dumont) is presented as an utterly ludicrous phenomenon, even if it is one that is immediately recognizable during this extremely desperate period after the 1929 crash. The intrigue in the film collapses the corruption of international relations by money into the corruption of politics by the pursuit of wealth through any means, however immoral or irrational. Sexual seduction joins with the usual proto–Beckettian absurdities and slapstick in which the physical body mocks the reasoning mind. As in farce, multiple improbable disguises, mirrors, and mistaken identities proliferate. Yet the relevance for 1930s politics could not be clearer, especially with reference to events in Germany and Prussia and to the political conditions after the crash that would lead, in 1932, to the rejection of Herbert Hoover and the installation of F. D. Roosevelt with his 'new deal'.

At a crucial turn in the film, we have no fewer than three people answering to the name 'Firefly'. Having locked Groucho in a bathroom, both Chico Marx and Zeppo Marx disguise themselves as Firefly, and both get into the bedroom of Mrs Teasdale, where they are looking for information that will be helpful to Sylvania. Just as Mrs Teasdale sees Firefly (Chico) leave the room, Firefly (Zeppo) immediately reappears, to Mrs Teasdale's evident consternation. 'I saw you leave the room, with my own eyes,' she says. The reply: 'Yeah? Well, who're ya gonna believe? Me, or your own eyes?' The problem is compounded yet further, and more farcically, when another Firefly (Groucho), having escaped, also now enters.

'Who're ya gonna believe? Me, or your own eyes?' is a line that encapsulates a particular problem, based on doubt and knowledge, that advances the plot of *Othello*; and it is of great relevance – politically as well as institutionally in the University – again today. For, today, this same problem consumes a huge amount of political debate, focusing on the question of whom to trust and whether we can be permitted to trust the empirical evidence of our own senses, our own eyes. Increasingly, it also becomes farcical, as is the case with Donald Trump, starting with the obvious assault on empirical evidence surrounding the size of the crowd at the inauguration, but building from that to really serious acts designed to consolidate ignorant prejudice.

Politically, in the USA, this 'Firefly orthodoxy' is being established in the name of 'ordinary' Americans. The desired effect is to persuade those ordinary people to dismiss or at least distrust all informed news. Informed news depends upon standard protocols of accuracy, validity, and truth as measured by empirical evidence. By contrast, the psychology that mobilizes 'ordinariness' works against this, to persuade us that such (accurate, validated) news is 'exceptional', made by and for 'exceptional' individuals, and of absolutely no relevance to 'ordinary' individuals.

One thing that follows and that is of profound relevance in our consideration of the contemporary condition of the University is precisely the scepticism about trust – and above all, about trust in the power of teaching, research, and learning. We face a historical situation when, as we saw, through the rise to prominence of Thatcherism and Reaganomics in the 1980s, a new economic neoliberalism of market fundamentalism has become normative. The sector leadership of the University has not only accepted the mantra 'There is no alternative', but has worked instead to extend the logic of neoliberal economics right into the heart of our intellectual life. It has embraced the very monster that it should exist to expose and question. All must now be monetized – and this includes not just our regular practices of teaching, learning, research, and so-called impact, but also the monetization of our very names and titles as institutions. We have our 'brand', our 'reputation', and – like the character of Michael Cassio in *Othello* – our 'good name'.

This has become the cornerstone of entitlement. It is utterly vacuous. However, a subscription to the value of the good name can also become a powerful populist political weapon, as it is in the hands especially of the contemporary extreme political right, who have taken on fully the legacy of an unchallenged neoliberalism and applied it to all aspects of social and private life. The effects of this on the University are enormous.

The mantra 'There is no alternative' is taken as read, as a statement that is now so obvious as to pass as ordinary; and anyone who proposes even the possibility of change is decried and told to 'be realistic'. Yet being realistic here means accepting things as they really are at this moment (the state of things as being ordinary) rather than acknowledging our ability to change the way things are (to 'take exception') – and our responsibility to change things when they are serving people badly. For the intellectual – and thus by extension for the University – the responsibility is not necessarily to change things ourselves, but to make clear, by teaching and research, that it is indeed possible to discover other ways of organizing ourselves and shaping the world and its history. Our intellectual task is to broaden the range of human possibilities. This is what I have insistently described as our role with respect to the edifying enhancement of freedoms.

It is perhaps precisely because our sector leadership has been utterly conformist in the past forty years or so that it has felt no compulsion to speak out and to articulate a logical account of the 'idea of the University', or to attempt to challenge 'the way we live now', to borrow Trollope's poignant phrase. Because it has conformed to the ideology of total marketization and market fundamentalism, there has been no need to explain the values for which the University stands. It has become utterly 'natural' to think of it as a servant of a neoliberal economy, one which 'naturally' establishes structural inequality (and thus resentment as the primary mood) in the social order. This now passes as an acknowledgment of the ordinary; and anything that disturbs this can be de-legitimized because it represents not just an 'exception', but rather an exception that is characterized as being the very enemy of the ordinary, and thus the enemy of ordinary people. This gives that basic resentment an object against which to vent its spleen: the University, the intellectual, knowledge, and the very activity of thinking itself.

If we are to understand why it is the case that this neoliberal version of the University is entering now into a period of crisis, especially since 2008 and the financial crash, then it makes sense to widen our historical lens a little. In doing so, we will find that it is – as is the case in my examples above – the fact of social or national conflict that plays a key role in determining how we imagine our higher education in its forms and functions. In this case, that conflict was, above all, the Second World War and its lingering aftermath through the Cold War.

The roots of our current anxieties about the University and its survival are to be found broadly in the period between 1945 and 1989. In that period, martial conflict gave way to cultural competition, between the demands of a so-called 'free-market economy' on one side and a demand for a more structured so-called egalitarianism, based on state interventions, on the other. We called this the Cold War. In time, the seeds that were sown through that long series of conflicts have themselves flowered, yielding the specific crisis regarding the state of knowledge, truth, politics, and ethics in these first decades of the twenty-first century.

We can indeed be glad that the martial conflicts of 1939–45 gave way to a different and ostensibly less violent form of conflict in the Cold War. We can be further glad that the damages caused by a Cold

War have given way to something that, again ostensibly, is even less threatening to human survival. First of all, war becomes displaced onto international sporting contests between competing nations. Then, we reach what looks to be a final 'resolution' of international conflict with the instauration of global and globalized 'free-market' competition. In this development, national boundaries themselves can be at least partly erased: it is no longer a question of France warring against or competing with Germany, say; rather it is Amazon competing with Google, neither of these latter having any specific geo-political or national location or identity as such. This mentality is what lies behind the thinking of those who once agreed with Francis Fukuyama that we are at 'the end of history', having supposedly resolved all conflicts under the sign of the free neoliberal market.

Yet the acceptance of the 'no alternative' mantra makes the resulting world marketplace an extraordinarily silent place. No voice other than those supportive of the market fundamentalism that governs our world can be heard. This has a major detrimental effect on the University, especially on the post-1968 University that I have described above as being characterized by the defence of free speech and dissent.

The point about a dissenting voice is that it calls into question the clichés of ideological – ordinary – norms. It casts doubt on the value of 'the name' as such, and especially on the name of those who mindlessly repeat those clichés without scrutiny or judgement. It says that dialogue and reason are worth more than the populist celebrity of a name, be it Trump, Thatcher, Oxford, Harvard, or anything else that has gained a reputation and that now stands on it without feeling any need to re-earn that reputation and that social standing. Silence is its enemy.

Does it follow that the voice of the critic must always be 'exceptional' in some way? Does it follow that the intellectual who intervenes in the clichés that constitute normal belief in our time must be regarded as an enemy of the popular or of the ordinary? A great deal is invested in 'ordinariness' in the current political climate. The tacit rationale is that democracy entails a respect for everyone equally and for all voices; and it follows from this that democracy is the group voice of people who are 'ordinary' and not exceptions to the rule, people who will neither make nor take exception to prevailing social, political, or cultural norms.

This is awkward in two ways. First and foremost, as I claim, it is patronizing: it fails, fundamentally, to address the extraordinary condition of every individual human single life considered in its singularity. Secondly, it permits someone to set herself or himself aside from 'the ordinary' in order to assess ordinary people precisely as ordinary; and in doing so, it permits that individual to understand herself or himself as 'exceptional', to self-declare as exceptional. The logic of populism that follows from this is inherently self-contradictory, as we will see in a subsequent chapter.

Here, however, the salient point is that the very category of 'the ordinary' is proposed and constructed in order to silence the dissenting voice, to make it seem outside and beyond what can be ordinarily accepted as the real. Dissent – the very cornerstone of learning – is thus degraded and silenced. It is an exception that will be used to justify the normative rule of a fallacious 'ordinary life' of the everyday individual. It thus precludes the possibility of allowing any individual to discover and reveal what is extraordinary within their very own 'ordinary' existence.

$$\backsim$$

It was during the Second World War, in 1943, that the eminent literary critic F. R. Leavis published *Education and the University*. Perhaps unsurprisingly – given this moment when the devastations of the war were obvious and when the visible enemy was Nazism with its pyres of burning books during the 1930s, superseded by the pyres of corpses of the slaughtered in the camps – Leavis felt that 'liberal culture' itself was under threat. Leavis considered the 'liberality' of a liberal education as a concept indebted to a Latinate root: *liberalitas*, meaning 'relating to the freeborn condition' of an individual. When he placed this alongside 'culture', he also consistently gave it a specific nationalist inflection, having inherited such a notion from the concept of *Bildung* as expressed in Humboldt's Berlin after 1810. One clear consequence follows, in which he placed England, the character of Englishness – and thus English literature – at the core of his idea of the University. As we will see, the project is to establish the 'exceptional' condition of English, of 'the English', and of those schooled in the 'exceptional' mode of literary criticism proposed by Leavis himself.

In some ways, his updating of Newman's *Idea of the University* in the opening chapter of *Education and the University* is his own war effort, and as such it stands as a defence of civilization against barbarism. Yet Leavis did not argue that the key threat to civilization here was the Nazis, but rather that it was the University itself. Leavis claims, first, that 'the idea of liberal culture has been defeated and dissipated'. Further, this has happened as a consequence of 'advancing specialization'. Then we get the shocking hammer blow when he says that the key driver of such specialization is the University itself: 'the production of specialists ... tends to be regarded as the supreme end of the university, its *raison d'être*'.[5] It follows from this, shockingly yet logically for Leavis, that it is the University itself that threatens liberal culture, and that it does so through a concentration on the production of 'experts' who specialize narrowly within very carefully circumscribed academic fields, to the detriment of a more general liberal culture.[6]

This specialization, according to Leavis, distracts the academic and the student from a more proper attention to the world and to the material conditions of everyday life (which I myself prefer to describe not as 'liberal culture' but as a 'culture of liberation'). It does this in two ways. First, it drives a wedge between the work of the University and the world of the general public; and it is precisely the necessity of bridging those two spheres that, for Leavis, is the very specific task that makes a University a University. 'An urgently necessary work', he writes, 'is to explore the means of bringing the various essential kinds of specialist knowledge and training into effective relation with informed general intelligence, humane culture, social conscience and political will.'[7]

Advanced specialization arrests the possibility of establishing that relation, yielding effectively a construction of society in which the world of the University exists separately from everyday life, the 'ivory tower' of dominant cliché. For Leavis, it is in the work of effecting

[5] F. R. Leavis, *Education and the University* (Chatto & Windus, London, 1943, repr. 1965), 25.
[6] It is unlikely that Leavis would have appreciated the work of G. E. Davie, who published *The Democratic Intellect* some years later, in 1961. That book contrasts the specialist education of the English Universities (especially Oxbridge) with the history of the generalist advanced education that has been the norm in Scotland. Davie argues convincingly that a generalist education is consistent with a democratized intellect, and in this respect Leavis might have agreed. Yet Leavis would have found this distasteful, given his own preference for an elite rather than a democratic education system.
[7] Leavis, *Education and the University*, 24.

strong relations between academy and history that 'we have the function that is pre-eminently the University's; if the work is not done
there it will not be done anywhere'.[8]

Further, in concentrating on specialist expertise the University in
this period prioritizes an abstract technocratic intelligence over a more
materially 'lived' experience.[9] Like one of his favoured writers, D. H.
Lawrence, Leavis was suspicious of the rise of technologies, here in
1943 referred to as 'the machinery' of modern life. He characterizes
the inexorable acceleration of technological advances as a historical
phenomenon that, by 1943, was increasingly distancing humans from
their sensibility, by mediating between their actual material life and the
world with which they would engage.

This is a revisiting of a familiar 'dissociation of sensibility' thesis that
has long been associated with the emergence of a disruptive modernity.
In this account, our modernity as individuals is proportional to our
distance from a hypothetical 'state of nature'. It was perhaps Schiller
who expressed the thesis in terms that are most pertinent here. In his
Letters on the Aesthetic Education of Man (*Über die ästhetische Erziehung
des Menschen in einer Reihe von Briefen*), initially published in 1795
and in the wake of the Terror in revolutionary France, he makes a
distinction between the ancient world and the modern. He asks how it
is that the individual Greek in the ancient world could act as a general
representative of humanity, whereas no single 'modern' man can do
so; and his answer is that whereas the ancient Greek was at one with
nature, the modern individual receives his substantive form not from
the harmonized world of nature, where all is at one, but rather 'from
all-dividing Intellect' ('der alles trennende Verstand').[10] It is intellect as

---

[8] Ibid.
[9] 'Experience' has long been of interest to educationalists, especially in the wake of
wars. See John Dewey, *Experience and Nature* (1925; repr. Dover Publications, New
York, 1998). Experience, in this context, might be re-described as the relation of
aesthetics to politics; and this is, indeed, how I understand it.
[10] Friedrich Schiller, *On the Aesthetic Education of Man*, ed. and trans. Elizabeth
M. Wilkinson and L. A. Willoughby (Oxford University Press, Oxford, 1967, repr.
1982), 33. I have written at length on this in my *Criticism and Modernity* (Oxford
University Press, Oxford, 1999), 177ff. The phrase 'dissociation of sensibility' itself,
however, derives from T. S. Eliot, in his 1921 essay 'The Metaphysical Poets': 'In the
seventeenth century a dissociation of sensibility sets in, from which we have never
recovered', and that was occasioned by 'the difference between the intellectual poet

such – thinking as such – that constitutes the 'disruption' that compli-
cates our relation to the world of nature.

In that hypothetical 'natural' condition, we were supposedly fully
immersed in the direct experience of living, as fully natural as the biodiversity of which we constituted but one element. The 'dissociation
of sensibility' arises entirely as a consequence of our self-consciousness,
an ability to see and to be interested intellectually or consciously in our
own position within nature. Such an intellectual exercise immediately
sets us also apart from nature, makes us exceptional with regard to its
otherwise ordinary condition; but it is this that allows us to think and
thereby to conceive the world differently from how we 'live' it as
pure experience. In such a hypothetical pure experience, a thought
would itself have been, in the words of T. S. Eliot describing this same
phenomenon, an 'experience ... [that modifies] sensibility', such that
one might 'feel ... thought as immediately as the odour of a rose'.[11]
In Biblical mythology, the meaning of the dissociation of sensibility is
characterized as the Fall; and, of course, the Fall is precisely occasioned
by an engagement with knowledge, an engagement that is already
marked intrinsically as 'Satanic'.

Of course, there are other philosophical precursors of this position,
including, probably above all, Rousseau, whose entire philosophy of
education depends on the regulation of 'nobility' with 'savagery' – or,
in less tendentious terms, 'nurturing culture' with 'natural being'. We
can see this as the fundamental root of a modern concern for the
relative value of epistemology against ontology: is it better just 'to be'
or 'to know that one is'? This gets its fullest philosophical conceptu-
alization in Heidegger's concern for ontology and for the primacy of
Being. Heidegger's ontology is, in one simple way, an appeal to find
some primordial condition of things and persons: this will constitute
their essence, as it were, before they 'reveal' that essence for understanding or epistemological instrumentality. This is also his 'question
concerning technology', because for Heidegger – though in terms that
differ enormously from those of Leavis or Lawrence – technology, too,

and the reflective poet'. See T. S. Eliot, *Selected Essays*, 3rd edn (Faber & Faber,
London, 1951, repr. 1980), 288, 287. The change happened, for Eliot, during the
English Civil War.

[11] Eliot, *Selected Essays*, 287. He is distinguishing between Donne and the later poets
Tennyson and Browning, who suffered from this 'dissociation of sensibility'.

distances us increasingly from these primordial or original conditions of Being. In this logic, technology also drives us away from truth.[12]

Such thinking permeates Heidegger's infamous Rectorial Address of 1933, 'The self-assertion of the German university'. This address, with its intrinsic appeal to German nationalism, not only seeks what Heidegger calls the 'essence of the German university', but also operates as a Nazi-sympathizing call to his students to 'will' that essence into historical reality. To do so requires a return to beginnings, which Heidegger will find in his linguistic diversions into ancient Greek. Through this, he proclaims the necessity of securing that mysterious 'beginning' which still 'endures'. 'The beginning still is. It does not lie *behind us*, as something that was long ago, but stands *before us*,' he said. The task of the University, he asserts, is to catch up with this beginning of all things – this natural Being as such – and to accept it as our destiny. That destiny, for Heidegger, is of the very essence of Nazism: it is to be the realization and, indeed, forceful assertion of 'the people's earth- and blood-bound strength'.[13] It marks the German out as exceptional, while at the same time reclaiming this exceptionalism as ordained and as an authentically 'ordinary' condition. Heidegger's German is exceptional in having a primary claim upon being ordinary and upon ordinary Being.[14]

What this does, in fact, is to sacrifice knowledge to being, and to suggest that the function of the University is to ensure the subservience of a self-consciousness that strives to 'know' things to an alleged more natural or original self that acts more or less instinctively. It subjugates 'knowing that we are' and 'knowing what we are' to 'being whatever' we are. Whatever.

'Whatever': the logic of the populist politician who asks 'the people' to rest their decisions not on thought or reason, but on their being,

---

[12] See David E. Cooper, 'Heidegger in Nature', *Environmental Values*, 14 (2005), 339–51 for a succinct and helpful detailed explication of this.

[13] See Martin Heidegger, 'The self-assertion of the German university', 1933 (German title 'Die Selbstbehauptung der deutschen Universität'), available at: http://la.utexas.edu/users/hcleaver/330T/350kPEEHeideggerSelf-Assertion.pdf.

[14] When any Nazi murderer excused himself by saying that he was 'just following orders', his tacit claim was that he was realizing this Heideggerian philosophy: he was following – and making real – his ordinary destiny: making the exceptional ordinary, routine.

their gut instinct. Typically, of course, this politician is a cynic who will then manipulate those instincts, giving them a vocabulary of cliché that will work as their legitimation.

The question is whether we have ever seriously escaped from this in any contemporary version of the University that seeks to relate it to a national character, or to the supremacy – exceptionalism – of one national character over another, as measured, for example, by something as banal, everyday, and 'ordinary' as competitive international league-tables. That competition underlies all others, and establishes a damaging and deleterious structure for all higher education worldwide.

Leavis argued that, in 1943, the human – disengaged from lived experience – engages not with the world but instead with 'the machinery' that stands between her or him and the world.[15] The war exemplifies this, as far as he is concerned, for the Second World War bore witness to huge technological advances in the machinery of killing, thus making the activity of killing highly efficient. Killing becomes a mechanical process, essentially a work that is 'neutralized' by its mechanical routinization. Like the bureaucrat in the office, concerned more with procedures and protocols of work than with the actual substance and content of work, the fighter is distanced from the content of her or his action, making killing easier and more efficient by distancing the fighter from the act itself. Leavis was fully alert to this, arguing that 'The war, by providing imperious immediate ends and immediately all-sufficient motives, has produced a simplification [of the complexities of modern life] that enables the machinery, now more tyrannically complex than ever before, to run with marvellous efficiency.'[16]

The University is in danger of becoming just such an efficient machine, and it is here that Leavis sees its silent allegiance to the very barbarism that it should be contesting. The higher education of his moment, he thinks, is failing because it is overly attentive to the efficient and machine-like industrial production of 'the desired

---

[15] It is worth considering whether, in our own time, it is bureaucracy and the cult of management that now assumes the role of this 'machinery'. I explore this in my *Complicity* (Rowman & Littlefield International, New York, 2016), esp. 27–52 and 64–9.

[16] Leavis, *Education and the University*, 23.

student-product ... a standard "educated man"'. In place of this, the task of a proper University, according to Leavis, is 'to produce specialists who are in touch with a humane centre, and to produce for them a centre to be in touch with'.[17] It is a secular version of a theological demand to re-create a state of nature in which all will be well and all manner of thing shall be well,[18] but a state also where the exceptional individual – here, essentially, Leavis and 'the English' – can stand apart from that centre while being a determinant of its form.

Although written over seventy years ago, the claims made by Leavis have an extraordinary resonance with our own contemporary moment. Leavis's complaints about over-specialization, for example, find their historical echo in what we must surely hear as the now shocking claim from the Conservative MP and former Secretary of State for Education Michael Gove that 'the people of this country have had enough of experts'.[19] Gove made this extraordinary, anti-intellectual, and populist claim as part of his campaign to ensure that the UK left the European Union. He thereby gave a simplistic vocabulary to 'the people' whom he was trying to manipulate and 'operationalize' in the campaign. In this respect, he was every bit as deceitful and cynical as Kellyanne Conway with her claims about there being a realm of alternative facts to which we can subscribe at will. What you say has no relation to belief, much less truth; it is simply a statement of ideological preference, and – after Gove – any evidence brought to the table is immediately to be dismissed. Trust yourself, vote your prejudice.

Our current institutional and governmental demands for a measurable 'research impact' are also inspired by the ghost of Leavis. Such demands are surely determined by a tacit claim that the University stands too aloof from the everyday lives of people in our society, too apart from 'informed general intelligence' and 'humane culture'. At the same time, however, we are also obsessed with ideas of 'efficiency'

---

[17] Ibid., 27, 28.
[18] The original of this phrase is to be found in Julian of Norwich, *Shewings,* ed. Georgia Ronan Crampton (Medieval Institute Publications, Western Michigan University, Kalamazoo, 1994), 72: 'Synne is behovabil, but al shal be wel, and al shal be wel, and al manner of thyng shal be wel.' The phrase is repeated in T. S. Eliot, 'Little Gidding' in *Four Quartets.*
[19] Michael Gove, in an interview on 3 June 2016 with Faisal Islam, available at: https://www.youtube.com/watch?v=GGgiGtJk7MA (accessed 23 November 2017).

and with the efficient 'production' of 'the educated individual' who will lead us in our global race in 'the knowledge society'. It is small wonder, given these contradictory impulses, that the institution is in existential crisis.

When Leavis wrote of the University as a 'centre' around which a society might orient itself, his focus was decidedly on the English University, and very specifically on Oxbridge. However, whether he knew it or not, he was essentially reprising that Humboldtian model in the Berlin University of 1810. Bill Readings describes Humboldt's conception of Berlin University as 'the university of culture'. This institution 'draws its legitimacy from culture', argues Readings; and at the core of this culture is a series of syntheses, most particularly the synthesis of teaching and research, and the synthesis of 'the institution and the individual'. These provide an arrangement that is uncannily like that advanced by Leavis, for in these syntheses we establish the University as that institution that 'gives the people the idea of a nation-state to live up to and the nation-state a people capable of living up to that idea'.[20]

For Humboldt, the 'centre' in question was the newly emergent version of the nation that constitutes modern Germany; for Leavis, the centre is not Britain, nor even England, but the much more circum-scribed, exceptional, and elite space of Oxbridge. In the extreme, it was Downing College, Cambridge, where he taught; and then, even more extreme, it was his own home, to which he invited favoured students. Between Humboldt and Leavis, historically and culturally, lies the Nazism of Heidegger's Rectorial Address and its attempt to reconcile the extraordinary with the ordinary; and we can never forget that one aspect of this was to make it ordinary and routine to burn books, and to dragoon cohorts of students into conformity with the 'ordinariness' of Nazism.

The key thing to note in this is that the University in all of these accounts is concerned with a version of 'distinctiveness' or of distinc-tion: the logic of 'the exception'. It may be the distinctiveness of the German national character, or it may be the distinction of an aesthetic and scientific elite as vested in the idea of Oxbridge. In either case, the University here establishes a hierarchy through the very ideas of

[20] Readings, *The University in Ruins*, 65.

discrimination, of setting apart, and of high intrinsic self-worth. It is very easy for this to mutate – as it does, historically – into a construction of the University as the site for 'excelling' and thus distinguishing itself from all social norms, thereby diverging from its surrounding social ecology. We arrive at what Readings calls 'the university of excellence', in which all and everything associated with the University is measured in terms of an increasingly vacuous notion of 'excellence' in all things.

↝

All of our contemporary stories of the excellence of our institutions – actually and simply, a pure ideology of excellence itself – relate directly to this background. The UK sector is now expected to contribute to Britain's prowess in being 'world-leading', which is our new term for an inflated notion of 'the excellent'. Within this, we find a demand for competition also entering the fray; and competition itself has a very specific inflection in our time, related to 'excelling' in a 'market' in order to boost financial standing and profit. Thus, the martial conflicts of the mid-century gave way first to cultural conflicts within the University, and finally to a competitive confrontation in which individual Universities compete for superiority, a superiority to be measured in financial terms.[21]

The contemporary University is now expected to play a significant and even central determining role in establishing distinctions between and among nations, as each supposedly strives to outdo all others in a competition that David Cameron, former UK Prime Minister, described as the 'global race'. That race, fundamentally, is a race to get our hands onto resources and, above all, money. While many University sectors seem to endorse this, they do not often attend to the fact that it is a zero-sum game: every winner in such a race produces a loser. The structural inequality that is a direct corollary of the logic of competition here is glossed instead as 'diversity', and is thus encouraged, sanctioned, and praised.

The obverse of this logic of competition – a logic that has become

---

[21] We might say that domination over land and territory gives way to domination over wealth. I write more about this in *Literature and Capital* (Bloomsbury, London, forthcoming).

normative for the University institution worldwide through the high visibility of league-tables and their associated cultures – is that the University exists in order to exacerbate all kinds of social, political, and economic inequalities, forever extending the gap between winners and losers until, eventually, the winner takes all and everyone else loses. This is our new 'ordinary' condition; and it is surely one that we have a duty to change.

In this quest after some intrinsic notion of 'excellence', each individual University, as well as the sector as a whole, has been driven into a mode of deep introspection. Instead of establishing a profound intimacy and relation between the world of the specialist and that of a general population, the University concentrates on its own standing as against other Universities. The 'world' with which it concerns itself is increasingly the world within its own walls, focusing (for example) on 'the student experience'. A concentration on the 'student experience', on making things pleasant and seductive for the student, shrinks the world and vision of the University and its teachers to the size of the seminar room or laboratory. It demands that we devote our primary concern to satisfying those students within our own institutions. It thereby requires that we dismiss or at least relegate any concern that our work might have a consequence for those who, for whatever reasons, are not in our seminar and laboratory today. 'The student experience' deliberately narrows our intellectual, social, and political ambit. It eliminates the world from our concerns. In this state of affairs, if we look out at all, we look out only to see other comparable institutions, in order to compare and compete.

It goes without saying that this leads us into a self-defeating irrelevance to the lives of 'ordinary people'. 'Exception' here means that we literally 'stand apart' and distance ourselves from the world and its history. Unsurprisingly, this then gets us into a desperate and catastrophic spiral: in becoming 'irrelevant' to the world as a consequence of this obsession with a supposed 'excellence' that produces funding and financial resource, we have to struggle to make the case that we are deserving of more funding, and this in turn deepens yet further the sense of irrelevance as we turn ever further away from material realities and the conditions of society in which we operate. In seeking to become 'exceptional', we find ourselves facing the threat of exclusion – exclusion from social and political importance.

An entire *Lebenswelt* – a mode of 'living in the world' – is reduced here to the merest introspection. Far from the Wittgensteinian claim that 'the world is everything that is the case', this position instead thinks that 'the world is everything that can be measured for competitive league-tables'. This is not a being-towards-the-world, much less even a being-in-the-world; rather, it is a being-placed-in-league-table-position. As a result of such banality, we exist solely in relation to other institutions. In short, it is as if we have established an intertwined and introspective network of 'ivory tower' institutions, floating free above the world and disconnected from it. We become divorced from a national polity in exactly the same way as the global multinational – Amazon, Google, Facebook, Starbucks – distances itself from paying its dues to ordinary people, in fact precisely and most comprehensively at the moment when we claim (like those global corporates) to be serving those same ordinary people.

This is the dark underside of all those claims that our contemporary institutions make for their global credentials: like those corporates, we have stopped paying our dues to the social world and the 'ordinary' people who subtend us and to whom we look for co-existence. We should be working towards the good society; but that noble aim has been long forgotten as we work instead towards legitimizing a rat-race of competitive acquisitive individualism.

The world University system starts to resemble a biological 'rat king': condemned to a slow death by starvation through an incestuous embrace of inwardness and self-regard. The University, in this arrangement, is entirely disjunctive with respect to material realities of everyday life. In this respect at least, Leavis had it right – but not just about the state of the 1943 institution, for this also describes the contemporary position.[22] It is a position in which the University fails its societies.

Leavis himself had foreseen all this, in fact though not at all in these terms, as early as 1930. At this time, his position in the English Faculty in Cambridge was very precarious. Just married to Queenie Roth, whose family disowned her for 'marrying out' of her Jewish faith,

---

[22] As I will show, however, he was far from right in many other respects.

he had no permanent position in the faculty, and was bereft after the death of his mother. He had also come close to suffering a nervous breakdown, having been virtually unable to write at all for some time. He took the opportunity to get himself back on the rails offered by a former student, Gordon Fraser, to publish a pamphlet entitled 'Mass Civilisation and Minority Culture'.[23] The pamphlet argues that it is only a small minority of people who can, at any given moment in history, fully realize the deep substance of 'life' itself: these are exceptional individuals. Among them, there are some who can articulate their experience: these are poets. Next, there are those who can engage substantively and appreciatively with the poetry, who can endorse the implicit evaluations of experience that are inscribed within the poetry, and who can communicate that to others: these are critics and teachers. There is here a clear hierarchy. Leavis writes that 'Poetry matters because of the kind of poet who is more alive than other people, more alive in his own age.' He goes on to gloss this idea of an exceptionalism as the condition of poets and of poetry, in terms that might now be regarded as somewhat chilling, stating that the poet 'is, as it were, at the most conscious point of the race in his time'. This is 1932; and Leavis is explicit that the poet here differs in this way from 'the ordinary man':[24] he is a kind of *Übermensch* in at least this exceptionalist regard.

Leavis argued that this 'minority culture' is utterly crucial to 'our power of profiting by the finest human experience of the past'.[25] The metaphor of 'profit' is not accidental here, and is related directly to money: 'The accepted valuations [of literature] are a kind of paper currency based upon a very small proportion of gold.'[26] It is upon this elite – essentially now a quasi-financial elite – that 'fine living depends, and without which distinction of spirit is thwarted and incoherent'.[27] Thus it is that we see that a logic of exceptionalism – which today is re-categorized as 'excellence' – is structurally central to a culture based upon hierarchical distinctions (the inequality of class), itself determined by a specific aestheticism ('fine living') and money (or 'profit' from the 'small proportion of gold' that is to be distributed highly unequally).

---

[23] See Ian MacKillop, *F. R. Leavis: A Life in Criticism* (Penguin, London, 1995), 113.
[24] F. R. Leavis, *New Bearings in English Poetry* (1932; repr. Penguin, London, 1972), 16.
[25] Leavis, *Education and the University*, 144.
[26] Ibid., 143.
[27] Ibid., 145.

In short: the wealthy live well by disproportionately gaining from the poetic resources of the world. They are the minority that has 'culture', while the rest of us masses have the lesser 'civilization'.

Given that the University deals in an education that is always post-compulsory, its status is already one that will be subjected to a special type of scrutiny. We find it broadly unobjectionable to educate people – by law – up to the age of eighteen; but a tertiary or 'higher' education is, by definition, not compulsory. There must always there-fore be a suspicion that it is surplus to requirements, that it is an additional 'extra', that – in some fundamental sense – it is actually 'unnecessary' and the site of a particular redundancy (the cliché is that the academic is lazy and, in the extreme, a waste of otherwise productive energy that is better directed at 'doing' things rather than 'thinking about' things). In some sense of the term, higher education must therefore be regarded as 'exceptional', an exception to the norms or governed by our logic of exceptionalism. Clearly, however, our societies do not straightforwardly accept such a proposition, claiming instead, often with great piety, that higher education is more necessary than ever. There is, here, a paradox – the paradox of exceptionalism itself – that requires further consideration, in terms of how it affects the institution and its constitution in a society.

As I showed in my discussion of the Browne Review in Chapter 2 above, while the University can be viewed as an optional extra for some, it remains compulsory for a society. Indeed, the entire historical trajectory since 1945 has been to make University if not compulsory then at least increasingly ordinary, as we have driven steadily upwards the numbers of students and of institutions that we have. In this sense, while it may still be an optional extra for some individuals, it is nonetheless absolutely necessary for a collective. That collective might assume the identity of a nation state (Humboldt, say), a city (Oxford or Cambridge, say), or 'civilization' in general (against the barbarism of war and violence, say), and so on. The important thing is that we have a conundrum here. Is the University an institution that is necessary or contingent; and is it an institution that serves to fulfil the identity of an individual or of a collective? I use this vocabulary – contingent, situation, option, and so on – to indicate that what we are facing at the current time is an *existential* crisis of the University.

These are also – as in existential situations – political questions;

and they relate to the condition of our society and of our individual relation to other people. In 1963, the Robbins Report on higher education squared this circle with a serendipitous phrase. What became known as 'the Robbins principle' argued that a place in a University education should be available not in fact to everyone, but rather only to all 'who were qualified ... by ability and attainment'. This, ostensibly a meritocratic principle, has been taken as a norm at least since the great University and higher education expansion of the 1960s. It indicates that the student must have demonstrated her or his suitability for University through academic achievement and potential ('ability' leaves open the possibility that a student has demonstrated a capacity for future attainment). That is to say: a qualification is what 'entitles' the student to a University place.

This only appears to settle the matter, however; and it does so by sidestepping the political issue. The political substance of the actuality is important. If we see the University as an institution designed for the advancement only of some individuals – those marked out as 'exceptional' by virtue of attainment or potential in whatever spheres – then it is indeed a superfluous institution, a luxury, when seen from the point of view of the polity at large. Indeed, this position (the one that sees the University as optional extra, additional luxury) essentially drives a wedge between the University and the polity as a whole, for the position presupposes that the University exists for the benefit only of those who attend, only for those 'inside'. There is no better definition of the University as irrelevant 'ivory tower', its utterly parochial introspection confirmed by our contemporary obsession with the student experience, as if students were some kind of tourist seeking an exotic authenticity in an otherworldly destination.[28]

If, on the other hand, we consider the University as a luxury for some but an absolute necessity for its general society as a whole, and thus prioritize its relation to the collective society, then we have an entirely different attitude that must prevail. No longer is the work of the University something that gives an exceptional identity primarily or merely to individuals (that identity being characterized as 'employable', 'rich', and so on); rather its concern is much wider, and has to address

[28] I analyse and criticize the myth of 'the student experience' in my book *For the University* (Bloomsbury, London, 2011), 36–67.

the collective from which it emerges as an institution in the first place. It thus contributes to the identity of the society itself. The distinction I make here underpins and allows us to make a political choice: does the University serve the self-centred and selfish identity of individuals, determined to distinguish themselves from the collective and from all others; or is the University an institution that serves a public good? Instead of 'the student experience', might we not consider 'the social experience', and decide what a University might have to say about that?

The former view (which prevails in our time) establishes the University as a site of individualist distinction, designed to increase all forms of inequality among a population. The latter establishes the University as an institution with social responsibilities. In the contemporary moment, our problems all arise from the simple fact that a political choice has indeed been made: following the Browne Review of 2010 the former view is taken entirely – and explicitly – for granted. In this respect, Browne simply endorses and makes explicit an ideological position that had been steadily gaining ground since the 1950.

This, in turn, derives from the evolution of secondary-level education. First, the 1944 Education Act (the 'Butler Act', after R. A. Butler, the then Conservative Education Minister, who drafted the Act) extended secondary education to a wider working-class constituency than before. By the late 1950s, the underprivileged children of this post-war generation were now receiving an education that might permit them to attend a University. Such an education was envisaged as a mechanism through which the underprivileged might be enabled to enter the middle-class professions; and thus the University became mobilized as a driver of so-called 'social mobility'.

However, if the University does indeed provide an education that stretches the abilities of those who attend, it is surely equally clear that this mobility is not limited simply to those working-class students who attend. The already privileged and the middle classes are also moving upwards socially through their education, since (presumably) they are given exactly the same education and mind-stretching exercises as the working-class students, although they have started from an already privileged and elevated position. Inequality is not only structurally embedded: it is exponentially extended through the myth of social mobility. Browne consolidates the unthinking banality of the 'social

mobility' ideology, once again without seriously examining what is at
issue in the cliché of social mobility itself.[29]

The ideology that piously drives the social mobility myth rests on
the assumption that to be working-class is so atrocious that anyone
in their right mind would want to escape from that condition. It is
based upon a contempt for the poorer members of a social order, and
it encourages the poor to be ashamed of their own class. Further, it is
based in a contempt for work itself (especially manual labour), and in
a self-regarding and self-serving middle-class ideology of *amour-propre*.
Shamefully, the University not only now endorses this demonization
of the working class, but also endorses an entire philosophical basis for
such an immoral attitude. 'Social mobility' says that a working-class
individual from a background of poverty can become a University
professor or VC. It has nothing to say about the fact that such a background of poverty persists.

The upwardly mobile individual in this becomes the cover for the
scandal that the University is structurally working in a determined
ignorance of social misery, as if it has nothing to offer to alleviate such
conditions. In short, the myth of 'social mobility' legitimizes a social
and political order in which the University excuses itself from having
any responsibility to address social poverty as a class issue. In accordance with the logic of privatization, poverty is a matter for atomized
individuals; and, given that we endorse 'social mobility', those who
remain poor must be to blame, themselves, for their condition.

The consequence of that is that the University, as now constituted
in our societies, becomes one of the major causes of social, political,
and economic inequality. The myth of social mobility ensures that the
University does not stretch minds; rather, first, it stretches the distance
between the student class and the rest, and second, within that student
class, it attenuates yet further any sense of equality, solidarity and cohe-
sion. The result is an ever-extending inequality; and we already know
that the result of this is that the top end becomes ever smaller (not just

---

[29] R. A. Butler had envisaged the Act essentially as something consistent with a particular brand of Conservative 'paternalism', through which the upper and (especially)
middle classes would kindly assist those lower in the social scale of things to escape
their condition. The tacit assumption here is that there is something shameful in
being working-class, and that anyone in their right intellectual mind would want to
escape from it.

the 1% but the 0.1%), while those at the bottom end, especially those not attending a University, find their poverty ever more damaging and limiting. In this account (again, the account of the University that prevails in our time) the University exists to worsen the conditions of a collective while encouraging a small group of individuals to amass wealth and distinction to themselves, at great social – and, in the end, personal – cost.

We can turn to look more closely at these costs; and we will do so by considering a novel, a text that is itself focused on the existential crisis of a student. Dostoevsky's *Crime and Punishment* has enormous relevance to our concerns, notwithstanding its provenance in nineteenth-century Russia.

↬

Dostoevsky published *Crime and Punishment* in 1865. Russia was still recovering from its humiliation in the Crimean War a decade earlier. Tsar Alexander was also under pressure to effect great and progressive social reforms to ameliorate the living conditions of the population; and he responded with two great changes. In 1861, he effected the emancipation of the serf class; and in 1864, precisely when Dostoevsky was writing, he brought about significant and substantial changes in the judiciary and in the system of law. This is the social and political background that informs the novel; and Dostoevsky pits the specific crime of the individualist Raskolnikov – an admirer of the great 'exceptional' figures of history and a proponent of exceptionalism itself – against a society in St Petersburg that is obviously ravaged by poverty as a formerly peasant and feudal-serf class seeks to make its way in a new economic and social dispensation.

Perhaps it will be unsurprising, therefore, that I will use this novel as a key to understanding how it is that the University – and specifically its identification with intellectual work, or with critical thinking as such – becomes subject to an intrinsic criminalization in our own time, thereby giving further weight to the damaging attitude that sees the very fact of intellectual work as somehow suspicious, and potentially working against the interests of the society that sustains it in its higher education institutions.

Raskolnikov is a student – or, rather, a 'former' student: like many today, he is so indebted financially that he has had to give up his studies, at least temporarily. My contention is that it is no accident that Dostoevsky makes this – an impoverished student – the central character in the novel. The relation between intellectual work and money forms an elemental part of the text's architecture. As the novel opens, we see Raskolnikov living in impoverished conditions in his attic, a dismal garret. While this might have become a romanticized version of the bohemianism that was much in the air elsewhere at this historical moment, here Dostoevsky insists on the realistic squalor of the character's life.[30] Throughout, and notwithstanding his desire to be exceptional, we will see that Raskolnikov is not all that unusual, for many in St Petersburg are living in similar conditions of poverty and misery, resorting to prostitution and petty crime in order to survive.

Raskolnikov does have one source of money: the old woman Alonya Ivanova, who acts as money-lending pawnbroker, and whom he murders. As Raskolnikov sees it, this woman is at once both a menace and a (literal) redeemer. She is a menace not just because she drives extraordinarily hard and mean financial bargains, but also because she hoards the money and the goods that she has. Yet Raskolnikov also needs her, needs to be redeemed by her, if he is to be able to have any funds at all. He will murder her; and, in at least one sense, this crime can be rationalized and (for Raskolnikov) in principle excused precisely by that rationalization. He will claim to have done the world a good, by ridding it of a woman who is regarded as a pestilential bringer of harm to all around her; and, at a more material and venal level, the rationale for the act (though it is not expressed as such) is that he will also steal her money and the pawned goods in her hoard after murdering her, thus alleviating his own precarious financial position, with the concomitant expectation that he can thereby return to his studies.

However, the most significant thing in this text is not the murder of Alonya, but rather the murder of her disabled and put-upon sister, Lisaveta, who is 'almost an idiot'.[31] The murder of Lisaveta is absolutely and entirely gratuitous: nothing in the novel's plot or even characterization needs it to happen. It happens precisely because it is what

[30] Puccini premiered *La bohème* in 1896, but it was based on Henri Murger's *Scènes de la vie de bohème* of 1851.
[31] Fyodor Dostoevsky, *Crime and Punishment*, trans. David Magarshack (Penguin, London, 1983), 80.

existentialism would call an *acte gratuit,* an entirely unnecessary action, but one that becomes itself a significant marker of a freely expressed choice of action, a choice to undertake a being-in-the-world. It is this murder that therefore relates to the idea of the exception.

With the murder of Lisaveta at the centre of this text, we have something that is utterly contingent, yet necessary as a fundamental condition of Raskolnikov's enactment of freedom and of autonomy. Above all, it marks Raskolnikov out as a particular kind of exceptional individual. He believes that his own exceptionalism essentially means that his action is not a crime in any usual sense, and that it therefore does not need to be balanced out or eradicated by a matching punishment. While this might make a rational (if odd and disturbing) sense of the initial murder of Alonya, it cannot speak to the case of Lisaveta.

Raskolnikov advances his thinking about this kind of exception in the scholarly article that he has already published, and that has been picked up by Porphiry, the examining magistrate who haunts Raskolnikov like his own conscience. The article explains Raskolnikov's view that the world can be divided into two orders, the ordinary and the extraordinary. He subscribes to a view that society is based upon this distinction and its intrinsic hierarchical elitism. The ordinary are docile and conservative: they know their place in society, do not rock any boats, and perform their function routinely and without much self-reflection.

The extraordinary are different; and they are different in ways that match almost entirely our contemporary image of the University. These extraordinary individuals are distinguished by their excellence in various ways. Most especially, they can bring into being 'a new word' and a concomitant new way of thinking. They are thus essentially like academic researchers, discoverers, innovators, and intellectuals. In practical terms (and in the specific case cited by Raskolnikov), they are those who resemble Napoleon. We can see this 'exception' more generally as an example of what will find its full philosophical description in 1883, in Nietzsche's *Übermensch.* For Raskolnikov, the exceptions have certain 'entitlements', one of which being that they are not subject to the normal economics of the law or of justice – that hypothetical 'balancing' of the specific event of a crime 'costed' against a punishment tariff.

The contemporary student, too, is one who seeks 'entitlement', seeking an identity and status qualified as 'bachelor' or 'master' or 'doctor', and seeking this usually 'with honours'. These titles are markers of specific kinds of exceptionalism, which we now call excellence, and which we promise to mark out in one very specific and explicit way. We won't mark it out with something as metaphysical or virtuous as 'honour', but rather with higher financial rewards in those better-paid middle-class jobs. While the entitlement may not place our students above the law in the real judicial sense, it does nonetheless place them 'above' others in our social hierarchies and inequalities.

However, there is indeed one way in which these entitlements do, in fact, place students 'outside' the law; and they do so in ways that characterize the intellectual precisely as some kind of criminal 'outlaw'. In this, as I will show, the only way for the student or intellectual to be accepted and rewarded socially is to conform utterly to the dogma and ideology that structure their existing society. It is when intellectuals criticize the existing state of affairs that they become delegitimized by a conservative society, and their thinking is regarded as suspect or even criminally menacing.

In *Crime and Punishment*, the exception – that extraordinary being of Raskolnikov's imagination – is one for whom the everyday law is strictly irrelevant. The extraordinary being might indeed be a Napoleon, as in Raskolnikov's preferred image; but he may also be like a fundamental and fundamentalist terrorist. Raskolnikov acts in a belief that it is fine to spill blood to achieve an ethical good or a positive political end; and this is indeed the existential crisis that Dostoevsky explores here, as elsewhere in his writings. Yet the question of terror is one also that haunts our Universities.

᠄

Terror stalks the corridors in at least two ways. The first is the obvious one in which the UK government – in line with governments elsewhere – considers the University to be potentially a hotbed of radical dissidence and political extremism. The second is that which is associated with a certain 'safe space' movement, in which the University is proposed as a place of refuge for students themselves who might be terrified, discomforted, or just discomfited by exposure to certain texts, narratives, or ideas.

In relation to the first terror here, the government would prefer to see the University as the site of a fundamental social conformity. The

The exceptional and the ordinary

103

current ideal is that the University should 'produce' a graduate that can be described as 'work-ready', and with the appropriate 'skills' that our existing world of business and commerce thinks it needs. This account of the University is one in which it exists purely as a mechanism for consolidating the ambition and desire of a mythic and allegedly homogeneous 'business', a 'business' that narcissistically sees itself as the totality of what constitutes 'society'. The task of the University is to feed the mill. It is reminiscent of Zola's great image in 1885 of the mine as voracious monster in *Germinal*, in which he describes Étienne Lantier, after the failure of a great miners' strike, watching as the miners start to go back down the mine-shaft: 'il retrouvait le monstre avalant sa ration de chair humaine … avec le coup de gosier d'un géant vorace' ('he saw again the monster swallowing its rations of human flesh … with a huge voracious gulp').[32]

In this, it is as if the world of business – the voracious mine – stands as the sole and fundamental reason for our social existence.[33] It is a hungry monster, needing constant feeding and attention, needing to be served at all times, making humanity itself subservient to its mechanical self-reproduction and self-sustenance. The University is proposed as the machine that will keep producing the necessary energy to keep business going. This is rife with problems and self-contradictions. The first relates to the idea that business needs constant innovation; and this is usually captured in the cliché of 'thinking outside the box'. This, however, is by now such a cliché that we can safely say that anyone who uses the phrase 'thinking outside the box' is actually fully immersed 'within the box'. 'Thinking outside the box' is precisely what everyone inside the box does; and, indeed, it is precisely now the qualification for getting into the box in the first place.

In short, what is demanded here is not innovation, but rather an ideological utter conformity to a vacuous idea of innovation, in which nothing new ever actually happens, and in which 'the new' is but an instance of the Nietzschean 'eternal return' of what has always been

---

[32] Émile Zola, *Germinal* (1885; repr. Fasquelle, Paris, 1972), 493. This bears comparison with the political aftermath of the UK miners' strike in 1984. See my *For the University* for an extended analysis of that strike and its effect on the University.
[33] This is the case even for the worker who seeks to advance himself through education: Étienne Lantier in Zola's *Germinal*, Jude in Thomas Hardy's *Jude the Obscure*. Charlie Chaplin captured the motif perfectly in his 1936 film *Modern Times*, where we see Chaplin himself being literally processed through the machinery.

the case. The exceptional new is reduced to the status of the ordinary conventional. Looking at it in this broad sense, we can see that this specific contemporary model of the University is much too close to Heidegger's for comfort – and yet, and yet, our sector is not only comfortable with it but keen to extend it even further. This is potentially disastrous – especially if, historically, we extend our 'new exception' to the point where, as in Nazism, it becomes ordinary, respectable, and routine and is carried through in the name of the ordinary people. In the 1930s, it led not just to the censorship-by-burning of books (books being seen thereby as the 'witches' of the twentieth century), but also to war and catastrophe.

Essentially, and considered in less grand-historical terms, it follows logically from this prevailing account of 'what the University is for' that 'business' stands to learn nothing whatsoever from the intellectual possibilities of new thought that a graduate might offer. The only 'knowledge' that is important here for business is the knowledge that fits comfortably with things as they currently are. It is little wonder, therefore, that UK business is not exactly 'exceptional'. As Stefan Collini has written, 'Future historians ... will struggle to account' for the fact that while British business is anything but a great success story, and while UK Universities are remarkably good, nonetheless 'the coalition government [of 2010–15] took the decisive steps in helping to turn some first-rate universities into third-rate companies'.[34]

What this further implies is that the government sees the possibility of independent thinking as itself always potentially dangerous, disruptive of the smooth operations of the social order as it stands and, within that, the smooth ongoing operations and processes of contemporary capital. It is uneasy at the thought that those who are currently privileged by this arrangement might be discomfited by a seriously new thinking. The consequence is the well-known attack on academic freedom and on free speech; but this is only one aspect of a much wider criminalization (and censorship) of criticism in general and, within that, of the very processes of independent thinking.[35]

[34] Stefan Collini, 'Sold Out', *London Review of Books*, 35:20 (24 October 2013), 12.
[35] It is worth remembering that an attack on academic freedom was also central to Heidegger's Rectorial Address 'The self-assertion of the German university': 'The much-lauded "academic freedom" will be expelled from the German university'.

The second new element that haunts us here is the terrifying of students themselves. The demand for 'safe spaces' is like a demand for refuge; and one paradox is that we witness this at a time when many countries reject refugees on the grounds that among them there might be some individuals who are themselves potentially terrorists who might menace their new hosts, us. One of the greatest paradoxes surrounding our contemporary University – and which is centrally relevant to the 'safe space' and 'no platform' arguments – is this: that it seeks to arrest the very process of thinking, its fundamental *raison d'être*. We might describe 'thinking' in these terms: thinking is what happens when something previously foreign or alien to our consciousness demands to be understood; anything else is not really a thought but simply an iteration or mere rehearsing of someone else's prior thinking.

If we accept this, then we must also acknowledge that thinking, by that very definition, is something that disturbs me. It asks that I re-arrange my mental order of things, to find a way of accommodating this new and alien element with my previously existing and established view of reality. The demand that we construe a University as a 'safe space' is, fundamentally, consistent with an oppression of thinking. Worse, it is also consistent with the racist suspicion of foreigners that it would prefer to excoriate. In the end, it is not the student who is protected here; rather, it is the society itself – and, locally, the University's neoliberal management – that is determinedly protecting itself from the possible disruption to its existing order that is promised by the introduction of foreign or alien – or simply new – thinking itself.[36]

Thinking is thus not only exceptional; it is also 'taking exception'. It is exceptional in that it does not happen as a general rule, but rather needs conditions that make its irruption – into the ordinary or the usual or the ideological – possible in the first place. It is surely the University, as the site of thinking and intellectual activity, that might and should provide such a condition. Thinking – together with the institution where, par excellence and by definition, it is supposed to happen, the University – is exceptional in that it must abandon existing rules and

---

[36] The argument about 'safe spaces' is, of course, more complex. For a fuller exploration of what is at stake, see Frank Furedi, *What's Happened to the University?* (Routledge, London, 2016), and the essays in Cheryl Hudson and Joanna Williams, eds, *Why Academic Freedom Matters* (Civitas, London, 2016).

regulations: it stands apart from whatever passes as the 'general rule' of things. In this regard, it is also fundamentally shaped by a critical attitude, and it stands at an angle to the existing state of affairs in the world. As a consequence, it must also seek to re-arrange the world in order to allow for the thought to be seen and explored fully. Finally, it is exceptional in that it 'takes exception' to things as they are, feeling some basic sense of resentment at the way the world is organized; and it seeks therefore to change the world.

If we consider the University to be the site of intellectual activity as such, then it goes some way towards a realization of Marx's famous 'eleventh thesis' on Feuerbach, written in 1845: 'The philosophers have only *interpreted* the world in various ways; the point, however, is to *change* it.'[37] And this, we might say, is the proper province of the University. This is the genuine meaning of 'academic freedom': a freedom whose key *raison d'être* is to be the foundation of all and every human freedom. After all, if the society is to learn from the work of the University at all, and thus to benefit from the thinking done there by the students who will enter the social order, it follows that the society itself must start thinking, taking exception, and thus changing existing realities. In a reversal of the spirit of Heidegger, the task might properly be seen as one that 'opens' the ordinary to the very possibility of discovering that the ordinary is always singular, always an exception to the rules and regulations that will otherwise not just 'govern' our lives but also restrict the range of our possibilities. Those possibilities must be there for all, and not governed by the demands and control of those who would secure market freedom for themselves, the better to privatize it.

Were this to happen – were we to have such academic freedom – then the University might be more genuinely open, in the sense that the society as a whole might avail of its work. This is the subject of my next chapter.

---

[37] Karl Marx, 'Theses on Feuerbach', in *Ludwig Feuerbach and the End of Classical German Philosophy* (Foreign Languages Press, Peking, 1976), 65.

4

Another brick in the wall

Between 1945 and 1989, there lies an extremely interesting semantic shift in the meaning of 'openness'; and 'the open' becomes a site of debate, both semantically and politically. We can trace this shift in looking at two conservative thinkers, Karl Popper and Allan Bloom. In 1945, Popper published *The Open Society and its Enemies*, a book that he had written while in exile from the Nazis; in 1987, Allan Bloom published *The Closing of the American Mind*, a book written in what, for Bloom, was despair at the condition of the University and the student movements that began in the 1960s and that signalled, for him, a dreadful lapse in established standards and norms for human culture.

We might add to this collocation, finally, the moment just after 1989, and partly prompted by the symbolic and substantive fall of the Berlin Wall that year, when Francis Fukuyama published *The End of History and the Last Man* (1992). The latter half of Fukuyama's title echoes what was to be the original title – *The Last Man in Europe* – for what became Orwell's extraordinarily prescient 1949 novel, *Nineteen Eighty-Four*. One interesting central element that should concern us in Orwell is the way in which Newspeak can essentially reverse the semantic content of words. In what follows here, I will be interested fundamentally in how an alleged democratic opening of the University can become instead a system of exclusion: an 'opening' that, contrary to what the word implies, actually erects 'another brick in the wall'.[1]

---

[1] In 1979, Pink Floyd produced and released their concept album called *The Wall*. The songs narrate the story of Pink, a character who, through a classic *Bildungsroman*

Popper advanced an idea of philosophical and general social 'open-ness' against all theoretical philosophies that are grounded in any form of teleology or essentialism. His contention was that such philosophies foreclose human possibility, that they are inevitably totalizing, and that they are therefore also invariably totalitarian in their political tendency. If an individual or even collective life is somehow 'determined' by its end-point or by the gradual revelation of some alleged internal 'essence', then, in Popper's account, it cannot be free. Fundamentally, Popper was a twentieth-century opponent of any residual form of the-ological 'predestination', an opponent of the kind of philosophy that thinks of the human as one who will fulfil a destiny that has somehow been pre-ordered and pre-ordained. For him, the individual who acts in accordance with a prior theory, a theory that essentially determines the content of those acts, cannot act freely.

His text, written in exile after he had left Austria in flight from the *Anschluss*, was made in the shadow of the Nazi persecution of anyone whom the Nazis considered to be 'essentially' Jewish; and Popper's grandparents were Jewish. His parents had already converted to Lutheran Protestantism; and so, through this, he would have been fully aware of the theological predisposition to subscribe to a variant of predestination in Luther's claim that salvation could be by God's grace alone. *The Open Society*, essentially, rejects both Nazism and predesti-nation in favour of a belief in social liberalism. It is this alone, Popper argued, that will keep history itself open, and that will help prevent a war that rests its justification in claims of innate or essential superiority of one group over others.

The idea of fulfilling one's pre-assigned essence or intrinsic selfhood – an idea that ghosts Heidegger's Rectorial Address, as we saw – must be rejected, Popper believed, if we are to avoid conflicts both personal and international. Popper criticized both Aristotle and Hegel in these terms. He rejects Aristotelian ideas that things find their 'natural place' in the order of things and of history. He rejects Hegel because he believes that a subscription to Aristotle leads to a Hegelian master–slave dialectic and, from that, to the inevitability of war.

narrative, erects a wall between himself and the world, education, and his feelings. Education is seen as something that makes its pupils into 'just another brick in the wall'.

Aristotle took the view that 'Every proof must proceed from premises.' This is fine, but opens us up to the problem of an infinite regress
when we ask for proof of the premises. To avoid this, Aristotle has
recourse to the claim that there are some fundamental principles that
must be self-evident, self-evidencing, and thus self-proving, and that it
is from these that we can derive every proof. It follows that 'according
to Aristotle, the whole of scientific knowledge is contained in the principles and it would all be ours if only we could obtain an encyclopaedic
list of the principles'.[2] Learning, in this account, becomes the gradual
revelation of the true essence of all things, which is, indeed, Aristotle's
definition of knowledge.

Hegel's historicism, argues Popper, derives from a similar belief
in essences. Our historical becoming, in Hegelianism, suggests that
'whatever may befall a man, a nation, or a state, must be considered to
emanate from, and to be understandable through, the essence, the real
thing, the real "personality" that manifests itself in this man, this nation,
or this state'.[3] To act at all, according to this, means to 'assert myself' in
terms of my essential selfhood against other selves; and therefore 'each
must strive to assert and prove himself, and he who has not the nature,
the courage, and the general capacity for preserving his independence,
must be reduced to servitude'. As for the self, so also for the nation,
which now has a 'duty to attempt the domination of the World'.[4]

One might reasonably ask what all this has to do with the University.
Part of the answer to that is hinted at in my previous chapter, discuss-
ing Heidegger's call to his students to fulfil their essence through a
commitment to the perverted German nationalism of the Nazi cause.
Another significant part of the answer is to be found in a different
account of a culture of openness, in Allan Bloom's *The Closing of the
American Mind* of 1987. For Bloom, it is a particular 'openness' – the
kind of openness envisaged by Popper, though Bloom nowhere refers
directly to Popper's work – that leads to relativism with respect to
truth and to value. His claim is that the American University, in
its engagement with relativistic theories of truth (seen especially, he

[2] Karl Popper, *The Open Society and its Enemies* (1945; repr. in 1 vol., Routledge,
London, 2011), 227.
[3] Ibid., 225.
[4] Ibid.

argues, in deconstruction), has given up on the search for what essentially constitutes the true, the good, and the beautiful. In opening us
to uncertainty, the American University (and especially its arts and
humanities faculties) closes our minds against the essence of the great
ideas and knowledge of the past and of the tradition. That essence is
to be found in the Great Books syllabus that had previously been the
staple of a liberal American education, he claims.

It is precisely the 'openness' to possibility, instability, uncertainty
and the possibility of changing things, therefore – as Bloom construes
it, the belief that all points of view or perspectives might have their
own account of truth – that gives Bloom a problem. He believed that
such openness yields a cultural relativism, which will have the effect of
making 'the American mind' simply a reflection of one entirely relativist
and contingent point of view, and not of an intrinsic set of fundamental
determining values. The singularity of what Arnold had thought as 'the
best that has been thought and said' yields place to a confusing multiplicity of diverse accounts of truth and value. It starts to look as if Bloom
fundamentally fears that the University in America is disuniting its state.

Here, in Bloom, 'the open' describes a relativism or scepticism
regarding value; and it is this that, for Bloom, entails an abandonment
of standards of evaluation, standards that he wanted to be calibrated
according to a specifically national American ideal and norm, and to
a hierarchy of values that took this as a central norm or ground zero.
This, obviously, is the first major shot in what has become known as
'the culture wars' in our University sector worldwide.[5] It is not often
noted that this culture war is itself but an echo of the nationalist martial
wars of 1939–45 (and also, behind that, of 1914–18), wars that are
rehearsed in the claims for the primacy of English for Leavis, or for the
establishment of national character in Humboldt.

Just two years after Bloom's book appeared, the Berlin Wall fell.
Fukuyama seized this moment to present the claim that the American
mind or culture – the culture of a liberal capitalism – had brought
history to an end. This, of course, is not the end of history envisaged

---

[5] Christopher Newfield, *Unmaking the Public University* (Harvard University Press,
Cambridge, MA, 2008), points out that the 'culture wars' and 'theory wars' were
initiated from within the right-wing politically, and that, contrary to what that right
wing argued, 'theory' did not fire the first shots at all.

by Hegel, not a moment when Spirit comes to full Absolute Knowing. Rather, it is a moment when American culture proposes itself as the winner of the final conflict of ideologies that had been going on all through the Cold War years.

This broad period between 1945 and 1989, then, sees what is essentially an ongoing diversion in which the martial conflicts of physical war are re-formulated: struggles now take place at the level of cultures, including economic cultures, in what is essentially a displacement of the violence of nationalist military conflicts. Further, this leads, through this diversionary displacement, to a confounding of the claims of economic liberalism with social and cultural liberalism. These are very different semantic forms of 'liberalism', yet they seem to coalesce around the one semiotic marker: 'liberal'. Fukuyama's text proposed an end to history by conflating culture (in the form of Bloom's American cultural supremacy) with the economy (in the form of American and market fundamentalist capitalism with its 'free' markets). Social liberalism becomes engulfed under neoliberal capital, and is subdued by the triumph of market fundamentalism. What Popper feared has come about: the totalitarianism of free-market fundamentalism, which believes that the 'essence' of all things is satisfactorily manifested in its price.

Popper's 'openness' becomes equated with a specific kind of freedom, the freedom from totalitarian essentialism and historicism. If we are indeed at the end of history, then this freedom is now identified as the freedom of capital in its current most advanced financialized neoliberal form. This, paradoxically, turns out to be exactly what Popper feared, though not in the form of Nazism. It is the totalitarianism of market fundamentalism, in which everything – including knowledge – is now for sale. Market price will allegedly reveal true value, for values can be found only through free trading, according to this logic. It follows that if we want to find the value of anything that is proposed as knowledge, we must find its price in the market.

This is the background against which we can now look at the Open and Closed University in very specific terms. First, however, we need to consider this in historical perspective, where it is best examined under the rubric of 'the excitement of the modern', or a more generalized ideology of modernization.

⟜

The difference between Popper and Bloom is a difference in attitude to our relations with our past and future. To put this in crude and basic form, Bloom wants to use the present moment of teaching and learning not just to become acquainted with the past but also to become fully informed by it. Whatever future eventuates from this will retain the tradition of well-established values. Popper, by contrast, demands that the future be unpredictable, in the sense that we can use our present moment as a kind of transition between what seems to be determined for us (the condition of life that we inherit) and what new possibilities we might invent for the future condition of society. This, essentially, is a crisis of 'modernity' itself, in which we are caught – as Hannah Arendt succinctly put it – 'between past and future'.

Arendt writes about the sheer difficulty of thinking, in the sense that anything that is genuinely an act of thinking involves an engagement with 'the new' as such. Thinking requires that we are aware of the past, but not determined by it: the future is what can be imagined and 'thought' precisely because it is not as yet established. We stand in the gap between past and future, and this can be an uncomfortable place. From Roman times, she argues, 'this gap was bridged by what … we have called tradition'; but the tradition has worn thin – as Bloom argues in his attempt to resuscitate it. Then when this 'thread of tradition' broke, writes Arendt, there arise problems that are to be faced not only by intellectuals but by all, because we are all now placed in an existential crisis, situated in a gap between past and future, without any clear signposts that will guide our behaviour or values. The consequence is that the gap between past and future is no longer simply the preserve of the intellectuals, 'those few who made thinking their primary business'. Now, instead, the problem of the present has been generalized, opened to all, as it were, such that it 'became a tangible reality and perplexity for all; that is, it became a fact of political relevance'.[6]

If this is an existential crisis for the individual, so it is equally for the political and social institutions that govern the lives of individuals. Our contemporary institutions are shaped by their historical moment; and this moment, today, defines itself always as 'modern' and as a moment of 'change'. It is a tiresome cliché of our time, especially among the

[6] Hannah Arendt, *Between Past and Future: Eight Exercises in Political Thought* (Penguin, London, 2006), 13.

business and managerial classes, that we are living in 'a fast-changing environment' with 'rapidly developing changes in the landscape', and that we must endlessly modernize in order to keep up. Senior University managers, especially when elevated to their positions in our contemporary institutions, always seem to feel a deep compulsion to eradicate the immediate past and to begin anew in some foundational – fundamentalist – manner.

The present moment becomes breath-taking when they claim that they are 'really excited' as they 'look forward' to 'delivering successfully' in all 'key areas' of the 'robust and rigorous quality assurance landscape', thus guaranteeing that an 'excellent strategy' will mean that we will 'welcome challenges' as we overcome them, ensuring that we are 'at the forefront' of leaning and teaching and research, 'going forward', usually by 'making a significant investment' in further managerial posts like those with 'pivotal roles' who will 'drive things forward' in 'the exciting growth agenda' of 'our new Education Executive'.[7]

Amid all this breathless excitement, the central policy is always related to change, innovation, and restless modernization of everything we do, at all times. We have started to resemble the 'modern' author who was satirized by Jonathan Swift in 1704 in *A Tale of a Tub*. That author, caught in the eighteenth-century conflict between the supporters of traditional 'ancient learning' and the novelties of 'modernity', sides fully with the moderns. Indeed, he is so modern that he must always live in the constantly advancing present; and this leads him to the ridiculous point whereby he is virtually erasing his sentences as he writes them, for each new statement supersedes the last. So modern is he, indeed, that each sentence is out of date even as he is putting the full stop in place.

In politics, the logical culmination of such ardent modernity is the consummate and pathological liar, such as Donald Trump, for whom every new sentence is a new departure and a new 'policy' regardless of what he may have just said. This mental state resembles the condition of a schizophrenia in which the modern individual is modern precisely to the extent that he or she is living in a constant present tense, with no continuity at all between discrete linguistic instantiations of 'I'. Not

---

[7] These phrases are all lifted verbatim from University websites – because you could not make it up.

only is this utterly irrational, but it is also politically troubling in that it dispenses completely with any idea of reasoned debate, rational argument, or the scientific validity of any claim with respect to empirical realities.[8]

It is almost certainly the case that the senior managers who parrot the rhetorical clichéd verbiage regarding their 'passion' and 'excitement' at all this new newness, to the point where this is 'what makes me get up in the morning', have also either lost touch with empirical reality (and thus are mad, like Swift's 'modern' author living in a schizophrenic continuous present tense) or are simply talking without believing the words themselves (in which case they are liars). Although one might hope that they are only liars, thus allowing for the possibility of reasoned debate, neither option here is good; both schizophrenia and lying imitate and rehearse the behaviour of a Trump – which also means that our senior managers are no longer amenable to rational debate at all. Yet they are leading institutions whose very function has a good deal to do with the enhancing of honest and open reasoned argument. This is awkward.

To govern by whimsy is to govern by brazen power: it is intrinsically authoritarian. I argued towards the close of Chapter 3 above that academic freedom is the ground of all human freedoms. Any institution that is governed by managerial whimsy has replaced the primacy of academic freedom with the demand for compliance and conformity, regardless of reason and regardless of any democratic impulse. It has no place in a University; yet the ideology of constant managerial and professional reform in the name of what is a spurious modernization has ensured that whimsy dictates – in every sense of that verb.

In the higher education sector, our present times, it is claimed, are nothing like the much slower and allegedly nearly static medieval and pre-medieval epoch. It would thus be an exercise in crazed nostalgic folly to expect our University institutions to be anything like those that opened in Fes, Bologna, Paris, Oxford, Aberdeen, or St Andrews.

---

[8] It is naïve to expect that politicians will tell the truth: lying has always been regarded as a fundamental aspect of political rhetoric. The difference here is that, at the present time, with the ideological demand for constant modernization, we have lost the possibility of engaging in rational debate. To question the politician about any statement that he or she makes is to question a past state of affairs and one that no longer persists. The very ideology of modernization disables criticism.

There can be no going back to any imagined halcyon days, just as we are faced with the horror that it may now be impossible to go back to equally imaginary halcyon political days when a politician's statements might be measured and judged against empirical realities.[9]

While it is true that we cannot return to the mythic golden age of the University, for the simple primary reason that such a golden age never existed in the first place, it is nonetheless equally mistaken to imagine that we can construct something entirely new, with no reference to any past at all. The myth of endless 'modernization' depends on a false construction of history, in which every moment as it arises makes some kind of total and irreparable break from its immediate past: every new moment is, as it were, a revolution, a radical break with our forebears and our provenance. Yet it is always 'justified' by the seemingly reasonable idea that it is only a 'reform' of systems that are outdated and that have not adapted well to our current fast-changing environment (an environment in which the only real change is that the rich seem to get ever richer while the poor remain always with us).

The most obvious manifestation of this in our University sector is in the demand for constant innovation, both in pedagogical techniques and in modes of research. Every day has to be a kind of ground zero, or 'year zero', in which we are called upon to re-think everything anew in the doomed effort to keep up with our fast-changing times, and to work as if we are completely innocent of everything that has gone before. Shockingly, this extends to an implicit active forgetting of everything that constitutes our own knowledge and experience. 'Structured active forgetting' has become the norm. Any knowledge we have was yesterday's knowledge; today, things have changed; today, 'anything is possible'.

This suggestion, clearly, is an equally deranged idea, in which hyperbole exceeds rational sense and veers into commercial branding of the kind that we might see in a University strapline: 'Come to Utopia University, where anything and everything is possible.' More than this, however, the 'anything is possible' mantra sits very comfortably alongside a meritocratic suggestion that, if individuals have somehow failed

---

[9] On this, see two essays by Hannah Arendt: 'Lying in politics', in *Crises of the Republic* (Harcourt Brace & Co., New York, 1972); and 'Truth and politics', in *Between Past and Future*.

in advancing themselves socially or economically, it is because they have not embraced their possibilities or taken the chances that such an open society and University has offered them. They have more or less rejected the possibility of success for themselves, in this meritocratic logic. They must 'own' their own failure.

Politically, this allows a society to say that the poor are responsible for their own situation, that they are themselves to blame for their poverty, that – in the current jargon – they 'lack aspiration', and so on. In the University, it allows us to claim that those who have not advanced themselves are responsible for their own under-development or alleged backwardness. It excuses our social institutional failures, and allows the privileged to claim that our systems are a success.

To say the least, these meritocratic propositions are debatable: we have known for a long time that circumstances delimit possibilities. Zola's novels are all about precisely this; and, when such literary naturalism is superseded by existentialist fictions such as Sartre's in *Les chemins de la liberté* or *La nausée*, even existentialist 'free' characters such as Mathieu or Roquentin struggle with what fate has dealt them as their hand of cards. The reason why our forebears did not fly to the moon was not that they lacked aspiration, but that the historical circumstances of their lives made such a thing completely impossible and probably even unthinkable. The past conditions us, even if not totally, in giving us the circumstances within which our lives and possibilities can be shaped.[10] Merit always conspires with the contingent arbitrariness of luck, good or bad.

It follows that, even in our contemporary and modernizing moment, there may be – must be – things that we can learn from the past. We might learn that we should not repeat the bad aspects or detrimental attitudes that prevailed in the past, for one thing. (If only.) We can learn, perhaps above all, that we can evaluate our institutions in direct relation to the societies that have historically subtended them, for there is a deep intimacy between the structure of our societies and the presiding norms that govern our institutions within those societies. We

---

[10] This is the opening of Karl Marx, *The Eighteenth Brumaire of Louis Bonaparte* (Foreign Languages Press, Peking, 1978), 9: 'Men make their own history, but they do not make it just as they please; they do not make it under circumstances chosen by themselves, but under given conditions directly encountered and inherited from the past.'

can learn that Shakespeare, for example, wrote the language that he did not because he was a failed twenty-first-century hipster or hip-hop artist, but because only certain linguistic possibilities were available to him, no matter how inventively he might have modified and re-shaped meanings.

Indeed, it is only because we know of this intimate correlation – bringing together into a profound intimacy a society, its normative languages, and the conditions that govern its institutions – that we can understand the meaning of our historical institutions as having existed in the past at all; and that is why we know, today, that we are not in the ninth-century University of Al-Quaraouiyine in Fes, or in 1412 St Andrews. It follows from this that we must understand the endless drive to modernization as being itself ideologically driven, philosophically anything but straightforward, and yet related intimately to the conditions of our own historical epoch, an epoch that is governed by a number of important post-war institutions and international accords.

The condition of the modernity of our time, especially among the advanced and pioneering economies, can be fairly clearly summarized in the light of this. Our modernity can be appropriately characterized by a specific inflection of 'the modern' that brings together ideas of a globally interlinked 'open' world, a world of open doors organized around the primacy of finance, the view that all human interaction is really a form of quasi-commercial or real commercial trade, and that this will produce peace (in the form of acquiescence or complicity). Within this, there is an attentiveness also to the 'fast change' of technological advance, broadly recognizable as the backdrop of neoliberal economics in which stock-exchange movements focus on high-frequency trading done by computer algorithms at speeds that could not conceivably be matched by sentient human individuals. Thought, as in any sentient being, takes time and delays us; for financial trading, that time is time wasted and could be used more efficiently to make more profit, thanks to the purely robotic actions of an unthinking and unreflective algorithm in a computer's software.

In social terms, and especially in the UK, the USA, and other advanced economies of the twentieth century, this new ideology was one that combined the demands for emancipation with the aims of scientific and social progress through the exploitation of new technology, perhaps especially the technologies of computing and of artificial intelligence, and certainly the increase in mechanical automation of all industrial production.

It is worth remarking that the contemporary realization that professional jobs can also be robotized stems precisely from the fact that those jobs have also reduced the possibilities of human intervention by making that intervention a mechanical exercise in which the managing of existing realities has become more important than participating in the *making* and re-making of such historical realities.

In 1930, Keynes had famously pointed to the ostensibly inevitable utopia of the fifteen-hour working week. Initially, this could be imagined precisely because of what were even then already achieved advances in engineering, computing, and the emerging science of robotics. As we know, one of the major issues facing contemporary accounts of politics that are predicated upon labour derives from the fact that traditionally working-class manual jobs can now be done much more cheaply by robots. It is also worth remarking that it is only when professional and traditionally middle-class jobs (medical, legal, pedagogical, and the like) face a similar threat from mechanized robotization that these advances become a social and political issue.[11]

The very novelty of technology is key to a further political and cultural shift that affects the present moment. Technology tries to domesticate – to make familiar and ordinarily available – new modes of living and working that are unusual, difficult to understand, and essentially 'foreign' to our contemporary norms. At this point, a new discourse emerges, in which 'the foreigner' becomes the scapegoat for the loss of working-class jobs; and the consequence is a determination to close borders, to build walls (thus reversing Berlin 1989), and to reject all forms of foreign thinking in favour of protectionist economic strategies.

Gary Younge offers a succinct analysis regarding the Berlin Wall and its fall that is relevant here. As he puts it, after 1989 and 'as country after

---

[11] The MOOC (Massive Open Online Course) is the first significant attempt to robotize the University. For one significant figure in the early development of the MOOC, Sebastian Thrun of Udacity, it was clear that by 2060 only around fifty actual Universities would remain worldwide. See his interview in *Wired*, 20 March 2012.

country shed its Stalinist overlords and went into free-market freefall, the case for their peoples' right to leave was eclipsed by the fear that they might actually come'. He exposes the piety of the post-1989 'free world', which welcomed the abstract fact of the freedom of those who had suffered from Cold War restrictions on movement, but which then also feared the material reality, in which 'we' might have to welcome the foreigner here. 'In the west their "freedom" was welcomed; their presence was not. While they were demolishing a wall, we were building a fortress.'[12]

The political closures – and these may extend also to intellectual closures, such as that lamented by Bloom – that are brought about in the wake of such protectionism, including above all economic protectionism and privatization, are a major cause of the refugee crises of the early twenty-first century. The interesting fact for us as we consider the University in the light of this relates to the whole question of 'access'; but that must also be considered in relation to matters of class, national supremacies or 'market competitiveness', and the 'protection' of the privileges of the already wealthy classes at the cost of the underprivileged working class and poor.

What Keynes knew in 1930 was that the social problem for the worker would no longer be physical exhaustion from overwork, but rather the question of how to cultivate a new sense of self from the amount of leisure time, time that might be given over to things like further or higher education.[13] Time itself would be freed; time and possibility would open up for many who had become used to seeing the foreclosure of their life-chances through the economic demands of labour itself. The correlation of these two things – the benefits of technology and a particular form of working class emancipation through education and intellectual advancement – led to a construction of modernity that, from the 1960s onwards, would be one characterized by greater personal autonomy and also, with that self-determination, an

---

[12] Gary Younge, 'Border controls are a sign we value money more than people', *Guardian*, 16 October 2017.

[13] It was André Gorz, above all, who undertook the serious thinking that this situation provokes. See, for some fundamental examples, his *Farewell to the Working Class*, trans. Mike Sonenscher (Pluto Press, London, 1982), *Critique of Economic Reason*, trans. G. Handyside and C. Turner (Verso, London, 1989), and *The Immaterial*, trans. Chris Turner (University of Chicago Press, Chicago, 2010).

increased democratic rejection of deference to established powers and
the assumptions of class-based privilege.

༄

It is through this that a new formation of the University comes about.
The University of the 1960s and 1970s becomes one that is cast precisely in terms of dissidence, criticism, and protest. The key protest
was against one remaining major imperialist war, in Vietnam. Protest
against this war, in the advanced economies, took a primary form of
student protest against governments. Such protests suggest that the
students of this time had a strong social and political sense that the
work that they did was of a piece with reconstructing the world as
a whole. They saw this in terms germane to the period as part of a
culture in which deference would be refused, non-advanced nations
should have a right to autonomous self-determination, and the idea
that 'might is right' must be contested, in every way and at every level.
In short, there was a generalized bolshiness with respect to all forms
of established 'authority'; and such self-assertiveness, especially of the
young against the established forces of a society, became a norm for
the intellectual classes. The era of unearned 'privilege' was to be placed
under warning; and the warning would be linked to the expansion and
further opening of higher education.

The conventional view in the UK is that this expansion – the opening of the University to a greater mass of students – derives from the
recommendations of the Robbins Report in 1963; and it is certainly
true that the report had a massive positive effect, and that it gave material visibility to the drive for a higher education system that would no
longer be confined to the privileged classes only. However, there was
another great innovation in higher education in Britain at this time that
had at least as much effect on this, and that was the establishment of the
Open University. The symbolic effect of this – the idea of a University
that was Open in every sense, right down to its name or title – was
enormous, signalling a real change in our attitudes to higher education
for a greater number of people.

The original idea behind this new Open institution is much debated.
Harold Wilson claimed the patent on it, as it were; but several others
had also mooted the idea at various times. Most notable among these
was Michael Young. Young was known for his satire *The Rise of the*

Meritocracy of 1958. Although the idea of a meritocracy was subsequently posed as a progressive social benefit, given that it challenged the idea of value supposedly inherited by class, wealth, or social status, Young's satire is profoundly critical of the idea. For Young, a meritocracy simply gave material substance to a different kind of social division, in which those at the top would claim that they 'merited' their position and thereby enjoy their new privileges without scrutiny or scepticism, while the disenfranchised and impoverished likewise 'merited' their poverty. The idea behind an Open University was very different from this.[14]

The first direct political reference to the idea came in a speech made by Harold Wilson in Glasgow on 8 September 1963, when he spoke in public for the first time about a proposal to inaugurate what was then called a 'university of the air'. He reiterated the idea a few weeks later – and it was adopted as a policy commitment – at his formal conference speech to the Labour Party when the party met in Scarborough. The emerging manifesto platform was one that would bring Labour to political power in government. This was the same speech in which he spoke of the importance of technology to the economy and to social life, usually referred to as the 'white heat of technology' speech.

Interestingly, even as early as in that 1963 speech, Wilson was already describing the talk of 'fast-changing society' as a cliché. That 'fast-changing world' has been with us a long time, and is certainly not the new environment that our managers claim as they drive us to modernization. Wilson referred to 'the cliché that we are living at a time of … rapid scientific change', adding that 'we are living perhaps in a more rapid revolution than some of us realise'.[15] He was speaking of what would later become our most recent developments in artificial intelligence, AI, when he spoke of how automation in its essence is not

---

[14] See Pete Dorey, '"Well, Harold insists on having it" – the political struggle to establish the Open University, 1965–67', *Contemporary British History*, 29:2 (2015), 24172 for an excellent detailed account.

[15] See report, 'Labour's plan for science', the full text of the speech given by Harold Wilson at Labour's annual party conference at Scarborough on 1 October 1963, available at: http://nottspolitics.org/wp-content/uploads/2013/06/Labours-Plan-for-science.pdf (accessed 12 January 2018). All subsequent quotations from the speech are taken from this source.

just about making cars, say, without human intervention. Wilson saw that 'the essence of modern automation is that it replaces the hitherto unique human functions of memory and of judgment'. He makes a political distinction at this juncture in the speech. On one hand, technological progress 'left to the mechanism of private industry and private property' will lead to 'high profits for a few, high employment for a few, and to mass redundancies for the many'. Against this, he proposes a different mechanism, which he is unafraid to call 'socialist', whereby we might harness technology 'for a progress ... directed to national ends'.

Education is to play a key part in this, starting from the abolition of the exclusionary principle and divisiveness of what Wilson called the 'educational apartheid' of the eleven-plus examinations, an apartheid that closed the doors of advanced education to a substantial number of children. Apartheid, of course, was based on a structural racism that proclaimed the essential superiority of one group of individuals over another; and all my arguments about this so far will be very important to remember in what follows below. Further, argued Wilson, we cannot afford a similar 'segregation' such as happens through a similar closing-off of opportunity at eighteen-plus either. It was in the light of this that he proposed to double the percentage of the age cohort attending a University, and also to inaugurate a 'university of the air'. This would represent a continuation of the impressive legacy left by the Attlee administration, which had already increased student numbers extraordinarily dramatically. Wilson's new Open University would be a full University, not dedicated merely to the obviously utilitarian and instrumentalist deployment of science and technology, for 'I believe that a properly planned university of the air could make an immeasurable contribution to the cultural life of our country, to the enrichment of our standard of living.'

It is difficult to exaggerate the importance of this Open institution. It was to be a full University, autonomously governed like every other campus-based University, with full degree-awarding powers. Although it would indeed have some limited plant – that is, an actual physical place – it would operate via the new possibilities opened up for distance-learning through television (and specifically, through the BBC). Its most radical foundational condition, however, concerned the entry requirements for students. There were none. It was – and remains – a University that anyone could attend, with or without any formal prior qualifications academically or technically.

For Jennie Lee (who was at that time Minister for the Arts) and Harold Wilson, an Open University made economic sense, for it would tap into the extraordinary resources and potential of people who, for various reasons, had not previously been in a position to advance their learning. These included those who, for reasons to do with their family background and economic circumstances, had to take on paid employment from the age of fifteen or sixteen, curtailing their formal education. They also included people who had served in the war, and whose education had been thereby interrupted or even aborted. With the coming of new technologies that would also increase the 'free time' of labour, they included people who would pursue study just to know things and thus to extend their own horizons, enriching the cultural life and improving the general standard of living in the nation. An Open University, in this form, would rehabilitate the human and humane functions of memory and judgement (and, by extension, knowledge and justice) that some advanced technology ostensibly endangered.

Yet the Open University was an imperative not just for these good economic reasons. Wilson and Lee saw it as an essential part of a social project, that of increasing opportunities for those disadvantaged by class and by background. As Pete Dorey writes, 'In this context, it was claimed that a university education should become "a right of democratic citizenship".'[16] It would no longer be the preserve of the already privileged, and it would thus help ease the class divisions and snobbery (as Wilson overtly described it) that scar modern societies, especially and above all in Britain. The University would be Open in order to ameliorate the social conditions of all, and would work to eradicate the social divisions that had been based in class division and its exclusionary principles. Those privileged classes had assumed their own exclusive 'right' to the University and to all that it promised; but now the social mission in the 1960s would seek to change that. It would do so by this linking of education with both democracy and citizenship: everyone could be a member of this new Open institution, this new and fully open study.

---

[16] Dorey, '"Well, Harold insists on having it"', 247. See also Ben Pimlott, *Harold Wilson* (Harper Collins, London, 1992), 513–18.

We have come some distance from this idea and ideal in our own time. The Open University was developed between 1964 and 1966 and opened formally in 1969. Today, a mere fifty years later, we find ourselves under a government that explicitly envisages the closure of a University, such closure being construed, completely counter-intuitively, as an indicator of the success of the institution.

The 2016 Higher Education White Paper, prepared by Jo Johnson as Minister of State for Universities in the Conservative administration, will help us to explain (though not necessarily to understand and accept) this bizarre and dispiriting logic and political position. The title of the White Paper, *Success as a Knowledge Economy*, indicates the expected attitude of bright optimism that takes the idea of a link between knowledge and economy as so obvious that it will require no scrutiny, no examination or consideration.

We must be clear here: this entails an understanding that it is utterly normative to consider that the very essence of knowledge is that it can be monetized, that it is above all an economic issue. Any other consideration of the value of knowledge becomes somehow an additional extra, a superfluity, and thus entirely unnecessary. Such an attitude goes all the way from Charles Clarke's philistine comments in 2003 (when he was Secretary of State for Education) to the more recent scandal of Patrick Johnston's comments in 2016, made from his position as VC at Queen's University Belfast. Clarke stated that 'I don't mind there being some medievalists around for ornamental purposes', arguing that State funding should be reserved for disciplines that were 'useful'.[17] Patrick Johnston, having failed utterly to learn from such philistinism, in fact essentially repeated it almost verbatim when he announced that 'society doesn't need a 21-year-old that's a sixth-century historian', going on to add insult to injury by stating that what society needs is 'a 21-year-old who really understands how to analyse things, understands the tenets of leadership … , who is a thinker, and someone who has the potential to drive society forward'.[18]

[17] See Will Woodward and Rebecca Smithers, 'Clarke dismisses medieval historians', *Guardian*, 9 May 2003, available at: https://www.theguardian.com/uk/2003/may/09/highereducation.politics (accessed 23 November 2017); and see also the fuller report in *Times Higher Education*, 16 May 2003.
[18] See Rebecca Black, 'Queen's University Vice-Chancellor Patrick Johnston: can we put my history blunder in the past?', *Belfast Telegraph*, 1 June 2016, available

The 2016 White Paper essentially decides to ignore the controversies that we might expect to circulate around this. In fact, the paper reiterates precisely the philistine belief that the UK's economy depends essentially on the successes allegedly to be gained by the instrumentalization of knowledge for economic purposes. All kinds of philosophical questions would normally follow from this; but they go unasked. One might ask whether the last thing that society needs is a VC who can think only as narrowly as Patrick Johnston, or a Minister of State for Universities who reveals himself to be as barbaric as Clarke. We can see the consequences of our predicament under these politicians as we read the White Paper and subject it to scrutiny.

Part of the idea of the White Paper and associated Higher Education Bill in 2016 is the determination to add further impetus to the drive for marketization of the University institution. In line with this, market logic dictates that there should be a substantial increase in the number of institutions, so that competition can be extended and more firmly and purposively concerted. As in athletics, say, a crowded field should produce more excitement – and more innovative ways of winning. We will leave doping aside for the moment – but only for the moment, for the University in our time has its own modes of 'enhancing performance' by indirect and even corrupt means (usually massaged and decriminalized as 'gaming the system'). This belief is encapsulated in the cliché informing us that, apparently intrinsically and logically, 'competition improves quality'.

Ostensibly, then, the White Paper envisages an expansion of the sector, with lots of 'new providers' as it calls them, each of which will enter into the rigorous competition not just for students but also for that prestigious title, 'University', that I discussed in Chapter 2 above. However, this new competitiveness comes at a heavy price. In paragraph 17 of the Executive Summary of *Success as a Knowledge Economy*, we find the clear reversal of the impetus that drove Wilson and Lee in the 1960s. There, at paragraph 17, we get the government's explicit acknowledgement that some institutions are expected to fail and to be closed.[19]

at: www.belfasttelegraph.co.uk/news/education/queens-university-vicechancellor-patrick-johnston-can-we-put-my-history-blunder-in-the-past-34763168.html (accessed 23 November 2017).
[19] All references to *Success as a Knowledge Economy* are taken from the web documents, available at: https://www.gov.uk/government/uploads/system/uploads/attachment

Paragraph 17 opens by stating that 'With greater diversity in the sector, more high quality entrants, and increased choice for students, our primary goal is to raise the overall level of quality.' There are some significant and unwarranted presuppositions here. The new institutions will extend 'diversity' and will axiomatically be 'high quality', yet it is not clear that these two claims are either logically necessary or linked in any way other than by an ideology that says, axiomatically and without any need for legitimization, 'more choice means higher quality'. That, of course, is also what the sentence claims – or rather merely asserts – when it implies that the obvious corollary of its logic is that the 'primary goal' of raising quality overall will be fulfilled merely by the introduction of these 'new providers'. Without any evidence to validate any of this, nor even the feeling that there might be any need to justify it, it must remain as a purely ideological statement. It is proposed as something that is as natural as the weather, and equally uncontestable and unamenable to argument. After all, you can bring as many horses as you like to a race, but if none of them can run fast, their sheer numbers and diversity do nothing to enhance the quality of horse racing: quite the contrary.

The consequence of accepting such an ideology unquestioningly is fully apparent in the very next sentence in paragraph 17: 'we must accept that there may be some providers who do not rise to the challenge, and who therefore need or choose to close some or all of their courses, or to exit the market completely'. Shoot the horses. This is treated with sanguine suaveness, as the paragraph explains that a Closed University is no bad thing. Indeed, with characteristic philosophical Optimism, the paragraph immediately follows this threat of closure by stating that 'The possibility of exit is a natural part of a healthy, competitive, well-functioning market and the Government will not, as a matter of policy, seek to prevent this from happening.' The knackers' yard is the guarantor of our stock: look at the rotting corpses, and wonder.

This crazed Optimism continues into the supplementary document, called 'Student Protection Plans', where we find (in paragraph 6) that 'While institutional closures happen infrequently in the higher education sector, as part of a diverse and innovative sector providers may need to stop providing a course or close a campus. Managed course changes and orderly institutional exits are a feature of a healthy, competitive and well-functioning higher education market.'[20]

This is obviously counter-intuitive in all kinds of ways. To suggest that failure is a natural sign of health is hardly rational: it is akin to suggesting that heart failure is a precondition of cardio-vascular and respiratory health in a human organism. It also implicitly endorses the idea that failure – and thus the 'Closed University' – is an absolute and structural necessity in demonstrating the incontrovertible health of the higher education system. Any such suggestion regarding the politics of higher education, it follows from this, must be, clearly, purely ideological, driven by unthinking cliché and not worked through as reasoned propositions.

This should be placed alongside Wilson's 1963 speech, for there, too, Wilson also acknowledges the possibility of failure. Yet the 1963 attitude is entirely opposite to the contemporary proposition. Raising the idea of a genuinely experimental science and technology programme, Wilson accepts that some projects may indeed fail; but 'many will succeed and in succeeding will provide Britain with new industries'. The failures here do not prove the success of the overall programme: they are failures, and in the cause of experimentalism – more usually called genuine research – we must accept them and learn (and teach) from them. However, the failed hypothesis in a laboratory, say, is no reason for closing the laboratory. Yet this is fundamentally the claim that is a tacit presupposition of the 2016 White Paper, which can now be exposed as a minatory document ensuring that the threat of failure – and its consequences in closure – will hang over every institution, every academic, and every student. The spectre of the Closed University, and all that that entails, haunts our laboratories and seminar rooms.

〜

[20] See: Department for Education, 'Higher Education and Research Bill: student protection plans', September 2016, available at: https://www.gov.uk/government/uploads/system/uploads/attachment_data/file/552724/Student-protection-plans-information-note.pdf (accessed 23 November 2017).

There are two important consequences of this comparison between 1963 and 2016. First, for Wilson in 1963, the key thing was to do something genuinely new and inventive, and not simply to do what we were already doing in a more capitalist-efficient way. To expose ourselves to the possibility of that genuinely new thing, we must take a risk. As he put it, there can be no point in adding a new 'gimmick' or 'additive' to 'some consumer product which will enable the advertising managers to rush to the television screen to tell us all to buy a little more of something we did not even know we wanted in the first place'. That is to say, the value of the University's research is that it will produce things previously undreamt of in all our philosophies, something genuinely new. Secondly, the comparison of Wilson's Open University with the present time reveals clearly what it is that lies behind the paradox of the present thinking in which failure is indeed the mark of success, and that institutions must fail. There is at least one specific aspect of the ideology that determines the paradox and allows it to be thought as if it were rational. That ideology is one that subscribes to the view that 'competition' boosts 'overall quality'.

It is important to be precise here. Competition might indeed improve overall quality in some commercial activities, in the manufacture and sale of commodities by 'providers'. A new hybrid car, for example, might provoke all car makers to improve their overall stock with the adoption of new hybrid models. However, it does not follow that each particular commodity – each new model – is always better. Logically, in fact, each particular case cannot be axiomatically 'better', for the simple reason that, for each particular to be 'better', every particular would also have to be 'better'. And, if every case is better, then, logically, they are all the same – and thus cannot be better than each other. In fact, as we know empirically, competition produces greater degrees of conformity – and thus a narrowing of choices – as each new provider mimics what has been seen as successful elsewhere.

The spurious and pious logic of 'diversity', as spoken of by Johnson, is self-contradictory. It starts from the proposition that competition makes *every* institution 'better' (improves overall quality), and simultaneously contradicts this claim for a general improvement with the supposition that some are better than others. We have seen such chop-logic before, of course. It appears in Orwell's satire on totalitarianism in

Animal Farm, where 'all animals are equal; but some animals are more equal than others'.[21]

There is only one way to square the circle in this Johnsonian logic of competition. Behind the claims about diversity, Johnson – and all those who subscribe to this logic of market competition in the University sector – must think that, for the happiness of all students, it is imperative that they are 'matched' with the most 'appropriate' or most 'correct' institution for them as individuals. We then find, indeed, that those institutions that manage to market themselves as the 'best' are those that will claim and retain the most privileged or 'best' students.

Translated from philosophical logic to empirical reality, this gives a society the 'rationale' behind the existence of, for example, 'The Russell Group'. This self-rewarding and self-selecting group of VCs exists, it follows from all this, for one key reason: the Russell Group is there in order to promote a structural inequality among institutions in terms of their value, prestige, or standing. That structural inequality is, in turn, predicated on the apartheid-style subscription to the idea that some students are essentially better – more equal – than others. We have not rid ourselves of the snobbery, the class-divisions or the dubious (politically potentially racist) cultural substructure that used to be attached to the idea of an elite Oxbridge education; we have just re-titled it.

Here, we can recall from my earlier observation the importance that Wilson gave to the idea of attacking snobbery. We should recall that he described it as a form of 'educational apartheid'. The logic of competition in the University sector is one that we can now see as being based on a structure of thinking – an ideology – that is precisely the same as that which governed ideas of essential and completely undeserved and unearned privilege in a racist State. Far from welcoming 'diversity', competition here prioritizes an alleged but tacit innate superiority of one class of people over others: the wealthy over the poor. It is completely the reversal of any idea of a so-called meritocracy.

The key issue in this, as is evident from the Russell Group's own official policy statements and videos, is that the group really still regards itself as intrinsically 'exclusive', being governed therefore by systemic exclusion and closure. This is the case notwithstanding its many and

---

[21] George Orwell, *Animal Farm* (1945; repr. Penguin, London, 1982), 114.

repeated claims that its doors are as wide open as they could ever be to anyone and everyone. They are precisely as 'open' as is the most expensive restaurant to the poor and hungry.

Looking at the group's self-advertising regarding such claims to openness, we can see that, fundamentally, its case is that the excluded have only themselves to blame for their exclusion. It asks those who are thus allegedly excluding themselves to examine their own failings. Maybe they have not 'made the right choices' in terms of the disciplines they wish to study. Maybe their qualifications are not in what the Russell Group disingenuously call 'facilitating subjects', meaning the subjects that it values above all others for no actual stated reason. Maybe they don't even apply because they lack the necessary aspiration. Maybe they did not make use of visit-days to help overcome the 'daunting' environment of the Russell Group hothouse. These – all made explicit in Wendy Piatt's publicity materials – can be very simply glossed and explained.[22]

'Making the right choice' of subject means choosing only what you've been successful at thus far, and thereby accepting that your fate was sealed at age eighteen or, indeed, when you 'chose' your GCSEs (a choice that was itself limited depending on your school's range of offered subjects, peer pressures, parental advice, and so on); or even, indeed, at eleven when you failed your eleven-plus exam; or – well, why stop now? – when you were born to the wrong parents and background.[23]

Choosing 'facilitating subjects' means doing only those disciplines which 'we', in the Russell Group, have decided to value over others, in a decision that is utterly in line with both a notion of essential academic hierarchies (physics higher than art, say; biology higher than sociology) and a craven conformity to whatever the government of the day suggests we 'need' (STEM subjects, say). The claim is that 'facilitating subjects' are facilitating because they 'open a wide range of options

---

[22] See Russell Group, 'Opening doors: understanding and overcoming the barriers to university access', 30 January 2015, available at: www.russellgroup.ac.uk/policy/publications/opening-doors-understanding-and-overcoming-the-barriers-to-university-access/ (accessed 23 November 2017).

[23] This is also consistent with the Conservative agenda to 'examine' children at ever earlier ages. Logically, they might just go the whole way, and adopt a eugenicist approach to education: maybe something like Huxley's *Brave New World*.

for university study'.[24] There are eight such subjects (English literature, history, modern languages, classical languages, mathematics, physics, biology, and geography). It is not clear how it is that these open more possibilities than, say, philosophy, art-design-technology, economics, music, drama – or, indeed, anything else. Yet they do bear a striking resemblance to the classification of disciplines that are called 'academic' and not 'vocational'. This classification is one that is instrumental in making a class distinction between 'workers by brain' and 'workers by hand', and it is one whose purpose is to occlude distinctions of social class while exercising precisely the judgements made on the basis of those essentialist distinctions.

Some potential students apparently lack the correct degree of 'aspiration'. Let us be as frank as possible here, and reveal the awkward and awful attitude that lies hidden behind the piety of 'aspiration'. To have aspiration implies (and perhaps even means) to adopt the correct or acceptable attitude of scorn and derision for your working-class background, and especially if that is economically or culturally impoverished. The unstated implication behind 'aspiration' is one that asks: who in their right mind would not want to escape from a working-class community, after all? The sooner we all escape, and thus abolish the lower classes, the better. Such a tacit logic is socially divisive in the extreme, and is instrumental in producing a culture of resentment as a fundamental norm.[25]

Finally, the advice saying 'don't be daunted by us' means that we know we are forbidding institutions. That is our very aim and ideal: we forbid entry to those who have failed in the three previous requirements above.

In any case, logic dictates that, if these are to be 'top' institutions or 'leading Universities' in the Russell Group's self-description, they must

---

[24] See Russell Group, 'Subject choices at school and college', n.d., available at: http:// russellgroup.ac.uk/for-students/school-and-college-in-the-uk/subject-choices-at-school-and-college (accessed 23 November 2017).

[25] The work of Richard Hoggart and of Raymond Williams is an appropriate counterpart to such an ideological position, indicating the worthiness of working-class traditions and communities, with shared values that are every bit as important as those held to be 'better' values by the middle classes. The entire attitude here is analysed well by Owen Jones in *Chavs: The Demonization of the Working Class* (Verso, London, 2011).

by definition be exclusive and anything but permissive. By definition, in a hierarchy such as they propose, not everyone can be 'top', and so they have to select. The way to get round this, according to Wendy Piatt and the group, is essentially to be more exclusive at an ever-earlier stage of education. This is, in a word, a reinstatement of hereditary privilege; and the Russell Group is entirely complicit with it; it simply doesn't care to acknowledge, openly, the innate snobbery that persists in UK cultures and education especially. Although they will not acknowledge it, the VCs who are the members of the Russell Group operate according to a logic of exclusion, placing a wall between them and the rest of the sector – and also the rest of the social world.

~

We live in what we might call 'the Age of the Wall'. The Berlin Wall famously fell in 1989; but since then, political and social walls have been erected or promised at an alarming rate. 'Peace Walls' continue to stand in Belfast; Israel builds a 'West Bank Barrier' some four hundred miles long; Hungary builds a wall along its border with Serbia and Croatia to exclude refugees during the 2015 migrant crisis; and so on. Famously, Donald Trump rested a large part of his case for election as President on the determination to build a wall along the southern border of the USA in order to ensure that Mexicans cannot enter the USA.[26] If the UK leaves the European Union, then it will have to build some kind of three-hundred-mile long barrier between Northern Ireland and the Republic of Ireland.[27]

However, I have suggested that we might learn some things from the past, even though we must be fully alert to these actual contemporary conditions. Let us begin not with the contemporary world, but rather with a pun from 1534; and we will see very quickly its relevance to our current condition, and to the idea of a democratically 'Open' University.

[26] This has been exacerbated further by his executive orders excluding individuals from seven other nations whose populations are mostly Muslim, and by his 'temporary' complete ban on refugees from Syria. At the time of writing, the legality of this is contested.
[27] At the time of writing, January 2018, the question of a border separating the Republic of Ireland and the European Union from Northern Ireland and the UK remains contentious.

It was in 1534 that Rabelais published *Gargantua*, in which we find the giant Gargantua building the 'anti-abbey', the 'abbaye de Thélème', for Friar John. Friar John had been Gargantua's accomplice in the ludicrous war that he had to fight against Lord Picrochole. The Abbey of Thelema is to be like no other monastery in the world, given the state of corruption into which these institutions have fallen. These monastery institutions were supposed to be the guardians of books, of entire libraries, and of thought and meditation: they were very like a University, in that they formed a focal point around which the most advanced thinking could be done, in the light of the traditions embodied in writings from the past. They were to be a kind of *fons et origo* of 'the good' in both thought and deed; and they were to serve as beacons of enlightenment or 'truth' that could be taught to the general society.

However, the satire on education that Rabelais provides in *Pantagruel*, the story of Gargantua's son, actually preceded *Gargantua*. Although it comes second in terms of the chronology of the narrative, *Pantagruel* was written and published before *Gargantua*, probably in 1532. It is clear, especially from chapters 7 and 8 of *Pantagruel*, that Rabelais was firmly of the view that the regular formal advanced education of the day – such as we have it in the influence of the monasteries – was in a state of utter decadence. The new Abbey of Thélème is to be radically different, in an effort to rehabilitate the point and function of learning as such. 'Thélème' is the French transliteration of the Greek θελημα, which can be translated as 'will'; and the motto that will guide this Abbey of Will is 'Fay ce que vouldras', or 'Do as you will',[28] 'As You Like It'.

In terms of the architecture, Thelema Abbey is to have no surrounding walls, according to Gargantua: 'il n'y fauldra jà bastir murailles au circuit'. Friar John agrees – and here comes the pun from which we might derive some instruction, for he says: 'où mur y a et davant et derriere, y a force murmur, envie, et conspiration mutue'.[29] So, 'where there is a wall both before and behind you, it follows that there is gossip [wall before and wall behind means wall-wall = mur-mur = *murmure* = gossip), envy, and a conspiracy of all against all'. Walls – which

[28] François Rabelais, *Oeuvres completes*, vol. 1, ed. P. Jourda (Garnier Frères, Paris, 1962), 204.
[29] Ibid., 189.

construct division and individuation – provoke introspective and parochial power-struggles, essentially. They are therefore the very opposite
of what is needed in an institution given over to free exploration, be it
in this abbey or in any modern institution in our own time.

Who could deny that the exclusionary walls that surround our
various University institutions or 'mission groups' breed exactly these
kinds of jealousies, resentments, 'conspirations', and struggles for preferential treatment?

Our contemporary institution is obsessed with walls and with discriminatory divisions and borders. Again, we proclaim our 'openness',
with our plethora of 'access agreements' and strategies for 'widening
participation'; but we certainly do not constitute an Open University
(nor, sadly, is the Open University itself any longer quite as 'Open' an
institution as it was first intended to be). Indeed, it is because we are
organized around ideas of 'closure' – the competitive logic that seeks to
legitimize the actual closure of institutions – that we need the institutionalization of 'access agreements' – open doors – in our constitution;
for such agreements will allow us to register as many students as we
need to justify our continuing existence. It is because we are organized
around a specific 'enclosure of the intellectual commons' that governs
the principle of exclusivity (which we call 'excellence') that we need
to invent the strategy of 'widening participation' as a countervailing
principle.

We remain fixated not just by a general 'war culture' as I described
that earlier, but also now by a general 'wall culture'. It is through the
combination of 'war and wall' that we are finding ways of continuing
the Cold War, itself an aftermath of 1939–45.[30] One speech that helped
set the terms for what we can call a 'Cold War culture' was that given
by Winston Churchill, under the title 'Sinews of peace', on 5 March

[30] In the UK, the phenomenon of Brexit is a good example of this. Throughout the
campaign, there were endless references to Churchill, to the war of 1939–45, and to
British bulldog stubbornness and national character. The Prime Minister 'triggered'
(interesting term) 'Article 50' to begin the process of leaving the European Union
in March 2017. Interestingly, in the middle of that month, Decca Records released
a 'new' album of songs by Vera Lynn, who is associated deeply with the 1939–45
war. Presumably, Decca scented a market at this time. See my 'Brexit: thinking and
resistance', in Robert Eaglestone, ed., *Brexit and Literature* (Routledge, London,
forthcoming).

1946. He was being awarded an honorary degree at Westminster College, Missouri; and he began the speech by making explicit the link between the name and title of the college – Westminster – and the political realm of politics in London's civic district of Westminster, where 'I received a very large part of my education in politics, dialectic, rhetoric, and one or two other things'. This is more than just a nominal link, for Churchill claimed that the college and the Parliament are 'the same, or similar, or, at any rate, kindred establishments'.[31]

The speech is best known for its depiction of an 'Iron Curtain' that 'has descended across the Continent' of Europe, stretching 'from Stettin in the Baltic to Trieste in the Adriatic'. The setting-up of this metaphorical wall establishes a clear political divide in the rhetoric of the speech between, on one side, Churchill's claims for a society shaped by a 'Christian civilisation' that values pre-eminently 'freedom and democracy' and, on the other, a world shaped by tyranny in which the great capital cities and their populations 'are subject in one form or another, not only to Soviet influence but to a very high, and, in many cases, increasing measure of control from Moscow'.

The speech establishes an identification of Western politics with a specific inflection of 'freedom and democracy' and aligns that, in turn, with the underpinning 'Westminster' linkage of politics to the University. It becomes a tacit presupposition of the speech that the University exists in order to further such freedoms and democracy as Churchill identifies, in his stated terms of free elections in multi-party states designed to respect and to further human rights, and opportunities for humans to develop their lives and potential to the full. This is set against a tyrannical polity, on the other side of the Cold War ideological structure and Iron Curtain, where 'control is enforced upon the common people by various kinds of all-embracing police governments'. In that context, Churchill argues that 'The power of the State is exercised without restraint, either by dictators or by compact oligarchies operating through a privileged party and a political police.'

Thus we have a series of cultural and political oppositions that shape

---

[31] See Winston Churchill, 'Sinews of peace', 5 March 1946, available at: https://www. winstonchurchill.org/resources/speeches/1946-1963-elder-statesman/the-sinews-of-peace/ (accessed 23 November 2017). All subsequent quotations from the speech come from this web source.

the modern and Cold War world: openness versus authoritarianism and tyranny; free expression versus policed speech; a supposedly genuine democracy on one side versus a distinction between State and 'the common people' on the other. It is small wonder that Churchill would identify with the former in all these oppositions. The question for us today, however, is how we have reached a position in which the latter, those various blocks to democratic freedom, identified here with a totalitarian State, have come to dominate and to shape the contemporary University on 'our' side of the Wall or Curtain just as much as on the other.

Of course, to say such a thing is to invite disbelief: obviously, we do not work under tyrannical authoritarianism; obviously, we are free to speak out and have a full academic freedom that allows us to criticize our own institutions and their leaderships; obviously, we are not opposed to the common people in any way. To that, all I might say here is: 'Really?' Historical events do not completely bear this out, in fact. We might examine the history more fully.

Prior to its fall in 1989, the Berlin Wall had been the clearest material manifestation of Churchill's metaphorical Iron Curtain, even if it was built some fifteen years after his speech. Its fall was presaged – and demanded – in another political speech. On 12 June 1982, the then US President, Ronald Reagan, spoke to a very large crowd at the Brandenburg Gate. Very dramatically, he described the Western side of the Wall as a domain shaped by people who 'welcome change and openness'. This was a clear invitation to Gorbachev, whose entire policy had been organized around the introduction of change (the 'restructuring' called *perestroika*) and openness (the transparency of *glasnost*). He was optimistically implying that Gorbachev was really (essentially) a Westerner, one who would welcome such change and openness. 'There is one sign that the Soviets could make', Reagan provocatively said, 'that would be unmistakable, that would advance dramatically the cause of freedom and peace ... Mr Gorbachev, come here to this gate; Mr Gorbachev, open this gate; Mr Gorbachev, tear down this wall.'[32]

---

[32] The text of Ronald Reagan's speech of 12 June 1982 is available at: www.history place.com/speeches/reagan-tear-down.htm; and video at: https://www.youtube.com/watch?v=5MDFX-dNtsM (both accessed 23 November 2017).

Seven years later, the Wall did indeed come down. In the inter-
vening years, between 1982 and 1989, the very meaning of 'freedom'
changed, however. Thanks to the economic primacy of Reaganomics
and Thatcherism, 'freedom' was reduced to 'choice' and, above all, to
consumer choice within a circumscribed commodities market. The
ideal of a freedom associated with the thinking of Churchill in 1946
(openness, free speech, democracy) was re-conceptualized as a newly
enhanced and revisited form of eighteenth-century commercial trading
based in *laissez-faire*. The moral and political dimension of freedom was
subjugated to a neoliberal ideology in which every aspect of our lives
is reduced to purely economic consideration, and qualitative value
translated into – reduced to – quantitative price. Through this decade,
everything became reconceived as a market; everything is for sale; and
the physical war of all against all is refigured as a commercial war of all
against all, renamed as 'free trade'.

It is important to distinguish such *laissez-faire* from the Rabelaisian
'Fay ce que vouldras' in Thelema. *Laissez-faire* subjugates moral values
and indeed all indices of virtue to monetary value alone. It trans-
lates matters that should be evaluated as qualities by translating quality
instead into the measurable metric of quantities. It does this through
a commercial activity that is driven by the idea of making financial
profit; and it prefers to do this in a privatized fashion. By this, I mean
that it prefers not to make any appeal to an over-arching State that
might regulate the commerce, or that might re-introduce issues of
quality, or questions of ethical value, or a sense that profits might
accrue to a community rather than to an individual.

'Fay ce que vouldras', by contrast, is oriented entirely around qualitative value: liberality, high learning, benevolence, virtue, and so on.
Its carnivalesque Rabelaisian no-walls and open-doors policy makes
it the complete opposite of the privatized institution: it is eminently
public and dedicated to a general and common improvement of life.
Those governing qualitative values operate as a silent regulatory system
– like a State – and subscription to them ensures that we can avoid a
state of natural war of all against all. Such wars are those we can see in
our own contemporary trade wars, trading tariffs, and frantic desire for
economic supremacy (national, personal, or in corporates). They are
also eminently visible in the league-table competition that increasingly
presides over and haunts our everyday activities: quality subsumed to

quantity, everything subject to measurement, and all finally coming down to a question of monetary profit in various ways.

We have seen the re-emergence of division occasioned by the spread of a rampant isolationism, itself built upon the ideology of competitive acquisitive individualism that was endorsed as a norm in the neoliberal 1980s. Not for nothing did Pink Floyd release *The Wall* in 1979, with its anthemic 'Another brick in the wall' as the image of a quasi-industrialized education (not to mention the injunction that the character, Pink, makes to himself to 'tear down the wall' and allow himself access to his emotional life properly).

The walls of a University campus were once typically covered in graffiti. Nowadays, they are much more likely to be clean and anodyne. They now are not the meeting-place for posters for every possible action and debate; rather, they either are blank like the office walls of corporates or they have advertisements for things related to 'the student experience': regulated societies and the like. The more important issue relates to how Open the University is with regard to its surrounding polity: the city, the nation, the world and its peoples. Is there a writing on the wall that we cannot see?

This will take us into a consideration of the rise of an anti-intellectual populism in our time, and how it affects the democratic principles – the being-together or *Zusammenhang* – that I suggested should be at the centre of a University education. In Chapter 3 above, I considered the idea of 'exceptionalism', especially in Dostoevsky's paradigmatic figure of Raskolnikov. The logic of 'the exception', when applied to ideas of inequality, raises interesting issues regarding democracy.

The relation of populism to democracy is the subject of the next chapter.

5

Inflation, democracy, and populism

I have suggested in earlier chapters that we are currently seeing a series of Newspeak manoeuvres in which some bizarre semantic reversals are taking place. In this present chapter, I want to examine one very fundamental shift, in which the University has played a decisive role. This is the shift from an alleged subscription to democracy into a mode of populism that is virtually the opposite of democracy. The shift in question manipulates the usual vocabulary and instruments of democracy for the anti-democratic purposes of advancing the interests of privilege.

We can begin from the counter-intuitive proposition, outlined in the previous chapter, that 'failure is success'. We can also begin not with an example from so-called 'high culture', but instead with a popular song. Long before he became a Nobel Laureate, Bob Dylan wrote 'Love minus zero / No limit' for his 1965 album *Bringing It All Back Home*. The song is usually considered to be a love song addressed to his then partner, Sara Lowndes. Each stanza compares 'my love' with the everyday, and notes a sharp distinction. In the first there is an opposition set up between mere everyday fidelity (being 'faithful') and the better and more substantial 'truth' (being 'true, like ice, like fire'). The second – the key one for this argument – makes a distinction between those who engage in open political debates (reading books, talking of situations, then drawing their conclusions 'on the wall', with graffiti) and 'my love', who, by contrast, 'speaks softly', for 'She knows there's no success like failure / and that failure's no success at all.' Speak softly: advice that would go unheard in today's bombastic and boastful University. The boastful bombast in the language of excessive success that shrieks from every institution's leadership office makes it impossible to hear what is actually going on, often in silence and often involving the silencing of less bombastic voices, the voices of critique that note failures.

Dylan's phrase – relating success and failure – is extraordinary. If we insist on having examples from 'high culture', then we might usefully align Dylan with Samuel Beckett, another Nobel Laureate, when he acknowledged a kind of inevitability of failure in his 1983 *Worstward Ho*: 'All of old. Nothing else ever. Ever tried. Ever failed. No matter. Try again. Fail again. Fail better.' This is one of the most often cited phrases used in relation to Beckett's work, often being used as if it were the most accurate description of his approach to writing itself. Less often quoted is the passage following it, where Beckett writes again of failure. This time, however, he writes: 'Try again. Fail again. Better again. Or better worse. Fail worse again. Still worse again. Till sick for good. Throw up for good. Go for good.'[1]

In this second appearance of the 'fail again' motif, Beckett adds a reversal, much like Dylan had done, where better becomes worse, and where 'Fail better' becomes 'Fail worse again. Still worse again.' The resolution in Beckett works when we go from the comparative – 'better' – to the basic, 'good'. There is, in both Beckett and Dylan, a sense that 'the good' has somehow always given way to 'the better'; and the logic of this is that 'the good' becomes a sign of failure, because it could always be 'better'. It might even be 'best'.

At first glance, this may seem to have little to do with education or the University. However, there is a structure of thinking here that will allow us to expose a specific attitude to the University (and to education more generally) in which we get not just that Orwellian Newspeak that sits behind the marketized view that 'failure is success', but also what I will call an Orwellian 'grade inflation'. Such inflation, however, has nothing to do with the annual allegations, especially in the UK, that we are giving too many first-class degrees or too many A★ grades at A-level, and so on. Rather, it has to do with a very different and much more sinister development, and one that endangers the very

---

[1] Samuel Beckett, *Worstward Ho* (John Calder, London, 1983), 7–8; Bob Dylan, 'Love minus zero / No limit', on *Bringing It All Back Home* (Columbia Records, 1965).

concept of the 'value' of the University as an institution. Why be good when you can be better; and why be better when you can be best? But then, what happens when everyone is 'best'?

Economic inflation was a serious problem worldwide during the 1970s. It hit a particular peak in the wake of the oil crisis of 1973, when the price of oil quadrupled. The oil embargo deployed by the Organization of Petroleum Exporting Countries (OPEC) in protest at US support for Israel was essentially a use of a key energy resource as a weapon of war. Its consequence for the world was an economic slowdown in growth partly brought about by the inflationary pressures resulting from oil scarcities. The world's major economies had already started to abandon the Gold Standard that had helped establish international currency regulations and international stability in the Bretton Woods accords after the 1939–45 war; and, in the new search for economic regulation, inflation based on the manipulated pricing of the earth's resources took off.

The interesting thing is that this period, when the Gold Standard was being abandoned, is also coincidentally the period that Allan Bloom identified as the period during which standard 'core' values were also being abandoned by the American academy.[2] The cultural and political relativism that, according to Bloom, started its rampant and aggressive progress through 'the American mind' really coincides with this period of economic uncertainty, instability – and a destabilizing inflation. The scenario here reiterates the laments that had been heard in the earlier complaints of Leavis, who saw the abandonment of a stable and standard 'humane centre' for all values as being disastrous for education. These descriptions of the academic world could also stand as model descriptions of the economic situation. The abandonment of the Gold Standard in the Nixon administration of 1971 in the USA started a process that leaves all national economies floating and relativized, their worth now dependent upon their transactional values. Likewise, the abandonment of Great Books leaves all University and academic disciplines floating free of any set standard for evaluation.

---

[2] Allan Bloom, *The Closing of the American Mind* (Penguin, London, 1987). To be slightly more precise, Bloom finds a turning point at the moment when the student revolts of the 1960s moved on into the 1970s. At the core of this is what he sees as an account of democracy that he describes tendentiously as 'a tendency to suppress the claims of any kind of superiority'. See esp. pp. 329–30.

In literature, for example, the conservative view was that this situation led to a wild relativism where 'anything goes', and where one individual's 'reading' of any given text or situation has to fight for validation against the 'competition' of another individual's 'rival reading' of that text or situation. In this state of affairs, it is not enough to be a 'good' reading, nor even a 'better' one: all have to claim to be the 'best' in order to gain cultural currency and capital, or to be deemed worthy of the 'invest-ment' of my time and attention. Spreading from within one discipline, the same now starts to apply to the sector as a whole. Every discipline could now claim to be 'the best', essentially. Next in the sequence after this, every institution starts to claim to be 'the best'. It is no coincidence that the first University league-tables date from a period at the end of the inflationary 1970s: the first such table produced was in the *US News and World Report* in 1983 as a list of 'America's best colleges'.

It is through this inflationary structure that we eventually reach a situation in which the language starts to become semantically self-contradictory, leading to the clear falsehoods from which we now suffer, in which something can be so successful that it even makes failure a success – or, in a slightly more acceptable linguistic form, so successful that it 'makes a success of failure'. The Orwellian undertone here should alert us to the political dangers of such inflation: it is consistent with an incipiently totalitarian political system, or at the very least with a profoundly authoritarian system and social structure. This, sadly, can describe many contemporary Universities, at least in terms of their internal governance. The older view of a University as a more or less democratic 'collegium' of scholars and students has now given way to a position in which 'the University' becomes identified as 'senior management' within each institution. The scholars, in this sense, become all of the status of adjuncts, even indentured servants; and they all become mere 'human resources', interchangeable even if each might claim, as a resource, a greater worth than others.[3]

↬

We might usefully ask: at what point did the word 'satisfactory', in educational discourse and policy, start to mean its opposite, 'unsatis-

---

[3] I describe this process, in terms of the details of University governance, in my *Universities at War* (Sage, London, 2015), 107–41.

factory'? When did it become unsatisfactory to be satisfactory? There can be no doubt that, in education, this Orwellian reversal has indeed occurred. It coincided with a period when we were encouraged to subscribe to the managerial dictum and myth of 'constant and continuous improvement' in all things. Such improvement, of course, can only lead to a situation where everything we do is intrinsically a failure, for we can always improve on it, and are compelled to do so immediately and without rest. We must therefore always change, innovate, and, above all, modernize by junking the past, including our own past achievements and experiences or knowledge. In this, we don't just have a form of structural in-built obsolescence; we also have a structure of systemic failure. Every new thing will in turn be shown, by tomorrow's new modernity, to have been unsatisfactory and inadequate.

This is useful to some politicians – as also to institutional managers – but of less use to academic staff, students, and public society as a whole. It breeds resentment as a necessary structural condition of all our professional and personal inter-relations. It encourages distrust of any form of success, including any success whose foundation lies in acquired expertise. It is supposedly a good thing, meant to keep citizens and workers alert and to remind us that we must at all times be open to change and a neo-Darwinian 'adaptation'; but in fact it simply keeps us open to manipulation at the hands of those who claim to be in charge of this endless 'modernization'. It also thereby sets up an internal hierarchy in institutions, whereby managers are axiomatically in charge of things, with workers (in this case, academic staff, students, ancillary colleagues) all chasing ever after the next new thing, however that is described and decided upon by senior management.

In managerial terms, this is what informs and shapes our contemporary sense that many academic colleagues and students are demoralized. In advancing this modernization agenda, management must always regard whatever we do as inadequate, since it is immediately out of date – even as we do it – and no longer relevant to contemporary modern needs. It goes together with a structural de-professionalization of academic staff, who are also reduced to being mere 'counters' or human resources to be expended in and through the process of modernization itself. This is not a good thing, and it is clearly extremely poor management – yet it is precisely what passes for 'best practice' in contemporary University governance, structured as it is in a fundamental hierarchy in which academic staff and students serve the administration: another Orwellian reversal of norms.

'Satisfactory' started to mean 'unsatisfactory', we can see, when we started routinely to describe our Universities as 'excellent'. Once everyone becomes 'excellent', it follows logically and semantically that 'excellent' becomes the new 'average', the whole linguistic system of description here undergoing an inflationary shift.[4] Now, in order to distinguish itself from this new average, this 'merely' average or 'bog-standard' (as Alastair Campbell might call it), a University must now proclaim itself as being better than excellent, as exceeding excellence itself, because mere excellence now must clearly display the failure of the merely average: we can't be just like everyone else.[5] We find ourselves in what is now 'the commonplace, and therefore compromised, quest for individual distinction and singularity'.[6]

To exceed excellence is, of course, logically impossible, but semantically intrinsically inflationary: the excellent can never be enough – never be excellent enough – if it has not yet exceeded itself. Thus the rate of inflation accelerates further and, next, we graduate to the 'world-leading' University, which, in due inflationary course, becomes the 'global' or 'globally leading' University.

Given that we have not yet reached the point where the stock-exchange in inflationary titles simply explodes into the 'planetary' or 'cosmic' institution, we rest now at the stage where, to distinguish itself as a serious University, an institution must now self-describe as being 'world-beating'. This is the new normal: the University as an institution

---

[4] Speaking before the House of Commons Education Committee on 31 January 2012, Michael Gove, then Secretary of State for Education, argued that all schools could become 'good', even though 'good' was defined as 'above average'. See the transcript, especially question 98 and reply, at https://publications.parliament.uk/pa/cm201012/cmselect/cmeduc/uc1786-i/uc178601.htm (accessed 23 November 2017).

[5] Alastair Campbell used the demeaning phrase 'bog-standard' when he was Tony Blair's press secretary in 2001, on the occasion of Labour proposing a reform of secondary-level education. See John Clare, 'Blair: comprehensives have failed', *Telegraph*, 13 February 2001, available at: www.telegraph.co.uk/news/uknews/1322418/Blair-comprehensives-have-failed.html (accessed 23 November 2017). Campbell disowned the phrase later.

[6] Pankaj Mishra, *Age of Anger* (Allen Lane, London, 2017), 13. Mishra's 'history of the present' traces the issue back to nineteenth-century *ressentiment*, the very 'resentment' that I describe here as structural in our contemporary society.

whose fundamental essence is that it 'beats' the world. Taken literally, of course, this also means that the University in this self-description leaves the world behind, trailing as some kind of 'after-thought', and as an after-thought appropriate to a 'loser' in some global race. These losers are those often now identified precisely if journalistically as 'the left behind', and they are then identified, for reasons of ideological manipulation, as 'the people' themselves.

To counter this charge of producing losers, even if only as a consequence of excessive success, the newest inflation describes the University as 'world-changing' — as if our Universities could not be content with engaging with the real world, but would just prefer to exchange it for another one. That other world is the parallel universe in which University management and communications sits.[7] The situation here recalls Brecht's famous poem of 1953 'Die Lösung', in which 'the people', having 'forfeited the confidence of the government', leave the government with a seeming solution, in which it might be easier for the government 'to dissolve the people / and elect another'. By analogy, our contemporary University is in danger of dissolving the reality of our world's contemporary condition and 'electing' or choosing to believe in another world, a fantasy world made of the imaginations of management and able to live up to the model that the University proposes.[8]

Inflated entitlement in this way serves to drive a further wedge between the University and its fundamental links to its hinterland in society itself. The University becomes a world apart (and thus, in due course, it is not out of the question that we will indeed see some 'cosmic' institution soon). It leaves material realities and social histories behind, while staring with great self-interest introspectively and narcissistically at its own world-beating excellence. This yields a malformation of a certain idea of 'autonomy', a malformation that suggests that, if the University operates according to its own laws internally (*autos nomos*), then, by definition, this excuses the institution from having a direct responsibility to the wider social formation, a social

---

[7] See my book *The English Question; or, Academic Freedoms* (Sussex University Press, Brighton and Portland, 2008), chapter 9 (pp. 137–47), 'Clandestine English'; and also my *Universities at War*, 118–24.

[8] See Bertolt Brecht, *Poems*, ed. John Willett and Ralph Manheim (Eyre Methuen, London, 1976), 440.

formation that depends upon the general regulations and agreements that constitute social and political law. In becoming rather literally like the mythical Narcissus, obsessed with self-image and 'reputation', it closes itself off from the world around it.

At the centre of this introspective institution, we find a further self-inflated source of many of our problems: the VC who feels his own title and entitlement are never quite enough. He becomes a 'President' instead, or a 'Chief Executive', whose task is also to be 'world-beating' in the inflated salary terms with which we have become accustomed as a corporate norm ever since the 2007–08 crash, if not before. As the most senior of the modernizing managerial roles, this inflated presidential role must keep leap-frogging everyone else in terms of a salary, such a salary operating as quantitative numerical indicator of alleged success. The institution, of course, may well be very successful; but it does not follow at all from this that the reason for the success is the presence of the VC. Academic staff, students, and ancillary staff have done virtually all of the material and hands-on work. As in the corporate sector, however, failures are always delegated downwards while those at the top always claim the successes.[9]

Language is important here. The standard explanation given for this inflated title and entitlement for our VCs is that, when they go abroad (primarily to the USA) no one there understands the meaning of the title. First, of course, this is simply untrue: are we expected to believe

---

[9] There are numerous examples; but one particularly brazen one might stand as a paradigm case: Nigel Thrift, former VC of Warwick. Interviewed by *Times Higher Education* on 15 January 2015, he was asked about rising VC salary levels and whether it was fair that VCs were criticized for accepting them. He replied: 'Warwick is coming up to a half a billion pounds turnover, has to land its finances on a coin year after year, gets less and less government funding and so must earn more and more of its own income, has to continue to invest in its infrastructure, and must keep on improving. University councils will look for people able to rise to challenges like this.' Translated into clear English, this means: 'Warwick staff do great things; and so I'm worth it', a combination of Narcissus and what we can call, after the advertisement, 'the *l'Oréal* defence'. See 'Q&A with Sir Nigel Thrift', *Times Higher Education*, 15 January 2015, available at: https://www.timeshighereducation.com/news/people/qa-with-sir-nigel-thrift/2017883.article (accessed 23 November 2017). The interview came a short time after Thrift had a 21% salary hike, while limiting all academic staff to 1%. On 16 October 2017, Janet Beer, VC in Liverpool and head of Universities UK, was challenged about VCs' pay and asked whether it was too much. Her reply was 'I don't know what too much is'.

that American and other foreign University Presidents, Provosts, and Rectors are all so ill-informed about our institutions that they have not even bothered to understand how we title the head of a University? After all, since our Universities are 'globally outstanding', presumably people across the globe have become acquainted with how we are run and what we call ourselves. Certainly, the reverse is not the case: we don't have VCs who, when they meet the 'President' in Harvard, say, linger under the mistranslated belief that they are having a meeting with POTUS that just happens to be taking place in Cambridge, Massachusetts. It is utterly disingenuous to try to legitimize self-aggrandizement in this way. Second, even if it were the case that the title of 'Vice Chancellor' is impenetrably obscure to foreigners, can our VCs not 'explain' to them what the title means? It would be a little like explaining to French speakers that the thing they call 'un arbre', we call 'a tree', while Italians speak of 'un albero' and Germans 'ein Baum'. For *vive la différence*, read instead 'vive ma propre différence, c'est-à-dire ma supériorité: moi, toujours et partout moi'.

Such cultural difference, however, cannot be permitted in a sup-posed global race or competition in which we are all ostensibly vying for superiority on the same racetrack, all supposedly commensurable with all those utterly unscientific international league-tables that fail completely to describe material realities. Failing to describe what's important, these tables describe as important the things they can count. The conformity of the language reveals here that there is now an underlying drive towards conformity that is itself governed by the logic of a spurious and manufactured fake 'competition' that produces success and failure – or, as is now clear, produces failure *as* success, thus starting the process of emptying words of their commonly accepted semantic content. The door opens to a language known only to bureaucracy, or Humpty-Dumpty, in which abstract terms can be used to mean, well, virtually anything and nothing.

When this happens to language, we enter a disturbing terrain both in terms of education and in terms of politics. It yields a bureaucracy that is always ahead of the game because, like Humpty-Dumpty, it claims that words mean whatever the manager wants them to mean. As Humpty-Dumpty claims in chapter 6 of Lewis Carroll's *Through the Looking-Glass*, 'When *I* use a word, it means just what I choose it to mean'; and when Alice suggests that 'The question is … whether you *can* make words mean so many different things', Humpty-Dumpty gives what is in fact the real knock-down argument that is pertinent here. He replies that 'The question is … which is to be master, – that's all.'[10] We might say here, in a modification of Wittgenstein, that 'to manage a form of language is to command a mode of life'.

Our semantic inflations are fundamentally about the seizure of control over what can be legitimized as meaningful. The question is one that sits right at the centre of our University arts and humanities disciplines, but one that has a percussive effect right through the institution and society.

⤸

In his essay 'Custodians and active citizens', Robert Hampson advances a concise summary of some of the positive values that the study of arts and humanities subjects in the University offers to a society. While he acknowledges the current demand from business and politicians that the University should train people in the relevant skills to grow the economy, he suggests some other values that should concern us because they are more fundamental. There exist 'other skills, less comfortable for business and politicians, which are important to the long-term health of the society in which we live'. Such skills include 'imagination and vision; a practice of critical reading attentive to language and its implications; an understanding of the narratives, myths and symbols with which we make sense of our lives or by which others try to persuade us; and the ability to bring wider temporal and cultural perspectives on the present'. According to Hampson, these are valuable – and useful – for one major fundamental reason: they make possible the production of 'citizens equipped to engage in the debates about values and social choices that should be part of a healthy democratic society'.[11]

[10] Lewis Carroll, *Through the Looking-Glass* in *The Annotated Alice*, ed. Martin Gardner (Penguin, London, 1970), 269. In contemporary UK politics, the equivalent seizure of power is reflected in the coup d'état captured in the meaningless 'Brexit means Brexit' of Theresa May, giving her the mastery in which she can claim whatever post-European Union arrangement she finds as the real and genuine fulfilment of the wishes of 'the British people': it'll be their fault.
[11] Robert Hampson, 'Custodians and active citizens', in Jonathan Bate, ed., *The Public Value of the Humanities* (Bloomsbury, London, 2011), 73–4.

Hampson was writing at a moment when the humanities were under explicit attack in the UK by courtesy of the Browne Review, which advocated the withdrawal of all state funding for these subjects in our Universities. Yet the UK was not alone in this. Similar predicaments faced – and continue to face – the arts and humanities worldwide. Martha Nussbaum opens her 2010 study *Not for Profit* with the observation that we are facing a worldwide crisis: 'No, I do not mean the global economic crisis that began in 2008 … I mean a crisis that goes largely unnoticed, like a cancer.' This crisis is the crisis in education that threatens 'the future of democratic self-government'.[12] Although centrally concerned with the US situation, where she derives much from a tradition that follows John Dewey's work on the relation of education and democracy, Nussbaum also calls extensively on the work of Rabindranath Tagore to explore similar issues in India and elsewhere. The crisis of education, for Nussbaum as for Hampson, is the cause of a political crisis that threatens democracy itself.

These are among the many eloquent, explicit, and widely accepted explanations of why the disciplines that we associate with arts and humanities earn their place in a University. In almost all such arguments, these disciplines find a special distinctiveness in their contribution to the advancing of democracy and well-informed wide participation in debates over key political issues is a society. They form the backdrop to what Nussbaum validates as 'deliberative democracy', a variant description of a liberal tradition of democracy that goes back to John Stuart Mill's account of democracy as 'government by discussion', a description often repeated by Amartya Sen.[13]

Although he was no lover of democracy, F. R. Leavis shared some of these views, arguing (as I noted earlier) that informed discussion and judgement sat firmly at the centre of his account of a liberal culture. The key difference between Leavis and these other views is that, for

[12] Martha Nussbaum, *Not for Profit: Why Democracy Needs the Humanities* (Princeton University Press, Princeton, 2010), 1, 2.
[13] The phrase was initially coined by Walter Bagehot. See his *The English Constitution* (Fontana, London, 1963), 159–60, 170–1. Mill essentially popularized its meaning. See John Stuart Mill, *Utilitarianism; On Liberty; Considerations on Representative Government*, ed. Geraint Williams (Dent, London, 1993), 115, 207ff. See also Amartya Sen, *Collective Choice and Social Welfare*, expanded edn, (Harvard University Press, Cambridge, MA, 2017), *passim*.

Leavis, the key judgements had to be made by those who were of the elite, those who figured as 'the exception'.

In our own time, it is clear that 'the elite' has become a term of abuse. 'Widening participation' is nowadays one key driver of the democratic credentials of the University. The claim is that by increasing the numbers attending a University, and, in addition, by operating a system that allows underprivileged individuals to gain access to 'prestige' institutions, a 'social mobility' will follow, in which working-class individuals and individuals from low-income homes will rise both socially and financially. The 'ordinary' individual and, indeed, 'the people' will be thus set free from the shackles that constrain their potential for a successful life. This mode of thinking, however, is structured around an equation of success with financial wealth, which in turn is equated with social standing. Indeed, to rise financially in the current climate is itself, *ipso facto*, to rise socially because it denotes success. The accounts of 'liberalism' and 'democracy' that underpin this might usefully be scrutinized.

In the USA, Allan Bloom shares a similar 'democratizing' idea, at least ostensibly. He offers a very dispiriting picture in which he claims that 'university officials have had to deal with the undeniable fact that the students who enter are uncivilized, and that the universities have some responsibility for civilizing them'.[14] The demise of liberal education, as he sees it, coincides with the period when 'the discussion of a unified view of nature and man's place in it, which the best minds debated on the highest level' is lost.[15]

This is Bloom's equivalent of Leavis's 'humane centre', to be calibrated according to an elite of the best minds. By this point, it should be clear that the issue is one that relates the managerial discourse of excellence and elitism to the ostensible democratization of knowledge and of our University institution that is advanced as a desirable social good. In short, how does a well-informed democracy relate to 'the people'?

When the issue is stated in this way, it is clear that it is not just education that is in crisis. The crisis – as I will show – is a crisis in democracy itself, a crisis caused by the advance of the demagogue who will

---

[14] Allan Bloom, *The Closing of the American Mind* (Penguin, London, 1987), 341.
[15] Ibid., 346–7.

divert the democratic impulse into a perverse populism. This is a crisis that has emerged worldwide, and that now figures as a major threat not just to the University but also to much more fundamental survivals, including the survival of the planet itself.[16] In what follows here, I want to consider the University's role in the damaging deterioration of democracy and the consequent endorsement instead of a populism that thrives on ignorance, anti-intellectualism, and the so-called 'post-truth' of 'alternative facts'.[17]

This is close to the ancient 'quis custodiet' question. If we argue that democracy depends upon being knowledgeable about the facts in any political or social situation, then how might we deal with the predicament that access to those facts might be unequally distributed? If we say that there are neo-Platonic 'guardians' or custodians of knowledge who can help guide us (or teach us), then how do we ensure that those custodians are acting not in their own privileged interests but in the interests of those of us who will learn from their teaching and from their research? Who guards the guardians? Today, our predicament derives from the fact that we have subjugated knowledge to the management of information; and the question becomes 'who manages the managers'? Within this, given the questions regarding semantics that I have raised here, the further question is 'who controls meaning?' How do we deal at all with the custodianship of knowledge, and with the curatorship of archival meanings, when we do not all have the equal access to the archive that might properly allow us to be Hampson's 'active citizens'?

⌇

There is a difference between 'events' and states of affairs or 'conditions'. Events either happened or they did not. The Holocaust happened. We

---

[16] The most important 'culture' that cries out to be addressed by the University is not now a 'national culture', nor even that of a 'social culture'; rather, it is the culture of the entire ecological environment itself. The ongoing trashing of this – often by a political class in thrall either to the short-termism of its own power or, more often, to the lobbying of corporates with financial interests in exploitation and corruption of the environment – is our greatest danger.

[17] It was Kellyanne Conway, senior adviser to Donald Trump, who coined the phrase 'alternative facts' to allow that administration to avoid culpability for the attempted validation of lies that are designed to keep people ignorant of actual facts.

may interpret the significance of that event or series of events; but we cannot reasonably deny the factual truth that it happened.[18] Conditions are slightly different from events. For example, it was a condition of sanity until early seventeenth-century Europe to believe that the health of the human body is regulated through the calibration of four basic humours (black bile, yellow bile, phlegm, blood). We know now that human health is much more complex than this, because the conditions of our knowledge now differ from the condition of medical knowledge that we had in the early modern world, even if our physiology (the events that make up our physiological living, our material body) remains the same. No matter how much new knowledge we gain, however – that is to say, no matter what the 'condition' of our knowledge is – there remain unchangeable facts, the facts of 'events': the Holocaust happened, and Nazis killed millions of Jews, Romany people, homosexuals, and intellectuals.

Democracy depends upon us using the first of these categories – the truth of events – in order to effect change in the second – our condition. In simple terms, we gain new knowledge from a clear awareness of the facts of whatever has happened before and an analytical understanding of those facts and events. We do this through the discussion and debate that constitutes proper teaching and learning, and that will lead to our new condition of knowledge. The legitimacy of such debate and of its contribution to the advancing of democracy is itself predicated on two other factors: (a) the increase of knowledge, itself deriving from research; and (b) the presumed equality among participants as they stand before that knowledge, in the sense that all can in principle have equal access to it.

If we accept the validity of this, as a mere part of the understanding of how democracy operates in the realm of knowledge, it is clear that the University plays a key role in the improvement of our human condition through the advancing of learning in dialogue and debate. However, this is precisely what is under a somewhat concerted attack at the present time. The democratic drive that underpins this pro-

---

[18] Obviously, there are those who do deny the Holocaust. However, they cannot be recognized as 'rational' in doing this. Either they lack reason itself, or they are simply liars. This is entirely different from the question of how historians interpret the facts of the Holocaust.

spectus is increasingly characterized as something that excludes 'the people'; and, in place of democracy, we find the rise of a populism that will eschew knowledge itself, and that will prioritize conditions over events. The result is a helpless acceptance that 'knowledge' is supposedly immediately accessible, and to be found in gut or animal instinct: in short, in crude and unexamined or unchallenged prejudice itself.

We find ourselves now at a historical moment when knowledge itself is increasingly regarded as intrinsically elitist, and we face the prospect of making social, political, and cultural decisions about how to live in a good society simply upon the basis of the validation of ignorance. The unacknowledged cultural position here is that 'the elite' have somehow appropriated knowledge for themselves; and the unstated but increasingly normative belief is they do this in order to maintain their privileges as an elite. That is to say: it is as if the elite have privatized knowledge and claimed it for themselves. If someone believes this, it is obvious that they will resist that knowledge, for they will regard the acceptance of it as a form of subservience to the elite, a form of deference that is anathema to democracy. This is a belief that is well founded, as my arguments thus far about the privatization of knowledge in the University have shown. Paradoxically, in this populism, knowledge does not mean power; rather, it means or implies disenfranchisement and submission to the power of someone else.

This is the triumph of belief over truth, of faith over reason. Better still, it is the triumph of 'what we want to believe' over 'what we know to be true'; and it involves a determination, therefore, to remain ignorant and to turn our eyes away from the exigencies of truth or of fact or of events. What validates this ignorance is its contagious spread across a community; and, provided we can share our belief with enough people, we can call it 'the will of the people'. In such a state of affairs, 'democracy' is reduced to 'voting', and even the truth of what has happened will be determined by majority preference in a vote.

The populist impulse mistakes (often deliberately) the interpretation of fact for the fact itself; it prioritizes condition over event, and desired belief (fantasy or wish-fulfilment) over truth. One key thing is required for this, and it is the dismissal of expertise. It is even better, for those who feel disenfranchised by the privatization of knowledge by the elites, if we can claim that expertise is itself precisely the phenomenon that has oppressed our preferred belief.

In this way, we bear witness to the triumph of populism over democracy. When such populism triumphs, it means that the University has signally failed in one of its key fundamental purposes. It depends upon the closing-off of the human mind to the real possibility of making actual changes to our conditions; and it results in a quietism that accepts the fundamental base and order of the world's condition as if it were fact. It yields the mantra of a supposed 'realism', the mantra that says 'There is no alternative' if you are Margaret Thatcher, or 'Resistance is futile' if you are a Dalek. When democracy is corrupted in this way, while still asserting a claim upon democracy, the political rhetorician has recourse to 'the will of the people', as if that will is entirely unified, without tension, internal difference, and nuance, and an expression of freely expressed and independent reason.

How, exactly, does this affect the University as an institution? First, the University – and especially its leadership – says that we must acknowledge realities and adapt ourselves to them. This yields a specific ideal through which the demand is that the University should conform to the world 'as it currently is', for it should operate humbly, deferentially, in the service of that world. Such an attitude presupposes that the world exists entirely independently of the University, that the University does not constitute at least a part of that world, and that 'the world is everything that is the case', all except for the University and the other social institutions that help to constitute that world or that indeed make it 'everything that is the case'.[19] The University and all other social institutions are thereby tacitly deemed to be intrinsically subservient to some other pre-existing reality, and are regarded as having a second-order reality at best. Those institutions, including the University, are now effectively disallowed from having any part in changing the world 'as it is', and must simply 'reflect' it and endorse its norms as given, or serve it unquestioningly as if it were its Humpty-Dumpty master. And, in our time, the 'world as it is' is the world identified by a specific ideology in which all existence is framed as a profit-seeking business transaction.

Second, the University thus mistakes whatever is the prevailing condition of the world as intrinsically unchangeable, because it is

---

[19] Ludwig Wittgenstein, 'Die Welt ist alles, was der Fall ist', in *Tractatus Logico-Philosophicus* (Routledge, London, 1922, repr. 1992), 30.

presented unquestioningly as a fact. It follows that, no matter what knowledge we might present regarding what has factually happened or what is factually happening in the world, it can always be reduced to the level of a mere interpretation of a condition. In any case, whatever we find is supposed also to endorse the norms that govern this allegedly unchangeable worldly state of affairs. In this way, for one simple example, human-made climate change becomes something 'debatable', notwithstanding the factual evidence regarding what is actually and factually happening. Likewise, it is taken as 'fact' that all human existence is motivated by a desire for success in our transactions; and, given that those transactions figure under the rubric of 'business', success here means the acquisition of profit through our 'investments'. This is what underpins those claims that a University education, regardless of the debts that a student might accrue, is a sound investment.

Third, in this spiralling sequence, the University now finds itself – and its construction of what constitutes knowledge – as something whose purpose and function is not determined by the pursuit of truth, but rather by the demand to conform to whatever is the case. It follows, logically, that the University should now exist primarily as a vehicle or instrument through which an individual acquires greater wealth than her or his less educated neighbour. Further, the determination of whatever constitutes the 'reality' of our world now lies not in the hands of intellectuals who might pursue factual knowledge; rather, it lies in the hands of those who can determine and control 'public opinion', those who control semantics and meanings.

At this point, two statements become axioms. First, knowledge is useless unless it produces financial profit or contributes directly to GDP in a nation. In the UK example, Jo Johnson's speech to HEFCE in October 2017 makes it clear that UK Universities will be 'rewarded' with investment proportionate to how well they manage to commercialize their research. Secondly, and even more fundamentally, it becomes safe and even normative to suggest, as did Michael Gove MP, that 'the people of this country have had enough of experts'.

A 'deliberative democracy', such as that advanced by Nussbaum, now finds itself in an awkward position. Such a democracy depends upon a well-informed citizenry, like that envisaged by Hampson. That is precisely what is now endangered through a political recourse to populism. The University, it follows, is also in an awkward predicament.

In acceding to the mantra of 'realism', it finds itself unable to contest conformities to the prevailing view regarding our condition, no matter how many inconvenient truths or facts it presents. Instead, it gives up its role in the advancing of democracy and endorses instead a bland and deferential conformity to public opinion: it becomes populist, no matter how heterogeneous, under-informed, or even misled 'the people' might be. After all, we are now in that position where 'the people' are encouraged to believe their feelings or whatever they prefer or want to believe, rather than allowing their minds to be changed by the facts of whatever is the case.

My contention here, therefore, is that the contemporary priorities of the University lead it to betray the very people whom it claims to be serving through its 'access' and 'widening participation' agendas. It betrays them by yielding place to the primacy of fantasy (what I might want to believe) over reality itself. 'Reality', if it is anything, is constituted in and by change; after all, do we not live in a 'fast-changing environment'? When the University preaches or practises conformity as its legitimizing principle, it thereby precludes the possibility of allowing or encouraging people to change things, or to be in control of that 'fast-changing environment'.

Pankaj Mishra argues that the politics of Europe underwent an extraordinary change as Europe entered into a specific modernity in the wake of revolutionary ideas of equality and fraternity. This opening 'transformed the relationship of ordinary people to time, space and their own selves – introducing them to the earth-shaking idea that human beings could use their own reason to fundamentally reshape their circumstances'.[20] This is one kind of modernity that the contemporary University seems to eschew.

In short, our contemporary 'University of Conformity' institutionally and intrinsically precludes the possibility of changing one's mind about how things might be in the world. Given, further, that 'changing one's mind' is a synonym for 'learning', 'research', and 'teaching', the University of Conformity undermines its own institutional form and purpose. It is never 'world-changing', nor even 'world-leading'; rather

---

[20] Pankaj Mishra, *Age of Anger* (Allen Lane, London, 2017), 52. It should be noted that Mishra, however, presents an extremely nuanced account of such modernity, indicating its negative aspects as well as its progressive elements.

it is 'world-following'; and what it follows is a populist idea instead of a democratic ideal. 'Democracy', as Mill once indicated, 'is not favourable to the reverential spirit'.[21]

'When the facts change, I change my mind.' So said Keynes. Except that he did not. It is interesting that it is not factually true to say that Keynes said this. It seems more likely – yet still not entirely certain – that he said something like 'When my information changes, I alter my conclusions.'[22] This latter is actually closer to what I am arguing here. 'My information' is, quite literally, what has 'informed me', or what has made me who and what I am. 'My conclusions' are subject to alteration, in the light of what must always be a continuous chain of new information, which is available to me for as long as I eschew being dogmatic. As long as we are alive, we are subject to new information, new formation of the self: that is, indeed, the very definition of survival or staying alive. As Keynes himself pointed out – in a criticism of economists who remained always optimistic that no matter how bad things were at any given moment, they would turn out well in the end or 'in the long run' – '*In the long run*, we are all dead.'[23] Survival depends on our being open to the possibility changing the way things are, now and in the short run, if we are to survive long enough to have a 'long run' at all.

The contemporary University is often presented as a 'business'; and the language of business can be at times deeply optimistic in this same fashion.[24] A standard mantra in contemporary business is that 'In every crisis there is an opportunity.' In layperson's language, this really means that we can always 'make the best of a bad lot'. My contention is that one fundamental principle for those who lead our Universities might usefully be to change the bad lot, rather than seek to profit from it.

~

[21] Mill, *Utilitarianism*, 347.

[22] See John Kay, 'Keynes was half right about the facts', *Financial Times*, 4 August 2015.

[23] John Maynard Keynes, *A Tract on Monetary Reform* (Macmillan, London, 1924), 80.

[24] Perhaps the most troubling rehearsal of this banality came from Alice Gast when she took over as President of Imperial College London. In avoiding the question of any responsibility on the part of her institution in relation to the death of Stefan Grimm, she claimed that professors are best considered as 'small business owners'. Alice Gast, interview, *Today*, BBC Radio 4, 17 April 2015.

We can understand this more fully by taking a further look at some conditions of democracy. David Runciman is extremely clear in aligning democracy with what I termed 'the open' in Chapter 4 above. He writes that 'Democracy always leaves open the space for competing views, unexpected reversals, unanticipated rivals. *It doesn't foreclose the future.*'[25] A similar description can be found in Norberto Bobbio. In *The Future of Democracy*, Bobbio cites a piece written by Franco Alberoni in the *Corriere della sera* on 9 January 1977, where Alberoni argued with great simplicity and succinctness that 'Democracy means dissent.'[26]

Alberoni had been Rector of the Università di Trento; and had developed, during the 1970s, a political philosophy that was founded upon mass movements. His early writing was a formulation of celebrity in which he studied 'elites without power', *Elite senza potere* (translated as *The Powerless Elite* in 1972). At that moment, the celebrity was considered to be important because of her or his relation to mass society; but celebrities lacked any serious political power. They stood as icons and as the focal points for much of popular culture; but they did not influence events in any significant manner. Today, however, this has been almost completely reversed, and we are in such an aestheticization of politics that it has become difficult to become elected as a politician – or at least granted authority and power in the cultural domain – unless one is already a television star, and preferably a star with populist rather than substantively popular appeal.[27]

For shorthand here, I'll suggest that the populist is one who appeals to the 'lowest common denominator' of human being, while the popular is one who attains a standing through an appeal to and recognition of 'the highest possible numerator' of human being. What is our 'lowest common denominator' in fact? The one thing we all share is that whatever the conditions of our lives, we are all heading towards the inevitability of death. Populism appeals to a life conditioned by

25 David Runciman, *The Confidence Trap* (Princeton University Press, Princeton, 2013), 240–1 (emphasis added).
26 See Franco Alberoni, 'Democrazia vuol dire dissenso', *Corriere della sera*, 9 January 1977; and Norberto Bobbio, *The Future of Democracy* (1984), trans. Roger Griffin, ed. Richard Bellamy (Polity, Cambridge, 1987), 61.
27 Peter Hennessy, *Establishment and Meritocracy* (Haus, London, 2014), 40, goes so far as to coin 'celebritocracy' to describe this phenomenon.

this fact. It thus organizes itself around a demand for basic survival, which – in its most fundamental form – relies upon violence. This is why populist movements not only praise war, but also head inexorably towards such conflict. Politics, in fact, is our highest way of circumventing the naked power and violence that might otherwise determine the sharing of worldly material resources.[28]

Populism such as this is abundantly clear in the phenomenon that we might call 'Trumpism', whereby a populist appeal to a series of untruths (underpinned by the most violently aggressive rhetoric) triumphs over democratic argument or political and reasoned debate. The US Presidential Trump 'campaign' was reduced to a mere slogan: 'Make America great again.' A similar effect is also found in 2016 in the UK Brexit campaign, which was also reduced to a slogan: 'Take back control.' In time, this latter becomes itself politics-as-sloganeering or the uttering and repetition of cliché: 'Brexit means Brexit'; we must respect 'the will of the people'.

Alberoni was associated with the Eurocommunism of Enrico Berlinguer; and this was a movement that moved steadily away from a conventional concentration on labour-based class-politics to a more Gramscian idea of hegemony – the consequence of this being the increased political attention given to cultural politics, as in feminism, sexual liberation, and the like. Democracy here becomes a cultural matter as much as an argument about labour and production. This, it was hoped, would lead to a 'democratic' (as opposed to a violent and revolutionary) transition to socialism. At this same time, the University was itself moving into the disciplines of cultural studies, semiotics, and 'theory'. These become part of the political superstructure, and, inevitably, they thereby involve the University as a central component or instrument in the formation of a democratic culture and society.

How has the contemporary neoliberal University responded to this? In the UK at least, the answer is clear: the joint commitment to 'access' and to 'widening participation' is to be the way towards establishing a greater sense that the University is not about adding further validation to the already privileged. Yet there are serious problems with this agenda, for the programmes governing 'access' and 'widening participation' do not, in fact, make any real or substantive appeal to the drive

---

[28] I write about this in detail in Chapter 6 below.

for extending democracy at all. Rather, they prefer the easier route of populist sloganeering, or the manufacture of cliché, whose purpose is to prevent serious consideration of thinking about how we might shape history.[29]

In the mid-twentieth century, roughly when Leavis was writing, a very small percentage of eighteen-year-olds attended a University. Predominantly, these were individuals who were already from wealthy or at least financially comfortable backgrounds. Since then, we have seen a steady shift towards a mass higher education structure. However, and notwithstanding the fact that, as I write in 2017, almost half of all eighteen-year-olds now go on to University study, we remain fixated on the idea that these are, in some ways, the 'wrong' additional people, for the evidence seems to suggest that we are simply admitting yet more of the already privileged.[30]

This is a classic example of 'crisis becoming opportunity' instead of 'changing the bad lot' that we are dealt. The bad lot in question is the fact of massive and growing social, cultural, and wealth inequalities. The 'opportunity' is for the less well endowed to 'improve their individual lot' by participating in the University and securing a degree. Why is this in any way suspect? What could ever be said against such an agenda?

The simple answer is to observe that the widening participation agenda is there in order to avoid dealing with the fundamental crisis, the 'bad lot' of mass class inequalities; and the clichéd repetition of the claim, made by every University, that it is engaged in 'widening participation' serves the purpose of precluding any discussion or debate about this fundamental 'bad lot'. Further, widening participation is grounded in two things: (a) an individualist post-1950s idea of aspiring to leave the working class behind; and (b) an unacknowledged

---

[29] We have all seen the clichés: widening participation and access, as here; student experience; dynamic approach; providing solutions; strategy; enablement; 'excellence is a given'; drive; enterprise – one might go on almost indefinitely, just by consulting the 'about us' page of any University website. Such clichés, through their mindless repetition, forestall any serious engagement with the matters they purport to describe.

[30] See the website of the Social Mobility Commission at: https://www.gov.uk/government/organisations/social-mobility-commission (accessed 9 January 2018) for more details and reports.

contempt for the working class – a contempt that serves simply to endorse a hierarchical social structure regarding the value or worth of individuals depending on their social class origins. These – noted earlier in this book – can now be examined in relation to the question of democracy and populism.

As is well known, the 1950s produced a very specific phenomenon, usually thought of as the 'grammar-school boys intent on storming the citadels of exclusive high culture'.[31] The phenomenon was held up as a prime example of 'social mobility', for it allows for some gifted or fortunate individuals from a working-class background to enter the domain usually reserved to the middle classes. Richard Hoggart was one such grammar school boy; but he wrote about this kind of rise with less than complete and unquestioning enthusiasm. He indicates that, through the 1960s expansion of higher education, 'The two main roles of a university were re-asserted: teaching in the atmosphere of research and vice versa.' This is laudable; and Hoggart welcomes it. However, he notes also that there is a 'third role to which some hold', and this role is 'that of turning a disciplined eye on society itself', a role that 'has never been accepted by most university people, let alone by politicians'.[32]

In this kind of structure, while good teaching and research might continue, the institution itself remains unchanged in its forms, functions, and identity by the presence of a different constituency. The consequence is clear and straightforward. Essentially, the individual student from her or his impoverished background is invited to join the ranks of the privileged. Having done or achieved this, the University absolves itself of dealing with the unpleasant fact that, where this individual came from, many more remain. That is to say: the working-class professor, as it were, becomes the token used by the institution to say that it need not address the wide social problem.[33]

David Greenaway, VC at Nottingham until his retirement in 2017, provides a key example, and one that is ideologically at the opposite end of the spectrum from that of Alberoni in the Università di Trento.

---

[31] Dominic Sandbrook, *Never Had It So Good* (2005; repr. Abacus, London, 2008), 183.

[32] Richard Hoggart, *The Way We Live Now* (1995; repr. Pimlico, London, 1996), 41.

[33] Declaration of interest and full disclosure: my own background is working-class and in the east end of Glasgow, in Easterhouse – a by-word for social deprivation.

Born into tenement life in Shettleston in the east end of Glasgow, he has a background that is not usually associated with becoming a professor or being knighted, as he was in 2014. Under his leadership, Nottingham has made a number of successful and outstanding efforts in the widening participation agenda, with massive percentage increases in the number of students coming from low-income families. He is explicit that education 'is about transformation', and equally explicit that Nottingham has a responsibility to transform the opportunities of 'everyone who can come here, independent of income and independent of background'.[34]

This sounds admirable; and is, indeed, a fulfilment of the widening participation and access logic. Yet, at the same time – and notwithstanding the fact that Greenaway also acknowledges that there does exist a social responsibility – these opportunities for transformation are being offered to individuals from low-income backgrounds, and are not primarily aimed at transforming the social conditions of those backgrounds themselves. The tacit presupposition here is that the education will be transformative for the individual students (while not being transformative in any way for their backgrounds), and it will be transformative primarily by lifting the income brackets of those fortunate individuals significantly. As is well known, this phenomenon also often produces existential conflict, as the individual finds herself or himself alienated from her or his original class while never being fully accepted into the newly acquired class.

Recently, Greenaway was the Chair of the Russell Group; and in this role he wrote a classic 'opportunity within crisis' statement in relation to the UK's Brexit vote. The academic community voted 90% for Remain, from which he drew two possible conclusions: 'either the academic world knows something the electorate doesn't or we're hopelessly out of touch'. Well, one might observe that, almost by definition, the academic world is supposed to know something the electorate doesn't. But 'out of touch' also? One reason for the perception that academics might be out of touch is the fact that the knowledge or expertise that they have – that which means they 'know something' – has essentially been privatized. Knowledge, when privatized as it

---

[34] See 'Interview with Prof Sir David Greenaway', available at: https://www.youtube.com/watch?v=vni9keS3C1c (accessed 23 November 2017).

has been in our neoliberal structures (including those of widening participation), is again, by definition, out of touch and beyond the reach of the 'ordinary' people who are excluded by that privatization. When we have a University that engages in the 'enclosure of the intellectual commons' in this way, it follows that almost axiomatically we will become 'out of touch'.

Shettleston in Glasgow was an area of terrible deprivation when Greenaway lived there for the first thirteen years of his life. Today, it remains an area where life expectancy remains stubbornly low (if you live there, you can expect to die at about sixty). We might well ask how it is that a 'leading' University such as Nottingham has done anything whatsoever to address this small fact. Greenaway suggests that Nottingham's great success owes much to 'the spirit of endeavour … that took me from a Glasgow tenement to vice chancellor of this university'. With himself as an example, he goes on to say that 'I'm keen to rediscover that sense of breaking free and exceeding expectations all over again. We all can.'[35]

The simple fact of the matter, however, is that we all cannot do this. The facts of Greenaway's biography are not necessarily replicable universally or even locally; and there are many factors restraining some individuals – in Shettleston, say, or in my own former home of Easterhouse – from 'escaping'. Much more important than Greenaway's 'escape' (or mine) is the fact that, structurally and politically, we can never address the problems that give the people of Shettleston such a truncated life span just by congratulating ourselves as individuals for how we have 'escaped'.

Then, further, why is there this need for such 'escape' in the first place? It is perfectly understandable that a working-class individual might seek to have a better income, say; but it does not follow that this ought to be characterized as an escape or 'breaking free'. In fact, Greenaway's lexicon suggests some level of contempt for working-class life and values, or some sense that the working-class individual suffers from an 'imprisonment'. It is reminiscent of the prisoner of war in those Second World War movies, who had a duty to 'endeavour' (Greenaway's word) to break free and to escape his imprisonment.

---

[35] All quoted passages here are from David Greenaway, 'Brexit might be the catalyst we've been waiting for', *Telegraph*, 22 October 2016.

This is at odds with the thinking of some others of those 1950s grammar-school boys, such as Hoggart or Raymond Williams. Like many others, both Hoggart and Williams saw some profoundly good values in working-class life; and they worried that a higher education was in fact driving a wedge between themselves and their class communities (putting them 'out of touch' with 'ordinary' people). That it can do so derives from that simple fact that, in Greenaway's understanding of widening participation and of social mobility, the governing presumption is that the knowledge I gain from attending a University is 'mine', and that the benefits that might accrue from it belong to me, as an individual only, not as something that I share with my community. It is an intrinsic – yet often unstated – privatization of the institution from within a privatization of knowledge itself.[36]

The picture here is one that is consistent with a populist view, and not with a democratic view of higher education. Democracy, as far as higher education is concerned, is about the giving and sharing of knowledge, not its privatization. It is about that 'third role' of the University as described by Hoggart, in which the institution engages a whole society, and wonders how it might improve things structurally and not just for the specific group of individuals who attend classes or work in laboratories.

It is very important to note here that I am not calling for a kind of 'politicization' of the institution. On the contrary, I am calling for its de-politicization. As things stand at the present time, the fact of the matter is that the University has already been politicized. The political agenda that it is currently supporting is precisely the populist agenda of market-fundamentalist economics, grounded in a fallacious idea of meritocracy that prioritizes the privatization of all human interests and the reduction of those human interests to solely economic terms.

We would do well to recall an observation made by Henry David Thoreau in his thoughts 'On university education' of 1854. There, Thoreau considers the relation between money and education. In

---

[36] It is noteworthy that Greenaway's first appointment to a professorship in economics was in 1987 at the University of Buckingham, the UK's first private University. It should also be noted that, although I concentrate on the specific example of Greenaway, I do so simply because he offers a good and clear example of the ideology that permeates the widening participation agenda. He is far from alone, for his thinking is utterly normative among senior managers.

particular, he addresses the idea of higher education as a form of investment for which the student pays or incurs debt. He argues that 'Those things for which the most money is demanded are never the things which the student most wants.' He notes that one of the most significant items in the student's termly bill is for tuition, yet for 'the far more valuable education which he gets by associating with the most cultivated of his contemporaries no charge is made'.[37]

That 'association' – albeit here with an 'elite' – is what a democratic education might properly seek. This means that widening participation rightly means not just bringing more underprivileged individuals into the University; rather, it means attending, by the work that is done within the walls of a University, to those 'outside' and to their needs. It means that the University as an institution must take on the task of associating more widely, more freely with its circumambient society. In short, it means the University undertaking its dormant responsibility of participating in widening the democratic franchise. Unless we do this, we leave the doors open to the vagaries of a mere populism that, in the end, fails to serve the very people whom it supposedly supports.

There is another complication in the politicization of the University that has further consequences for any suggestion that it might serve to democratize a society. The problem in question relates to nationalism. In his *Education and the University* of 1943, Leavis actually rehearses Thoreau's position, almost exactly. He, too, likes the idea of a community, albeit again the community of an elite few in a Cambridge college. The curricula of a University course, he argues, 'give opportunities' but the main benefit comes from 'the stimulus derived from the general ambience' and from 'the education got in that school of unspecialized intelligence which is created in informal intercourse – intercourse that brings together intellectual appetites from specialisms of all kinds, and from various academic levels'.[38]

Yet we should recall that, for Leavis, the general purpose of the

[37] Henry David Thoreau, *Walden* (1854), ed. Owen Thomas (Norton, New York, 1966), 34.
[38] F. R. Leavis, *Education and the University* (Chatto & Windus, London, 1943, repr. 1965), 28.

kind of University education that interested him was fundamentally to do with the advancing of a specific idea of being 'English'. It was, in fact, the wider context of the English nation that would benefit most directly from the leadership of the elite highly educated few, those who were properly attuned by virtue of their inner essence to the 'humane centre' of all values, a centre to be found specifically in English literature and even more particularly in the English literature seminar led by Leavis himself – and nowhere else. These would lead the 'ordinary' people through their own intrinsic standing as 'exceptions': Leavis's students would be a kind of avant-garde, the custodians of all values, centrifugally dispersed from Downing College. Within England. For England.

There is, it seems, a national limit that determines the scope and ambit of the benefits accruing to a University education. That limit is the limit circumscribed by the idea of 'the people', sometimes described – as in Leavis – as the masses, but always as 'the masses' of a specific nation. In the UK context, this has assumed a special importance, and one directly related to the position of David Greenaway discussed above, and also to the 'vanguard' position of Leavis. Leavis, in fact, was entirely consistent with a current of 'exceptionalism' that still prevails in the sector, worldwide. Whenever there is any suggestion that a barrier might exist between nations that might threaten an institution's expansion of overseas student numbers, the response is always the same. All institutions claim that they want to ensure that they can recruit 'the brightest and best' – the exceptional and already privileged – from across the globe; the rest of 'the masses' go unacknowledged. This has serious repercussions.

On the morning of 18 September 2014, the then UK Prime Minster, David Cameron, stood outside 10 Downing Street to make a speech in the aftermath of the referendum on Scottish independence. The result of the referendum was that the Scottish voters elected, by a majority of 55% to 45%, to remain within the UK. Cameron welcomed this, saying that it now effectively settled the matter of independence for Scotland: it was now definitive that it would not happen. Then he went on immediately to say, 'I have long believed that a crucial part missing from this national discussion is England.'

Suddenly, the entire tenor of the question of Scottish independence turns and becomes focused on England: 'We have heard the voice of

Scotland', he said, making it clear that the vote was definitive. For anyone versed in English literature, this stance surely recalls a very specific precursor. It rehearses the same attitude as that displayed in Cordelia's abrasive and dismissive comment to the Duke of Burgundy in the opening scene of *King Lear*. Burgundy is disappointed that, having been disowned by Lear, Cordelia will not bring a rich dowry and lots of land to him in marriage; but as he is saying this, Cordelia interrupts, to say, 'Peace be with Burgundy' – meaning 'We have heard enough the voice of Burgundy.' Cameron's statement dismisses Scotland at this point, and instead makes a stunning declaration of English independence. An enormous semantic inversion occurs here: the rejection of Scottish independence from the UK becomes, immediately and seamlessly, a claim for and an endorsement of English nationalist independence.

At this point, then, the entire political debates and campaigns over Scottish independence between 2013 and 2014 are essentially dismissed and silenced. Instead, a new position is suddenly outlined; and it is one that will shape the English nationalist politics that will lead, eventually, to Greenaway's hopes for the opportunities afforded by Brexit and a proposed leaving of that other union, the European political union. Cameron turns from Scotland: 'We have heard the voice of Scotland – and now the millions of voices of England must also be heard. The question of English votes for English laws … requires a decisive answer.'[39] This essentially constituted the firing pistol for the race towards a populist upsurge in English nationalism that heralded the Brexit vote, a vote not supported in either Scotland or Northern Ireland. The status of the Brexit campaign as fully and completely populist was made clear: 'We have heard the voice of Scotland' became 'We have heard enough from experts.'

Populism says that we should ignore the possibilities of knowledge, the possibility that a knowledge of facts might change our minds. Knowledge itself is elitist, because, being privatized, it excludes 'the people'. 'The people' therefore must vote according to their feelings and, indeed, must rest their vote as much as possible upon a vaunted and willed ignorance, lest their views be contaminated by reasoned debate.

---

[39] The full text of David Cameron's speech of 18 September 2014 is available at: www.bbc.co.uk/news/uk-politics-29271765 (accessed 23 November 2017).

Thus during the campaign to leave the European Union, we had a whole series of 'vox pop' interviews celebrating racism, xenophobia, and the like, all unquestioned: racism and prejudice going entirely unchallenged and uninformed by any attempt to produce knowledge. Yet the views of 'the people' were themselves not something naturally occurring: they were the views that conformed to the prevailing winds of the ideology, and those winds were explicitly English nationalist, formed and 'informed' by a series of extremely well-funded right-wing individuals and organizations.

It is a commonplace to state that Brexit (and, in the USA, Trump) arose because 'the people' are disaffected by 'the elites'. Yet the views of the people were themselves constructed by and through the will of a specific elite, that being an elite who piously and disingenuously proclaimed themselves to be merely the servants of 'the will of the people'. This particular elite rode the wave of English nationalism (or of American exceptionalism and protectionism) to deride the elites who were allegedly damaging the lives of the people: the elite of the intellectuals, the researchers after true facts. These political states of affairs derive fully from an anti-intellectual populism in which the University is marginalized precisely because it can indeed claim – as David Greenaway should acknowledge – 'to know something that the electorate doesn't know'.

The problem is that, in its present constitution, the University has marginalized itself, by going along with the ideology that such knowledge is a private matter, to be used for purposes of acquisitive individualism, or greed, and not for the widening of knowledge that can be shared in the interests of a democratic engagement that constructs our society. Given this, no one would indeed trust the intellectual, because this intellectual has fundamentally betrayed her or his vocation. This, fundamentally, reveals a substantial problem regarding democracy when it figures under the sign of a prejudicial nationalism; and it is a problem worsened by the prevailing view of what our Universities are for.

↜

Colin Crouch has noted how the democratic political impulse rises and falls across history. He notes a specific high point for democracy in the middle of the twentieth century, a period when Nazism and fascism, 'the final great movements of resistance against democracy', had been 'defeated in a global war'. This was also a moment when economic conditions made it possible to realize some democratic goals, when 'a certain social compromise was reached between capitalist business interests and working people'.[40]

In the terms of my own argument here, we might re-phrase this as a desirable compromise between a University and working people. And this might indeed be appropriate, given what has happened to both the University and to democracy itself since this high point. Crouch notes how one specific form of democracy has become normative, to the exclusion of other conceptions of the democratic society. The form that prevails is the form of 'liberal democracy', and it is succinctly defined. It has particular relevance for the University when the normative and populist account of the University is that it is, essentially, a business. A business is usually involved in 'production' of some kind, and always with the requirement that the production in question yields financial profit.

Liberal democracy is 'a form that stresses electoral participation as the main type of mass participation' first of all. It also formally affords 'extensive freedom for lobbying activities, which mainly means business lobbies'. Above all, it is 'a form of polity that avoids interfering with a capitalist economy' and that thus has 'little interest in widespread citizen involvement of the role of organizations outside the business sector'.[41] This form has become the norm worldwide since the 1980s under Reagan in the USA, where 'US concepts of democracy increasingly equated it with limited government within an unconstrained capitalist economy and reduced the democratic component to the holding of elections'.[42]

Where Reaganomics went, Thatcherism eagerly followed and Thatcher's acolytes pushed further – with damaging effects on the University in both jurisdictions. In both, the University's 'democracy' became constituted solely in terms of its status as an engine of the capitalist economy; and, in both Thatcherism and Reaganomics, that economy was focused entirely on the fundamentals of individualist profit.

---

[40] Colin Crouch, *Post-Democracy* (Polity, Cambridge, 2004, repr. 2007), 7.
[41] Ibid., 3.
[42] Ibid., 11.

Democratic participation in the formation of a social polity is now reduced and even trashed fully. Instead, we find that our institutions must simply comply with – and not scrutinize, analyse, or provide an understanding of – the over-arching and prevailing ideology of a neo-liberal agenda, one that places the desire for individual gain at the root of all motivation and all action. Without a spirit of community, there can be no democracy. The turn to nationalist populism has become the poor substitute for such a community; and democracy disappears over the horizon of the nation state itself. When the University stands as one such key institution that has been hijacked by such nationalist populism and individual greed, then it, too, becomes a major contributor to the problem, and not the motor of its solution.

I suggested above that democracy depends upon a presumed equality among participants as they stand before the disinterested extension of knowledge that comes about from academic research into events or factual states of affairs. However – and by way of conclusion to this present chapter – such equality itself cannot easily be presumed. This is especially so in a University system that is dedicated to the enclosure of the intellectual commons, and to an ideology that is itself determined by the priorities of privatization, including the privatization of knowledge itself.

Clearly, a complete condition of human equality in all things is unattainable by definition. It is unattainable by definition because the condition of being human is one of continuous change; and there can exist no global system that might regulate and calibrate such change in such ways as to render human individuals as 'fully equalized' at all times and in all places. Indeed, we might go so far as to say that such total equality is also undesirable, for it is the flipside of a completely dystopian version of a society where individuals act in complete conformity to some supposed 'standard' or 'model' individual.

Colin Crouch puts this succinctly when he writes that 'The tension between the egalitarian demands of democracy and the inequalities that result from capitalism can never be resolved, but there can be more or less constructive compromises around it.'[43] In our current social and political dispensation, the University has arrived at one specific compromise: it has almost entirely 'compromised' the standing

43 Crouch, *Post-Democracy*, 79.

of knowledge itself, by making it subservient to material inequalities of wealth. It has resolved the tension described by Crouch simply and straightforwardly by caving in to the inevitability of the inequalities that arise from unbridled capital; and it has forgotten entirely the egalitarian demands of democracy.

↩

One way in which our sector has tried to find a compromise between the inequalities of capital and the demand for democratic egalitarianism lies in the commonly held idea that education – and above all higher education – is a vehicle of social mobility between classes. The mobility envisaged by this is carefully circumscribed, of course: it refers always to a social mobility to move 'upwards' in terms of social class and capital. The downside – that mobility might work both ways and push some down, or simply keep them down – is conveniently ignored. The report *State of the Nation 2016: Social Mobility in Great Britain* offers us a way of understanding the issues here. It indicates four key factors obstructing upward social mobility: an unfair education system; a two-tier job and professions market; a structurally imbalanced economy; and a housing crisis.[44] It is the first two of these that are most important for the present argument.

The 2016 report points out that 'despite some efforts to change the social make-up of the professions, only 4% of doctors, 6% of barristers and 11% of journalists are from working class backgrounds'. All of these professions usually require nowadays some level of advanced higher education; but places on the required courses are not unlimited. Access to the profession in question thus becomes 'selective', necessarily as a consequence of the economic structure that governs these professions themselves. As I pointed out with reference to the case of David Greenaway above, we cannot all become doctors, barristers, journalists, or VCs.

How, then, to select? If the prestige of the institution where one does one's first degree becomes a proxy for the evaluation of individuals, it

---

[44] Social Mobility Commission, *State of the Nation 2016: Social Mobility in Great Britain*, available at: https://www.gov.uk/government/publications/state-of-the-nation-2016 (accessed 23 November 2017). Subsequent references come from the documents on this website.

follows logically that it will be predominantly individuals who attended a prestige University who will also gain access to the advanced levels of the professional training. Further, how did those individuals get into the prestige institutions in the first place? As the report makes clear, this is due to the existing class structures that govern our society as a whole. Thus – and this is not addressed in the discourses about social mobility – unless the University finds a way to contest that presiding structural division, and as long as it operates in the mode of conformity to what is 'realistically' the case, then – quite logically – we will never be able to achieve anything like a substantial process of upward social mobility. In fact, we will fail to address the problem at all, while conveniently hiding behind a set of social mobility aims that will act as a means of diverting blame for our unequal and undemocratic society away from politicians.

At this point, we can begin to see two things. First – and, to be fair, the report says precisely this – a good deal of what crushes the life-chances of the poor and the underprivileged relates simply to the fact of their origins, the point from where they set out. The question of an individual's 'origin' – where they set out from – assumes a great importance, and even a primary importance in determining where they will end. Just as importantly, it will also determine and circumscribe a good deal of the substance of their life: it will establish the framework of their possibilities. Despite our culture of supposed fast-change, they will almost certainly end up not too far from where they began: disenfranchised, disregarded by elites, used and abused by the powerful, and poor.

Second, we can also see that this, in turn, presupposes a quasi-natural condition of our society, giving the presiding image of a nature or natural condition of things in which there will always be a structural inequality between wealthy and poor. If this is understood to be, or is taken fully as, a natural condition, it becomes, *ipso facto*, difficult to contest. To contest nature is to be 'unnatural' or perverse in some way. Conformity to political 'realities' moves into a second-order conformity, one in which we are constrained to conform to this supposedly natural condition. At this meta-level, the so-called political reality is suddenly related to the question of our individual origins, and the reality is now deemed to be an entirely 'natural' condition, and thus unquestionable. It just is how it is; and it becomes reasonable to accept it, endorse it, consolidate it, and even extend it.

The University – as a University of Conformity – exists, in this state of affairs, primarily to exaggerate and extend the fundamental inequalities (of wealth, of opportunity, of prestige and standing) that scar our society in the first place. It is a tacit ideology of the 'natural order of things' – an order predicated on an acceptance of inequality without regard for democracy and without being regulated by a democratic drive – that becomes the fundamental obstruction to any social mobility. Worse than this, the ideology of an education that accepts and condones 'the natural condition' actually stands in the way of our ability to extend, via a higher education, all human possibilities. The ideology of 'nature' here, deployed for political purposes, precludes or at least diminishes human freedoms and the ability of humans to re-shape their environment.

When examining the conditions governing democracy, Norberto Bobbio considers the distinction between 'representative democracy' on the one hand and 'direct democracy' on the other. This is an important distinction, for it offers us a way of addressing the question of the institution and its relation to democracy instead of simply thinking of democracy in terms of the supposed equality of individual participants. It permits us to ask questions about the democratic society itself, and about the University's relation or contribution to such a polity.

It also allows us to address, fairly directly, the substantial distance between democracy and its perversion into populism; and, again, we will see that the University has mistaken the former for the latter, to detrimental political, social, and cultural effect. Bobbio points out that, in societies where democracy is ostensibly the political norm – such as we find it in most of our advanced economies – it is still the case that many individuals will from time to time feel inadequately or improperly represented. When democracy 'has been extended to more areas of society than ever before, the call most frequently heard is for representative democracy to be replaced by direct democracy'.

The parallel in a University institutional and social setting can be shown simply. The various participatory agendas that we have – social mobility, widening participation, access – all in the name of enhanced democratization of knowledge and of society, all work on the assumption that unless you attend a University (direct representation, as it were), you cannot participate in the benefits. On the other hand, if we have a different model of the University – one in which knowledge is used for the common good – with the enclosure of the intellectual commons re-opened, as it were – then we can have a system whereby everyone can benefit even if not everyone attends; but the corollary of this is that those who attend have to act as 'representatives' of that wider and common set of public interests.

Bobbio finds the source of his distinction in Rousseau's argument that 'sovereignty cannot be represented'[45] – and this is also consistent with Rousseau's sense that a democracy is an ideal condition to which we should rightly aspire, but which remains unrealizable in some hypothetical pure form.[46] The obvious response to this feeling that we lack sovereignty is to extend democracy, to the point where it becomes direct – which would imply, of course, government by continuous referendum. To take this to an extreme, we would all be so busy voting that there would be left nothing – no action or policy – to vote about.[47] In the University, we would all be so busy garnering individual financial profit that we would end up in a fully atomized society of private individuals unable and unwilling to share in anything and thus unable to form a society at all. That, of course, maps exactly where the current disposition is taking us.

As Bobbio points out, however, direct democracy itself cannot provide the solution here. In fact, we might go so far as to say that there is nothing as undemocratic as direct democracy. Bobbio's argument is that direct democracy requires that every citizen becomes a participant in all decision-making. The human being becomes – or is reduced to – the 'total citizen'. This – which seems to resolve Rousseau's question regarding the calibration of the demands of man and those of citizen in favour of the complete prioritization of the citizen – is not a

---

[45] Bobbio, *The Future of Democracy* (Polity, Cambridge, 1987), 43. He is quoting Rousseau from *Social Contract*, ed. E. Baker (Oxford University Press, Oxford, 1960), 262 (book III, chapter 15). For the original, see Jean-Jacques Rousseau, *Du contrat social* (Flammarion, Paris, 1966), 134.

[46] For Rousseau, the conditions necessary for democracy would include a very high degree of equality among participants, in a very small state where everyone can meet, debating issues that must remain simple and not complex.

[47] Many will recognize this as a rhetorical tactic deployed when one side senses it is losing an argument and makes an appeal to a vote to resolve matters. This quickly becomes a vote about whether we should indeed move to resolve the conflict by a vote, which, in turn, will require a vote about a vote about a vote, and so on. The idea was satirized in Monty Python's 1979 *Life of Brian*.

good thing. Bobbio writes that 'The total citizen and the total state are two sides of the same coin, because they have in common … the same principle: that everything is political.' The consequence of this is that we witness 'the reduction of all human interests to the interests of the *polis*, the integral politicization of humanity, the total transformation of human beings into citizens, the complete transposition of the private sphere into the public sphere'.[48]

There is a final turn here in relation to the University. Our contemporary condition is one whereby, instead of the total politicization of humanity that was of concern to Bobbio, we have instead established the financialization and monetization of all humanity and the reduction of all human interests to the interests of money or of capital. If we wish – as individuals – to contest this, then we need to contest the institutions that render it a normative condition; and one key such institution must be the University, for it is there that we can consider how to establish a more genuine condition of democratic human engagement through learning from research, and through teaching each other as part of that learning.

For Bobbio, a simple extension of the franchise (our 'widening participation') – while necessary – is not a sufficient condition for the proper extension of democracy. We must also attend to an extension of places in which people can vote. By this, he means that we need to extend 'social democracy', and not just (perhaps not even) 'political democracy'. This is important to my argument here, in that I am claiming that the University as an institution is one such place or location where such a social democratic will can be properly engaged.

This does not mean necessarily that we should organize ourselves internally by voting (with elected VCs, Deans, Chairs, and the like), although that would be an extremely good thing in itself. Rather, it means something more far-reaching: it means the University taking a stand as an institution for democratic social life, and thereby attacking the incipiently totalitarian condition in which the University endorses the monetization of human being and the financialization of all values.

---

[48] Bobbio, *Future of Democracy*, 44. For a fuller examination of the political damage caused by the implied destruction of privacy here, see my *Confessions* (Bloomsbury, London, 2012, repr. 2013). Hannah Arendt's *The Human Condition*, 2nd edn, introduced by Margaret Canovan (University of Chicago Press, Chicago, 1998) is fundamental to any argument regarding the calibration of private with public life.

To those who will respond that this is an explicit politicization of the University, the proper answer is that, in encouraging democracy, this position also subjects its own stance to further questioning. It does not preclude others from arguing that the University should be non-democratic or anti-democratic. In this respect at least, it differs from a corruption and betrayal of the University's fundamental principles – reasoned thinking, dialogue, the search for a good society based in the extension of justice and of freedom – from which we currently suffer.

A totalizing monetization of all values and interests – like the complete politicization of all life such that humanity exists only as citizens – produces apathy and disengagement. As Bobbio argues, 'The effects of an excess of politicization can be that the private sphere reasserts itself. The other side of the coin to extending politicization into many areas of decision-making is political apathy. The price exacted by the *engagement* of the few is often the indifference of the many. A corollary of the political activism of the famous and not so famous leaders in history is the conformism of the masses.'[49]

Such apathy and conformism is precisely the kind of quietism that neoliberal politics needs, as a means of ensuring that 'there is no alternative' to the current – 'natural' – conditions of wealth inequality. When the University becomes complicit with total financialization and the privatization of all human interests – especially that of knowledge – then we enter a crisis in which its very survival *as an educational institution* is in doubt. Thus the University finds itself, now, in an existential crisis regarding its very survival.

In my final chapter and section below, I suggest what is to be done.

---

[49] Bobbio, *Future of Democracy*, 56–7.

Part III

Survival

6

Origins, originality, and the privileges of nature

There can be little doubt that the University – indeed the entire infrastructure of all our educational institutions – has become a battleground in recent times. In extreme form, this affects jurisdictions beyond the UK much more negatively than it does here. Recently, we have seen academics being arrested and jailed in Turkey, for instance; we have seen students attacked in a whole series of places, including South Africa, Australia, and the USA. Violence such as this involves the laying bare of some intransigent pressures. However, there are many ways in which – short of falling into direct action and violence – the institution of the University has found itself embattled, in the UK as elsewhere. Something fundamental is behind this. Actually, something sinister is behind it, as can be seen when the battle takes the form of conflicts over academic freedom in which colleagues are threatened and silenced; or when they are seen to be a threat to 'law and order' within the institution through the simple fact of their thinking unconventionally; or when they are deemed to interrupt the 'smooth operation' of the institution if they question anything within its governance, or if they fail to fill in a bureaucratic form or undertake an administrative function in a manner approved by senior management.

Indeed, in the case of the UK, this sense of being embattled is very general across all of education. At primary and secondary levels, schoolchildren have been treated by our political class and by the educational institutions themselves essentially as pawns, to be deployed in conflicts over types of school and modes of education. The whole plethora of different modes of education – 'free schools', public schools, state schools, 'academies', and, haunting us as always in the UK, the return of the grammar school – provokes a deep uncertainty and scepticism among children and their parents. League-tables then become used as crude shorthand that will allow a citizen to discriminate between 'good schools' and the merely 'satisfactory'.

At tertiary level, things are not much better. There, too, a league-table culture dominates policy and strategy in all University and other higher education institutions. Prestige is at stake in this, and it under-pins the new currency that governs the demand for profit. Students are in grave danger of becoming fodder for the voracious appetite of the algorithm that flattens and devours all serious differentiation of value, burying serious value (and ethical values) under quantitative measure and the tyranny of number. Number operates here in tyrannical fash-ion because it is thought to be something absolute, something with which it is always impossible to argue. Two is always greater than one; first always trumps second, axiomatically and by definition. What this hides is the specificity and particularity of the things being enumerated. Two is indeed always greater than one; but what if the two are mice and the one is an elephant?

Such nuances are, of necessity, ignored in a bland flattening-out of all difference. Proceeding in wilful ignorance of such specifics and particularities – that is, in wilful defiance of what constitutes our real conditions – all energies are directed now towards the league-table position as an essentially superficial indicator of a supposed actual standing. Yet everyone within the system – and probably especially those who professionally 'game' the system in order to come out on top – know that the entire game is bogus. It is bogus for the primary reason that it pays little heed to the realities of value that actually form the shape of teaching, learning, or research. These, in the end, are all subsumed under numbers; and one number dominates all things: turn-over. It is this that, in the end, marks the playful-sounding 'gaming the system' as a mode of fundamental corruption that is steadily rotting the system as a whole.

The commercial world also finds league-tables useful, for they oper-ate as a shorthand means that allows employers or professional bodies to arrive quickly and efficiently at an evaluation of candidates for positions in work or professions. This, of course, becomes problematic, since it is based on bogus – or at least irrelevant – information in which quality has been re-transcribed as quantity. The corruption has serious consequences for the whole of the social framework, together with its transition from a democratic culture into a populist one. This proxy evaluation, further, affects the whole of our society: the general public starts to use the proxy evaluations made by league-tables as if they reflect a substantive reality. In turn, this affects both governmental policy and the general structure of our social and cultural systems as a whole. It affects how we live together.

This is what we must now examine more fully, because there is a further slippage between populism and an ideological belief that there is a 'natural order' of things – an order that is given to us as our determining 'origin' – in our societies, to which we ought to conform. This – a question concerning the 'origin of our species' – is where the whole issue of survival as a fundamental issue becomes important. This is not just about the survival of the institution, important though that is; it is about how the survival of the institution can help in the ecological battles over nature itself that are threatening to endanger many forms of biodiversity and that, in the end, will destroy the air that we breathe. At stake is the University as itself a specific kind of social, political, and cultural authority: an origin or originator of a mode of life, one that involves a constant seeking of enhanced human possibilities that will deal justly with the environment while retaining the possibility that we can democratically share in the survival of a public good.

In this closing chapter, we will look at the University and its relation to nature, to the origins of a social life; and we will examine how it might survive and offer the possibility for us to go on, to continue, to initiate, while retaining a relation both to nature and to culture.

~

Hobbes considered what happens in a profoundly 'original' state of nature; and it is unpleasant and far from the idealized paradise of a theological Eden. When he wrote *Leviathan*, in 1651, England was coming out of a period of prolonged political division: a series of civil wars in which Hobbes had witnessed everyday life as a 'war of all against all'. This is a phrase that should have resonance for us: what is a 'war of all against all' but a 'world war'? In the past hundred years, we have had two such wars; and, in the wake of these, we now have an international tension worldwide primarily over the resources that the natural world might yield. Those resources are not just the obvious resources of oil or mineral wealth, but are also resources such as water or clean air to breathe. The war of all against all in our time also therefore describes life as a condition of more or less vigorous competition for resources, for survival, and for pre-eminence. As I have argued throughout here, the key resource that shapes our contemporary geo-political order or international system is the resource of information itself. This places the University at the very centre of contemporary conflict; and it is here that we can start to re-assert our authority and our *raison d'être*.

We might equally well describe this war in the clichéd words of David Cameron and other politicians as a 'global race', through which we aspire to win – with the corollary that others will lose. In terms of the local consideration of the University institution most pertinent here, some will 'exit the market', in Jo Johnson's menacing phrase. Hobbes realized, famously, that in such a state of nature, life itself ends up being 'solitary, nasty, brutish, and short'.[1] It is also worth noting that, when Hobbes formulated this desperate phrase, he was also profoundly aware that when a society is founded in a war mentality – that is, when war or its lesser form, competition, is a presiding driver of all energies – then there is no place for justice: 'To this war of every man against every man, this also is consequent: that nothing is unjust. The notions of right and wrong, justice and injustice, have there no place.'[2] In such a 'competitive' environment, presumably the 'new provider' can expect that there is a good chance that her or his life will itself be conditioned like this: nasty, brutish, short-lived. This does not have the feel of something that is either healthy or ethically desirable. It is also at the most fundamental odds with the founding propositions from which we began this entire enquiry: what might the University do to extend justice in the constitution of a good society?

In at least one respect, such an appeal to a natural condition of things is entirely consistent with one specific political ideology and preference. To base evaluations of individuals or of institutions in relation to some mythical 'original' condition – given to us as if by an unquestionable biological necessity – has its objective correlative in the determination

[1] Thomas Hobbes, *Leviathan*, ed. Edwin Curley (Hackett, Indianapolis, 1994), 76.
[2] Ibid., 78.

to diminish the size of the State as such. The consequence of this is the neutralization of politics, a consequence that further hampers the proper activity of the University and of the intellectual, for it presupposes that the University has nothing to do with the polity, given that the polity is here rather emaciated. If the University has any relation to the polity – as even its contemporary managers insist – then when political considerations are removed from the polity, the possibility that the University can contribute to a political good is also thereby circumscribed, or neutered.

If the 'better' ground zero against which we measure value is given by an original nature, then institutions that have been constructed by humans must of necessity be misleading and represent a falling away from that condition. In our time, we might immediately recognize this as the political ideology of neoliberalism, in which the State and all creative and constructive human activities become subservient to markets, and where the evaluations of any creative activities are referred back to their market price. This has the all the clarity given by the tyranny of quantitative number, while hiding from view the more substantial issue of qualitative value. Worse: as with some latter-day Rousseau, it suggests that to be social at all is to deviate from a natural condition and is therefore suspect.

Dave Eggers satirizes this in *The Circle*. Two of his central characters, Mae and Francis, make love. Francis asks Mae to rate his sexual performance. She replies with qualitative descriptions: 'good', 'fine', and so on. Francis, however, finds this unsatisfactory and lacking in clarity because they can argue about the precise meaning of those words. Indeed, some might want to say that such argument constitutes the very basis of being social at all, and that this is the essence of a sociable being-together in the world. Impervious to this, Francis asks to be rated numerically, because the precision of number precludes ambivalence. Needless to say, he is not happy until he has been rated at 100%. If he were a University, this would be re-translated into those inflationary terms I discussed earlier: 'excellent', 'world-leading', and so on.[3]

The point here is that Francis, in demanding the clarity of

---

[3] See Dave Eggers, *The Circle* (2013; Penguin, London, 2014), 380. I discuss this in more detail, investigating its relation to democracy, in *Complicity* (Rowman & Littlefield International, New York, 2016), chapter 5.

quantitative measure, is determinedly eliding ambivalence and uncertainty. In doing this, however, he is also closing down the possibility of any future relationship between himself and Mae in qualitative terms. To remain in love, as it were, is to remain curious – the word is cognate with 'caring' – and to be in that condition that Keats admired in Shakespeare and that he described as 'negative capability'. Our social-being together, as the basis of any democracy, depends upon keeping arguments going, refusing absolute clarity in anything, and remaining in sceptical doubts while nonetheless continuing to act in a committed manner. In a specific sense, absolute clarity and certainty, in which there can be no doubt, is itself akin to the operations of violence and force, whose purpose is to finalize debate, to propose a 'final solution'.

Neoliberal politics, it follows from these arguments and this fictional example, is, paradoxically, a rather complete attack on the very existence of politics. It does not just attack the size and power of the State, but in its aim to shrink the scope and ambit of the State's operations, it constitutes a substantive attack upon the glue that holds a society together. Earlier, I referred to the essence of market-fundamentalist economics as a state of mind, endorsed by Milton Friedman, in which greed is the primary motivator for all human activity and societies. However, beneath greed there lies a yet more fundamental emotion, and one that is known to a people who, like the people of England when Hobbes was writing, are in a condition of war. That emotion is fear.

Peter Borish, a market investor who, almost alone, predicted the major financial and stock-market crash of 1987 (thereby making a fortune), argues that 'fear always trumps greed'. He explains that 'when it comes to trading, it's supply and demand for money … and when people are fearful, rationality goes out the door'.[4] When humans invent and develop a State, they do so for precisely the same reasons as Hobbes advanced when he makes an appeal to a transcendent power, subscription to which can help regulate conflict and avoid its reversion to crude force and violence. A significant part of the point of establishing a State is to diminish the emotion of fear in its people. In doing this, reason can operate at the heart of politics – or, in my terms here, the

---

[4] Peter Borish, interviewed on *Today*, BBC Radio 4, 19 October 2017.

University can assume its proper position, as an intellectual conscience at the heart of our search for a good society, based in justice instead of fear, violence, and greed.

The State operates as a regulatory authority that will calibrate the competing demands of opposed individuals. In doing this – and provided that the individuals in question acknowledge the authority of their shared State – the State and its fundamental existence as a political institution arrest the otherwise constant violence that would make life solitary, nasty, brutish, and short. In this view, politics exists in order to prevent us from having recourse to forms of physical violence to resolve competing interests. Unlike warring competition, it assuages our fears and allows for cooperation and cohabitation in an ecology whose key issue is that of enhanced survival.

If we consider this in the more localized concern of the contemporary University, the question arises of where we might find our own 'state', our own over-arching authority to which all individual Universities would subscribe in the 'global competition' for resources, students, prestige, funding, and so on. The answer is disappointing: our common ground and purpose lie in international league-tables. This is disappointing for the simple reason that we know them to be corrupting of knowledge and of truth, for they work by systemically reducing qualities and re-describing them as quantities. They are like Francis in *The Circle*, looking to the crudity of number to capture the reality of lived experience.

Further – and exactly as in *The Circle* – we find ourselves in the position of Mae. We are initially reluctant to subscribe to such numerical quantification and standardization, but then, gradually and through an insidious incrementalism in which we give one seemingly inconsequential inch after another, we come to comply fully with the very thing that is destroying our basic purpose. The reason we might want to resist this, and to be alert and attentive to the incremental small changes that lead us gradually but completely astray, is that we know that the league-table numerical transparency is an extremely poor and misleading substitute for the truth of what happens. The mode in which we comply is, as in the case of the coerced Mae, eventually to claim perfection – 100% – in all that we do. These practices combined produce a good example of corruption.

This whole thing is, in fact, quite simply reversed. All that it takes is

for the institutions that come out 'top' in the league-tables to disavow
their value, in as public and sustained a fashion as possible. To do that
is simply a question of the political will of our most senior leadership.
The survival of what is good in the University depends upon the
exertion of such a will. It may mean having the courage and principles
to take a stand against corruption; but if our leadership lacks those
qualities, they should not be leading our institutions. Anything else is a
betrayal of the intellectuals; and that is also a betrayal of the intellectuals
by those very individuals who began as intellectuals but who jumped
ship to become managers, often for personal advantage.[5]

However, the real gain in doing this would come when the 'top'
institutions – let's say the leadership of the Russell Group for example
– explain the eminently reasonable case for disavowing this culture.
League-tables, they would have to say, endanger the fundamental
interests of both citizen and University in the search for knowledge.
They take data, and use that data to provide information. However,
the information is not yet knowledge, especially given that it is always,
of necessity, partial. That means that it is also always prejudicial. We
reject this – the Russell Group might say – because we reject prejudice,
or judgements that are made prematurely and without sufficient care
for knowledge and truth. We reject the idea that the general public
should be misled by prejudice.

The first added gain, therefore, were we to follow this route, would
be to rehabilitate the idea of knowledge as something that is more
important than information. Further, we would also be demoting the
culture of prejudice – judgement based on ignorance of the demands
of knowledge. In this, we would be rehabilitating an ethical stance for
the extension of justice.

Given all this, the pressing question is really extremely simple: who,
in the institution of the University, and with the ideal of the good
society at heart, would not want to do this?

As things stand, now, we are encouraging and even engendering
a culture of prejudice. Our transcendent authority – our 'state' – is
itself corrupt; and we corrupt ourselves in complying with it. Even

---

[5] A minor personal anecdote, but true: when I returned to the UK in 1995, a
colleague who was a VC at the time gave me career advice, pointing out that the
managerial route (Pro-VC, Deputy VC, eventual VC) is 'where the money is'.

worse, our institutions behave in a corrupting fashion themselves, by pretending (and sometimes, claiming) that the numbers and gradations produced for our institutions can be consensually agreed as if they were true and not manufactured by the distortions that are forced by the figure and shape of specific and contingent algorithms. Finally, they being allegedly 'true', we stand over them as somehow in line with the natural order of things. Competition for positional advantage here corrupts our practices (a corruption linguistically purged and purified as 'gaming the system'). The system of competition itself treats our 'state' as one that is supposedly naturally occurring, when we know it to be a human-made failure and a perversion of actual and qualitative realities.

The second thing that we might productively do, in this situation, is to call into question the idea that 'competition' – competing for the 'top' position – is a motivating force that drives our concerns for justice and knowledge. Knowledge is not a matter for competition. To make it so is, of necessity, to privatize it – which means to deny other people any access to knowledge itself. Once more, by definition, a University simply cannot be a University if it does this. The sole reason for the privatization of knowledge is its commercialization: the determination to restrict access to knowledge so that I can benefit financially from that restriction. To do this is essentially to claim a patent not for specific commercial inventions but for all knowledge.

Once more, it is a simple business to change this. All that it takes is for a University sector leadership – including representative institutions such as unions – to disavow the idea that a University is a business. It is manifestly dishonest to claim that a University is a business, for the simple reason that the search for a good society precludes any activity that, of necessity, requires that a good society will determinedly keep its citizens in willed exclusion from knowledge. The commercialization of knowledge that follows on from its patenting is the phenomenon that permits the ideology of 'competition' to gain its false credence.

None of this is to say that the University as an institution can be excused from the demand to work properly and seriously. The problem derives from the ideology, stemming from the 1980s, that sees the norms of commercial business as being the only way to justify existence and identity. The time was one when, structurally and politically, the University, in common with all other public-sector institutions, was being starved of financial support: the conservative invention of

the curmudgeonly figure of 'the taxpayer', in the form of a resentful
and pusillanimous Scrooge-like miser, was instrumental in generating
a contempt for anything that was directed towards general public
service.

Trying to ride the spirit of the moment, some individual VCs who
were enticed by their potential intimacy with political power, and who
spied the possibility of advantageous and preferential funding for their
own institutions if they openly supported this ideology, enthusiastically
re-described themselves as 'Chief Executive Officers' and sought to
introduce private sector commercial norms into their institutions. In
doing so, this leadership started the process of betraying the University
in its fundamentals. Worse, they also betrayed the very society that, at
the time, still supported them financially, by their structural acquiescence to the ideology of patented knowledge, whose effect is to osten-
tatiously deprive that public of access to knowledge. When knowledge
is essentially privatized and patented in this way, then it fulfils the myth
that fundamentalist religion ascribes to it: it is associated with a fall
from nature, and it must therefore be subject to control. It cannot be
accessible to all, because it is dangerous.

What this ignores, of course, is that the real danger that it presents
is a danger to established modes of privilege. In the 1980s, the sector's
leadership inscribed the University fully into the role of protecting and
extending privilege, precisely at the moment when it was claiming to
be doing the opposite and 'widening participation'. To change this,
and to start to rehabilitate the University, all it will take is for the sector
leadership to distance the institution from the norms of business and
commerce, to regain a space of intellectual autonomy – from which
the world of commerce might indeed continue to benefit, of course.
However, more importantly, even if that benefit continues, it will not
be at the cost of the complete suppression of the ideals of using that
intellectual autonomy in the quest to extend good judgement, justice,
and the range of human possibilities for all.

As Jimmy Reid most famously put it in his Rectorial Address in
Glasgow University in 1972 – in a speech that was explicitly compared
to the Gettysburg Address – 'a rat race is for rats'. He went on to say,
'We're not rats. We're human beings', and he advised his audience to
'Reject the insidious pressures in society that would blunt your critical
faculties to all that is happening around you, that would caution silence

in the face of injustice lest you jeopardise your chances of promotion and self-advancement.'[6] We should remember not only how well received this speech was worldwide – and thus how much it helped legitimize a very particular role for the University – but also that it has as much relevance now as it did in 1972. It is the sentiment of this speech that neoliberal market-fundamentalist economics has striven to silence ever since Reid spoke that day in Glasgow. It would be a simple matter for us to re-assert the values: simple, and popular. It would recall us to our proper activities, and would widen our participation in the social sphere entirely. That is where we need to widen participation, in fact. It would get us out of the claustrophobic narrowing of all our activity into financial profit.

Reid's speech was about 'alienation', which he defined as 'the cry of men who feel themselves the victims of blind economic forces beyond their control ... the frustration of ordinary people excluded from the processes of decision-making'. When, as Reid put it, 'Profit is the sole criterion used by the establishment to evaluate economic activity', we get to a situation where 'our hard-won democratic rights' are threatened. 'The whole process is towards the centralisation and concentration of power in fewer and fewer hands'; and those who are in control are our great corporates and similar institutions, and who thereby wield that power, 'exercise a power over their fellow men which is frightening and is a negation of democracy'. He concluded his speech by quoting Burns, in a poem that stresses 'the truth that man is good by nature'.

This is an appeal to nature, and to a realization of a culture of social benevolence, whose advancement is the primary aim of the University, and whose operation will allow us to fulfil, in our social being, the proper task of extending that goodness and extending what the meaning of 'nature' actually is or can become.

~

We have not yet done with the state of nature as a power and as the measure of all value in education. In 1762, Rousseau opened his

---

[6] The full text of Jimmy Reid's speech of Friday 28 April 1972 is available at: http://liberalconspiracy.org/2010/08/15/a-rat-race-is-for-rats-were-not-rats-jimmy-reids-speech-in-1972/ (accessed 12 January 2018).

exploration of education in *Émile* with the observation that 'God makes all things good; man meddles with them and they become evil.'[7] This opening gambit rests on the presupposition that humanity exists in a fallen condition, that we are a kind of 'stain' on the otherwise pure condition of a theologically determined order of the world. It is as if our ecological footprint is intrinsically damaging to a purer natural condition. Yet it is not the case that Rousseau proposes that we return to some pure, clear, and simple original condition. His position remains much more nuanced and, indeed, makes room explicitly for the political as a counter to the (anti-political but market-fundamentalist) claims of nature, that ideological perversion of nature to the profitable ends of acquisitive individualism.

Education, Rousseau asserts, has three motivational sources: it 'comes to us from nature, from men, or from things'; and to be well educated is to find a harmony among these three elements, these three 'teachers' as he calls them. Tensions among these three educational motivations yield a situation in which we are faced with a predicament, according to Rousseau: 'you must make your choice between the man and the citizen, you cannot train both'.[8] This can best be understood not in the usual terms whereby Rousseau ostensibly laments the fact that our social being-together requires an element of repression of our authentic feelings. Issues of personal hypocrisy as a condition of society, while relevant here, are not primary for the purpose of the argument regarding the politics of a University education. Rather, the focus ought to be on this tension between 'man' and 'citizen'. As we saw at the end of Chapter 5 above, in the discussion of direct democracy in Bobbio, it has a profound contemporary relevance, relating directly to the political position of the University as social institution.

The education that comes to us from nature, for Rousseau, is related to 'the inner growth of our organs and faculties', and it is fundamentally related to survival itself. It helps us to deal with the problem that we are 'born weak ... helpless ... foolish' and it gives us, correspondingly, the three correctives of 'strength ... aid ... reason'. It is fundamen-

---

[7] Jean-Jacques Rousseau, *Émile, ou de l'éducation* (Flammarion, Paris, 1966), 35 (translation mine): 'Tout est bien en sortant des mains de l'Auteur des choses, tout dégénère entre les mains de l'homme.'

[8] Ibid., 37–8 (translation mine).

tally 'beyond our control'. Indeed, for Rousseau, the only educational mode – or teacher – that we can seriously control is the education 'from men'; and the fundamental goal of education is nature itself, the discovery and celebration of 'Nature within us' or 'natural tendencies'.

Rousseau represents a particular moment in a utopian philosophy of education in which there will be some effective and full reconciliation of the social and political citizen with the 'natural' human being. It is as if education will lift human beings from their mythical 'fallen' condition – fallen into knowledge and fallen into society and civilization – and allow them to regain a condition in which we fulfil a destiny by merging epistemology and ontology. Yet this is really a reiteration, once again, of the 'dissociation of sensibility' thesis that has dogged a theory of education right through modernity. In Rousseau, however, it takes an explicit political form. The task is to reconcile the citizen and the infant.

When Benjamin Constant came to think about this, in his lecture 'The Liberty of the Ancients Compared with that of the Moderns', he was able to re-phrase it. What is the relation between 'the individual' and 'the society'? It is a fundamental question regarding the relation between the political system of democracy and the condition of nature itself. To put the question very crudely, does the individual participate in a democratic culture in order to benefit and prioritize herself or himself (her or his natural condition) over other points of view; or does the individual adopt the viewpoint of the many, 'the polity', and vote in a more altruistic and holistic (political) fashion? Does the individual respect her or his own 'nature' and obey her or his own natural instinct for self-preservation and self-advancement; or does she or he see that such self-preservation is actually conditioned by the preservation of the whole society?

To put this in terms germane to this present argument: is democracy a purely political system, or can it be reconciled with the natural conditions of biodiverse life and natural ecology? With respect to the University, this becomes the question of whether the University itself acts as a political institution (and in favour of political democracy) or eschews the political in favour of the idea that each individual fulfils and acts upon the interests of her or his own individual self-serving nature. As I have shown, the institution today prefers the latter of these positions, and it thereby identifies itself as being 'neutral' in terms of politics. It serves the 'natural' desires of each individual. Yet such 'neutrality' is itself, as we have seen, a tacit but fully committed political position, favouring the ideology that suggests that our natural condition of one of acquisitive individualism. The consequence is that the University silently endorses that neoliberal right-wing ideology; and it defends itself from criticism by pretending that this is not ideological at all, but rather both neutral and 'natural'. It allows us to overcome the mythical fall into knowledge and to rediscover our original impulses; and the contemporary University takes a neutral position with regard to this. It serves our nature. It encourages us to conform to that alleged natural condition.

Such conformism is precisely the kind of quietism that neoliberal politics needs, as a means of ensuring that 'there is no alternative' to the current – 'natural' – conditions of wealth inequality. When the University becomes complicit with the total financialization and the privatization of all human interests – especially that of knowledge – then we enter a crisis in which its very survival as an educational institution is in doubt. It is in this way that the University finds itself, now, in an existential crisis regarding its very survival. This is also why my emerging recommendations in these pages, as to 'what is to be done', are important. The most important aspect of this, however, is that the recommendations are, in fact, quite tame, and are thus, in their minimalism, an urging towards actions that are easily achieved. All that is required is some act of political will. This, however, is what is lacking, for our contemporary institution has subscribed to a specific ideology of the natural in which political will has no place. We must simply carry out our pre-ordained functions within an existing and given ecology.

↩

Perhaps the most important aspect of our neoliberal market-fundamentalist agenda and its bland acceptance as a social and political norm (a state of nature) is the attack on politics, for it is this that underlines everything else and that constitutes a specific damage and wrong for the University. The kind of 'liberal culture' that forms the bedrock of a 'deliberative democracy' takes it for granted that, although teaching is a core concern for a University, it ought not to be didactic or prescriptive. The classic account is that the University must not advocate for any particular politics; but must simply provide enough bland and supposedly neutral information and modes of non-influential critical thinking to allow individuals to make up their own minds about any and all issues. This is the University as 'neutral', and thereby supposedly liberal: it 'liberates' thought and also liberates students precisely by the very act of liberating that thought.[9]

This allegedly neutral position is consistent with a particular view of public service. The logic is that, if the public pays for some service such as education, then that service should not be hijacked for the individual will of its 'providers' or sellers. This disregards the fact that no one actually 'provides' education: it is not and cannot be a product as such. The language of 'provision', 'delivery', 'the education offer', and the like is all consistent with a very specific political position, but one that attempts to hide behind a supposed neutrality, behind 'nature' itself. The same logic applies to, for example, the BBC's neutrality in the UK, where neutrality or impartiality is reconstituted as 'balanced' reporting of opposed points of view. In fact, the demand for such reporting has a very precise historical source, and one of its roots can be traced to arguments within the University during the 1970s and 1980s.

Allan Bloom rests his case concerning the role that University has placed in 'closing the American mind' on what he describes as the triumph of a specific kind of relativism that he traces to deconstruction. 'Deconstructionism', he writes, 'is the last, predictable, stage in the suppression of reason and the denial of the possibility of truth'.[10] This, although factually untrue as a description of deconstruction, allows Bloom to claim that it suggests that 'there is both no text and no reality to which the texts refer'.[11] From this, he suggests that the entire movement of Continental philosophy or 'theory' provides no rational grounds for subscribing to the truth of one account of events over any other interpretation of those events or facts. Further, he implies that the 'reality' that we have supposedly lost can be somehow neutrally described (and that the Great Books did that), or that it is a natural

---

[9] It is as if there is a slippage between 'the natural' and 'the neutral'. Neutrality is considered as if it were a position of brute nature, not yet modified by an intervention that would lead us to a specific political – or any other form of – commitment.

[10] Allan Bloom, *The Closing of the American Mind* (Penguin, London, 1987), 379.

[11] Ibid.

condition of things (that, again, while being 'natural', is also contained within Great Books, within a mode of writing).

Although Bloom is wrong about the detail here, he is nonetheless correct in suggesting that, throughout the 1970s and 1980s, there was a 'culture war' going on in the University. As Christopher Newfield compellingly argues, however, it was Bloom and his right-wing neoconservative supporters who declared that war, and they did so through the misrepresentation of 'theory' as something that divorced the University (and especially its arts and humanities disciplines) from any claims regarding worldly realities.[12] In point of fact, 'theory' (to retain this term as a useful shorthand for the emerging modes of critique that called conservative values into question) was useful precisely to the extent that it demonstrated that the reality of things as they stand now need not be an eternal and unchanging state of affairs, a state or force of unchanging nature. The point is that theory allowed us to see that things that are not working for the majority of people in a society might be changed, the better to work for more people. Essentially, Bloom and his acolytes (Kimball, the now disgraced D'Souza, and so on) were asking us to admire and accept as inevitable the injustices that were inscribed in their understanding of what the Great Books allegedly stood for. Essential values were to be found in those Great Books, as in the dominant ways in which they were read; and we could like it or lump it. This was nature, and there was nothing to be done about that – except conform to it, admire its hierarchical structure, accept the inevitability of its structural injustices.

What we can now add is that Bloom and his conservative allies claim a knowledge of those worldly realities as being 'naturally' knowable, graspable if only we would divorce ourselves from the knowledge that deconstruction might give us, with its forensic examination of meanings and semantics. The allegation made by Bloom-the-victim – as a key part of his strategy – is that theory had supposedly already triumphed and that, in this triumph, it had ditched the idea that we might have knowledge of the truth regarding any events or facts. The strategy therefore required that the conservative view, allegedly silenced under the triumph of theory, should now re-assert its natural authority.

---

[12] See Christopher Newfield, *Unmaking the Public University* (Harvard University Press, Cambridge, MA, 2008).

Notwithstanding the fact that his description of deconstruction or of theory is fallacious, it remains a description that is useful for Bloom and for neoliberalism generally. As described by Bloom and other conservatives in the culture wars, it yields a position that would be consistent with the rise of a particular demand that opposing views regarding 'the truth' be fully represented, and that we might be always justified in being sceptical of anyone who claims to make a truthful proposition. The resulting drive towards the normalization or naturalization of 'neutrality' would allow readers or the general public to decide – 'decide for themselves' – which side in any competing views was more 'natural' and more in line with the world of nature or with the world as it 'really' is. It was just that one of the available decisions would be in line with nature, while those that advocate for social change would be regarded as erroneous and as a dangerous deviation from the natural condition of general affairs.

The demand for such neutrality, emanating from a right-wing politics that asserted falsely its own 'victimhood' at the hands of a supposedly rampant political leftism, was itself fully ideologically charged. Its purpose was to discredit any criticism of neoliberal ideology that might seek to question the inevitability of a conservative ideology. Conservative neoliberalism was to be presented as being as natural as the weather, and as uncontestable. The point was to try to ensure that any and all doubts regarding this could emanate only from untrustworthy sources, from sources that had themselves given up on truth.

Truth, however, is not a question of balance at all. We should here recall the distinctions I made earlier among the categories of 'data', 'information', and 'knowledge'. Truth just is what it is: it is 'data', what we are given as fact and event, as visceral as the wetness of my skin in rain. Likewise, 'knowledge' is not 'balanced' either: on the contrary, knowledge is 'decisive'. Knowledge is based on judgement, but it becomes knowledge only at the point when the judgement becomes 'critical': that is, only when a decision-moment is reached.[13] I decide to raise my umbrella, say. In between these, however, lies 'information'; and it is this that is subject to 'balance' because information is always specific to a particular point of view, a particular bias. If nature is also

---

[13] 'Crisis' and 'criticism' derive etymologically from a Greek root, *krino*, meaning to judge, to decide.

aligned with data – with what happens – then it, too, is not balanced. It is either raining or it is not. My trivial example here has much wider reverberations when it is writ large. To say, for example, that the Holocaust did not happen is not an 'alternative view' of the truth, much less an 'alternative fact', but is rather a statement that has no truth content at all. It is a lie.

Once the University gets caught up in this and becomes, itself, subjected to the same right-wing ideological pressures characteristic of the demand for 'neutrality', the effect is substantial. In pretending to subscribe to neutrality and in succumbing to the pressure to avoid any form of didacticism, students are increasingly left without a standard against which to make judgements. As a consequence, logically but in a mode of desperation, they are forced to turn in to themselves, to introspection, and to various forms of identity politics. At least their identity – their origin and natural condition – is given to them as a set standard, as a fact and as a fulcrum around which they can weigh opposing accounts of 'the truth' in the search for some intellectual or personal – private – equilibrium. Their own nature thus becomes the standard against which they can calibrate various accounts of events; and truth can (and must) now be judged in relation to how well certain statements confirm my identity and give me succour and solace.

The institutional response to conservative ideology in the culture wars was adjusted to fit exactly the parameters that were in fact set precisely by the conservative agenda. That is to say: resistance to, or questioning of, the 'ideology of nature' is itself already contained within – and circumscribed, restrained, or limited by – the ideology of nature itself. The University, especially in its arts and humanities disciplines, offers degrees, courses, and modules that are themselves organized around a tacit appeal to nature or to origin and original being. They proclaim themselves as political, even as 'challenging' of all orthodoxy; and they are – but they are political in the sense that they conform exactly to the parameters given by neoliberalism itself and are fully circumscribed within that neoliberal polity. When neoliberalism includes or even becomes its own challenge, or when it successfully internalizes the challenge to itself, the effect is a yet further privatization of 'the truth'. Truth is now itself ghettoized.

Tony Judt was clear on this. In what at times is a dyspeptic critique of the University in the USA, he pointed to the increasing number of courses that are on offer in ostensibly diverse areas of study. Such a multiplicity of these types of degrees lends weight to the idea that the University is contesting any homogeneous or unifying single account of the truth; and in this, the University seems to accept and endorse diversity. In principle, therefore, this looks good, and maybe even critical, politically radical. The examples that Judt offers as typical are such as 'gender studies, women's studies, Asian–Pacific–American studies', and the like.[14] Judt's objection to these is that such programmes encourage students 'to study *themselves*'. Politically and educationally this is damaging to our societies, because in this narcissistic introspection students and Universities find themselves 'simultaneously negating the goals of a liberal education and reinforcing the sectarian and ghetto mentalities they purport to undermine'. We arrive thus at a fully undemocratic – even anti-democratic – situation whereby our students, 'in the wake of a generation of boastful victimhood … wear what little they know as a proud badge of identity: you are what your grandparents suffered'.[15]

We are here rehearsing at the micro-level precisely the anti-democratic introspection of the University at the macro-level that I described earlier. The resulting culture of an education that celebrates identity politics or that takes it as its starting (and finishing) point is then easily transposed into two things: first, the privatization of identity, known more appropriately and fully as the atomization of a divided society; second, the primacy of our historical position as a natural given, as given by nature and not culturally modified or subject to change.

In short: the apolitical world of the neutral University is neither apolitical nor neutral: it provides exactly the breeding ground for neo-liberal ideology. Any actual good that a University does, in the way of teaching or learning or research, now operates in spite of the governing and presiding ideology.

---

[14] We are here not far removed from the prevarications of Polonius in *Hamlet*, Act 2 scene 2, as he tries to cover all kinds of theatre: 'tragedy, comedy, history, pastoral, pastoral-comical, historical-pastoral, tragical-historical, tragical-comical-historical-pastoral'.
[15] Tony Judt, *The Memory Chalet* (Heinemann, London, 2010), 202. See also my *Confessions* (Bloomsbury, London, 2012, repr. 2013), 18–20 and *passim* for a detailed engagement with this issue as it affects literary study.

In the light of this, what, again, might we do? What happens when the seemingly most radical routes out of 'natural neutrality' and its culture of acquiescent conformism turn out themselves to be complicit with what they ostensibly want to critique? One possible answer is to ask the University to highlight the idea of difference instead of identity. If we are to attend keenly to the initial premises of research – that it is about the extension of the range of human possibilities – then the goal of research, logically, is to make a difference, to change things. The point is to make that which I thought of as my identity different from what I took it to be. In simple terms: the University is and should be a site for the changing of my mind, and with that, the changing of the world. It is where we find things undreamt of in our philosophies.

Yet, at this point, defenders of the contemporary position will no doubt indicate that this is precisely why we have something called the 'impact' agenda: the financial rewarding of research that demonstrates a clear impact beyond the supposedly closed walls of academia. However, this agenda fundamentally commercializes thinking: it rewards – and directs the University towards – research that is made available to the commercial and business communities in our society. Not only does it prioritize purely instrumentalist research, but it places that research in the service of commercial profit-seeking activity. The philosophy that underpins this is one that actually claims, if tacitly, that the world of commerce and of business has already found what it is that constitutes the good society; and it is the task of the University to serve those interests, to help commercial and business activities to do their work even better and more efficiently, more cheaply.

This is a bizarre reversal of roles. It assumes that commerce has thought things out, found the recipe for the good society, and that, in the wake of this, the University sector must learn from these business interests, must confound or confuse them with the general moral interests of justice, democracy, and freedom, and must then devote all intellectual energy towards serving this business interest. That is to say: the University is here hijacked for purely sectoral interest. The more generous way of understanding this would be equally satisfactory: it is simply to state that the neutral University has eschewed any interest in thinking about the good society, and has consequently taken the view that it has nothing to say or to offer to the advancing of the corollary interests of justice, freedom, and democracy.

Once again, can we not simply expose this and reject it? After all, President Eisenhower did exactly this in the USA in 1961, when he warned against the rise of the military-industrial complex. When the University found itself increasingly in the service of the industrial production that served the military, it diverted science away from the pursuit of disinterested knowledge and instead required the intellectual to work in the service of nationalism, of nationalist corporates, and of money as such. The fundamental point that I make here is the simple one that our contemporary parallel with this places the University in the position of being sectarian, serving merely sector interests. It is thus, once again, not only narrowing the range of human thought and possibilities, but also behaving in a prejudicial fashion and in the interests of pre-judgement. The prejudice that it serves is the prejudice given to it by the 'reality' of the world as seen from the sectarian perspective of profit-seeking finance and commerce.

It is in the interests of society at large, in the interests of the majority in the social world, that we explicitly reject this. If mediated properly, as something that places the University and the work of the intellectual at the disposition not of purely sectoral interests, and as an institution that works against prejudice, the rejection would again be popular and compelling. Further, it would entail a change in the direction of our sector and in the society as a whole. The first task is the simple one, of making a public rejection of the impact agenda, and explaining why that is a good thing to do.

If we hold to this, then the task of the University now is to assert its role as one that refuses to serve the world as it currently stands. In opening that world to the possibility of thinking differently, of changing our minds about things, of changing ourselves and changing the world, we establish a proper intimacy with the world. The University is no longer separate from the world, no longer an 'ivory tower' secreting things away; rather, it exists in a deep intimacy with its community, as a University that becomes fully immersed in its society. It is no longer the case that we are asked to 'respond' to the demands of existing commerce and business; rather, it becomes our business to be the fulcrum point around which all thinking takes place.

Such an approach would yield a genuine 'university of the air', for it would be a realization of the institution as something that is not tied to place or specific plant. The University would thereby become an institution essentially governed by the materialization of an idea; and, in this respect, it would become like the Rabelaisian Thelema, an Open University: genuinely open, and the site of an opening of minds to the range of possibilities that our research is ever extending.

↬

It is a simple fact that our survival – in every sense, from the survival of the species all the way through the survival of our social institutions and down to our personal biological survival – depends upon our interventions into the world of nature. Some might want to resist the claims that Marx and Engels made in 1845 when they wrote *The German Ideology*. Yet they too begin their propositions from the facts given to us by nature: 'The first premise of all human history is, of course, the existence of living human individuals. Thus the first fact to be established is the physical organization of these individuals and their consequent relation to the rest of nature.' They go on to ask what is the distinguishing characteristic of human individuals, and find that 'They themselves begin to distinguish themselves from animals as soon as they begin to *produce* their means of subsistence, a step which is conditioned by their physical organization. By producing their means of subsistence men are indirectly producing their actual material life.'[16] This claim is rehearsed again some seven years later, and constitutes part of the opening of *The Eighteenth Brumaire*, where Marx argues that we make our own history, but not under conditions of our own choosing.[17]

Marx, too, has some recourse here to the claims of nature; but he points out that survival – subsistence – depends upon human intervention into that pre-existing and constraining nature. In this sense, there can be no absolute or complete division between nature and culture, between biological existence and politics: our political being is itself how we manifest and realize our nature. This marks the enormous difference from the neoliberal view, a view that is essentially conditioned by forms of nostalgia. In the University – as the cases of

---

[16] Karl Marx and Friedrich Engels, *The German Ideology*, ed. C. J. Arthur (Lawrence & Wishart, London, 1970), 42; also available at: https://www.marxists.org/archive/marx/works/download/Marx_The_German_Ideology.pdf (accessed 12 January 2018).

[17] Karl Marx, *The Eighteenth Brumaire of Louis Bonaparte* (Foreign Languages Press, Peking, 1978), 9.

Bloom, D'Souza, Kimball, and others make clear – this is nostalgia for some mythic golden age of a harmony with nature where all is at peace and all truth is known.[18] The only such natural condition, in fact, is the state of death. That is the destination to which neoliberal views of the University will lead our institutions. Like other fundamentalisms, especially religious fundamentalisms, market fundamentalism is also death-oriented, in that it is oriented always towards a final solution of predicaments. The market provides that final solution, regarding the value of all things, by a dissolution of everything that might matter into the seeming certainty of a price, government by number.

We have two forms in which nature and politics thus coalesce. The first relates to the survival of the planet; the second relates to fundamentalist calls to a natural or original condition. We have become increasingly accustomed to such fundamentalisms in some religions, be it in the death cults associated with some Islamic fundamentalisms or the equally damaging cult of pious pain and sacrificial suffering in fundamentalist Christianity, for examples. The question that might appropriately be asked is whether our contemporary societies have adequately resisted such death-oriented impulses within our social, political, and cultural organizations and ideologies. The answer is that they have not. We have simply made a choice among fundamental-isms; and, for many who would be secular rather than religious, that choice has been directed towards support for market fundamentalism.

This places us in a particular predicament when it becomes also the dominant choice of our Universities. Such market fundamentalism is a zero-sum game: the success of one institution comes at the failure and death of another. The logic becomes clear: it is precisely the logic of market competition, which aims to eliminate all rivals and to establish a monopoly. In this case, it is a monopoly on knowledge and truth that is being asserted, essentially by the government of the day, which – under neoliberal conditions – is itself often guided by the invisible hand of business and commercial interests. The status of the thinking individual in this becomes seriously disfigured and damaged: the aim is to get to the end of such thinking itself, and to ensure that the only meaningful existence for the human is as a 'human resource' to be exploited.

---

[18] See Dinesh D'Souza, *Illiberal Education* (Free Press, New York, 1998), and Roger Kimball, *Tenured Radicals* (Harper Collins, New York and London, 1990).

Before Marx, Shakespeare had also considered the relation of reason or thinking to the world of nature. His dramatization of a fundamental conflict – and not at all the harmony – of thinking and nature forms a central part of *King Lear*. One of the most cruel scenes in the history of dramatic literature comes in Act 2 scene 4 of this play. A brief analysis of the central components of that scene will illuminate the argument for us.

Act 2 scene 4, essentially, continues the exploration of the very question with which the play opened. 'How much do you love me?' is Lear's basic question to his three daughters as the play opens. The court ritual as the play opens is shaped by the fact that the Duke of Burgundy is in the wings, and he awaits and expects to be offered the hand of Cordelia in marriage, and the dowry of land that will come with it. Lear makes a game of this; but it is a game whose playing produces only pain when his authority and control of the rules of the game are questioned by Cordelia's own 'zero-sum', her repeated 'Nothing'. Lear seeks to measure out quantities of land to the three daughters in a supposed direct proportion to the quality of love. This is precisely that bogus translation of quality (love) into quantity (dowry, money, land) that afflicts the contemporary University. It leads to disaster.

This is a scene marked by a horrible cruelty, in which Lear will be stripped bare. The flawed economics that dominates his thinking will leave him so utterly impoverished that he ends up fighting for basic and biological survival at the close of this scene and into the following one. This is a market economics that is utterly recognizable in our time: it says that a quantity of land will be returned clearly and consistently in proportion to a quality of love given. Quality becomes quantified, and essentially monetized.

Lear wants to stay with one of his daughters, in accord with the arrangements he made at the play's opening. He has 100 knights in his retinue. Goneril tells him that she will accommodate only half that number, 50. He turns to Regan; but she halves Goneril's offer to a mere 25. Lear's response is based on a crude economics. He turns to Goneril and says, 'Thy fifty yet doth double five and twenty / and thou art twice her love.' Goneril and Regan, however, are not finished: the reduction and stripping must go on, as if in some mad austerity-drive, to the point where it will leave Lear isolated completely and left to the vagaries of nature itself. The numbers go down incrementally, as

Goneril says, 'What need you five and twenty, ten, or five, / To follow in a house where twice so many / Have a command to tend you?' To this, Regan adds, curtly and before Lear can speak, 'What need one?'

It would, perhaps, be thought a crude simplification to read this as a straightforward allegory regarding the contemporary relation between the State and the University in terms of the economics of funding. Jo Johnson's logic – that of the Closed University – is absolutely pertinent, however: 'What need you five and twenty' eventually falling into 'What need one?' Yes, this is a crude parallel; but it is also completely appropriate. This is especially so given the crudity of the austerity logic in economics itself. It is exactly the same logic – quantification of quality by bogus measure – that is at work in the play and in our polity today. As is the case with Lear, further, the entire institution nationally is threatened with its demise at the hands of those who have now assumed power. Critics of my argument will say that this is exaggeration; but, while it is true that a large number of institutions will remain, nonetheless they will not be serving the function of a University. Instead, they will be 'organizations' or 'businesses' – edu-businesses trading in commoditized bits of information, or modules of unitized study purchased by discrete individuals – organizations whose task it is to extend a specific narrow politics that is designed to sow inequality and to lead to a structurally divided society, a society so divided that it will be eventually fully atomized. 'What need one?' will be eventually answered in the play's most fundamental word, 'Nothing'.

However, it is Lear's own explosive response to this predicament that is yet more telling here, for it explicitly relates the quantified rationality of number to the quality of life itself. In his reply to 'What need one?' he cries out, 'O, reason not the need; our basest beggars / Are in the poorest thing superfluous'. The economics of neoliberal austerity reduce the human condition fully, taking it beyond that of the lowliest beggar: 'Allow not nature more than nature needs / Man's life is cheap as beast's'. The logic that Lear discovers here in the speech is that nature is not subject to quantification and measure. It demands the intervention of grace, the intervention of the shaping hands of humanity, if we are to survive at all – as even our contemporary scientists and ecologists will agree. And, when intervention is lacking as it is here, its victim – Lear himself – promises terrorism: 'you unnatural hags, / I will have such revenges on you both, / That all the world shall – I will

do such things – / What they are, yet I know not: but they shall be /
The terrors of the earth.'

In this closing section of this book, it is imperative that we consider
the relation of an ideology of nature to the conditions of world terrorism. The relevance of this to an argument about the condition and survival of the University may not immediately be apparent; yet it is quite
fundamental. In a neoliberal social and political constitution, anything
that deviates from a 'natural order' is suspect. It is suspect because any
intervention into the natural order – the world as it currently stands – is
seen as a threat to that order. Reason – the very activity of thinking
itself – is itself just such an intervention. Reason allows for us to think
about the world as other than it is, and it thus presages the possibility
– and even the necessity – of changing the way things are at any given
moment if we are to survive that moment and to project ourselves into
a future. This is so because the one thing that is guaranteed by acceding to the laws or order of nature is the inexorable fact of death. By
contrast, survival – which is taken here as an axiomatic good – requires
that we think about how to manipulate the existing world of nature in
such a way that we can defer the moment of death.

There exist some fundamentalisms and extremisms, however, that
do indeed prefer the cult of death to the determination to survive.
Some of these, as I noted above, are predicated on religions, some of
which glorify suffering. Others are predicated on the claim to some
kind of ethnic or religious superiority, based upon the search for the
'authentic' or original text or other source for beliefs. This rehearses
the idea that, within a text – be it Bible, Koran, poem, or philosophy –
there exists the 'ideal' absolute truth – nature itself – in the voice of an
'author' and of an absolute authority, a single authority that supposedly
transcends every historical or material condition.

This, too, is deathly, for it opens the door to the conflicts that
shape hermeneutics. The conflict of interpretations is an absolute good,
unless and until someone claims that their interpretation is unquestionable, for then the tendency is not to engage in critical debate but to
engage in violence. The 'death of the author' leads, as Barthes rightly
said, to 'the birth of the reader'; but he did not follow the logic here
to one of its most seriously damaging conclusions. When a specific
reader claims that he or she has access to the sole truth of the text – a
truth supposedly validated by the claim that this reader has access to

an 'original' or 'natural' condition of the text – then the only possible consequence will be the awakening of violence, through which this reader will silence and quell the forces of any rival. The subscription to original textual truth is itself death-oriented. It leads to a prioritiza-tion of information (here, textual interpretation) as an absolute and as uncontestable because natural; and meanwhile, knowledge – which is dependent on doubt and democratic dialogue – goes ignored.

While some fundamentalisms like those described here are theologi-cal, others are based on capital. These latter find the fundamental truth of things in the signs and texts of wealth. The signs might be money, of course; but they might equally well be the ownership of land, say. In this context, it is the private ownership of knowledge that is at issue. In a University that is structured around the privatization of knowledge, we have a straightforward mode of fundamentalist capitalism, which we attempt to dignify by transcribing it as 'intellectual capital' or 'cul-tural capital'. In the consequent market fundamentalism that governs even these modes of capital, we inevitably arrive at the logic whereby some individuals might 'exit the market' – or die, in other words.

As Lear knew, thinking itself – the basic operation of reason – poses a real and substantial threat to the presiding ideology that claims nature as its foundation and as the guarantee of that ideology's legitimacy. Speaking out presents a yet more direct and overt threat to such an ideology. This is especially the case when the words that are spoken out present a challenge, as in Cordelia's 'Nothing'. We do not need to go to the extremes of jurisdictions such as Turkey to bear witness to a menacing situation whereby academics, thinkers, and intellectuals of various kinds find themselves subjected to various modes of silencing. The same happens everywhere, even if not yet going to the extremist actions of jailing the academic staff or, even, killing students (Giulio Regeni in Egypt, for example) or journalists who seek to provoke criticism of the natural order of things (Anna Politkovskaya in Russia, say).[19]

This – a totalitarian culture of violence – is the political consequence

---

[19] For details of these cases, see, for examples: Reuters report, 'Italian student killed in Egypt: Giulio Regeni "showed signs of electrocution"', *Guardian*, 14 February 2016; and Julia Ioffe, 'Alexander Litvinenko and the banality of evil in Putin's Russia', *New York Times Magazine*, 21 January 2016.

of the ideology of nature or origin. In avoiding politics, it leaves a Hobbesian war of all against all as the only way of resolving difference. This is as much as to say that the kind of social contract that we have – that is to say, the fundamental condition of our living together, communicating with each other, distributing resources, and so on – is a manifestation of 'the political' as such. Further, we have politics, therefore, in order to avoid a 'natural' fall into the violent resolution of conflicts by war, and to assure ourselves of sustainability and survival, personally and ecologically.

Famously, Clausewitz saw the intimacy of war and politics, and suggested that 'war is a continuation of political commerce … by other means'.[20] However, the two – war and politics – are not related to each other in a straightforward mathematical commutability. The statement does not say that 'war *is* politics' or that politics *equals* war. That is for the simple reason that, as a continuation of politics, war always marks the end and failure of a political contract or agreement. We should also always remember Clausewitz's fundamental opening remark that 'war is an act of violence intended to compel our opponent to fulfil our will'.[21]

We might usefully suggest that politics – and the civilization or being-together that it engenders – is what we have in order to avert the 'natural' condition of an 'original' condition of the war of all against all. Its point is to permit survival in the face of a potential primal violence; and it is for this reason that we must, in our University institution, resist any recourse to the false and deathly ideology of any fundamentalist claims to the 'truth of nature', to which only the select have access. Those select are those who have successfully privatized knowledge, privatized the University, and commercialized all human existence by reducing it to a monetized idea of quantitative value, where 'success' is measured in amounts of dollars, euros, rubles, pounds, yen, renminbi, and so on.

One way of considering survival is to think in terms not just of legacies, but also, more fundamentally, of intergenerational relations.

---

[20] Carl von Clausewitz, *On War* (1832; Penguin, London, 1982), 101. He later writes that 'war is nothing but a continuation of political intercourse, with a mixture of other means': ibid., 402.
[21] Ibid., 101.

In our contemporary financial arrangements for higher education, we are structurally indebting the next generation, arresting or limiting the range of their possibilities, and fleeing a potential conflict – as in *King Lear* – between parents and children. In the interest of preserving the privileges of the current mature generation, who themselves have benefited from higher education, we have decided to refuse to invest financially in the higher education of the next generation. We have disinvested, and have told the next generation that we prefer to pre-serve our own personal wealth rather than share our wealth in order to commit to the wellbeing of our children. As we step aside from such commitment, we commit our next generation to the Hobbesian war of all against all, as they struggle for survival in a state of nature.

That is clearly shocking. It is easily changed. Our sector leadership is completely aware of the economics that would indicate the desirability of committing ourselves to higher education as a public good, paid for from general taxation for public benefit. The advanced economies, especially that of the UK, can very easily afford this. Such a commit-ment is the most direct way of establishing shared interests between present and future, based upon the fact that past generations committed themselves also to the present generation. It is an establishment of social relatedness in its most basic and desirable form.

The canard that is usually thrown against the case for such a provi-sion is twofold: (a) that while we could afford this in the days of elite higher education for 5% of the population, we cannot afford it in the days of mass higher education, when nearly 50% of the eighteen-year-olds attend an institution of higher or further education; and (b) that the funding of higher education from general taxation disproportion-ately favours the wealthier middle classes, and requires the poor and under-advantaged to subsidize the education of the wealthy.

We can take these misleading suggestions in turn. We made the shift from a taxation-funded higher education to a tuition-fee subsidized system in 1998, when the then Labour administration introduced what it called 'top-up fees'. In 1998, it was not 5% of the age cohort who went into higher education: it was 39%. We have not made a sudden shift in the figures at all in recent times, or over the period when we have shifted almost entirely from a tax-funded system to a tuition-fee funded system. The additional numbers that make up that extra 11%, since 1998, are not enormous. They most certainly do not justify the logic of Browne in 2010 in determining the withdrawal of all State funding for arts, humanities, social sciences, and a large proportion of STEM subjects. That was a political decision based on two things: ideology (the desire to shrink the State) and the preservation of economic privilege (or preserving the wealth of the already wealthy).

The second claim is that a tax-funded system entails the poor subsidizing the wealthy, since it is largely the already well-off who attend a higher education institution. There are at least two issues with this. First, it holds true if and only if a government fails to implement a fair and progressive taxation system. Tax is a measure of an individual's commitment to the public sphere and to the common good. Some individuals find themselves economically advantaged, for all kinds of reasons, in their society. The logic of a fair and progressive system says that those individuals should commit themselves more to the society that has sustained them in that position. That is to say: the wealthier pay more, in proportion as they have benefited (and many, of course, benefit simply from luck, not from individual earned merit or from their own attendance at a University). The position I advocate – funding higher education from a progressive taxation system – yields a situation that is completely the opposite of having the poor subsidize the wealthy. That position, in which the poor subsidize the wealthy is, as I have shown in these pages, precisely the situation that we are currently in, thanks to the University's complicity with the marketization and privatization of knowledge, which systematically transfers what should be commonly shared knowledge and its associated wealth into the controlling hands of a small number of individuals. Those who decry a tax-funded system are simply pious hypocrites, determined to protect their own wealth and privileges against the demands made by a commitment to the public sphere or to the society that sustains them in their wealth.

Next, to suggest that any change to that current tuition-fee funded system would necessarily – as in the cliché – entail imposing such an unfair burden of taxation on the poor is to admit failure in another fundamental sense. If the problem that we have is that it is only the already privileged who attend, or who disproportionately attend, then surely that is the issue that we should address. Instead, in claiming that tax-funded systems impose unfairly on the poor, we are saying that we will not address the fundamental issue, we will maintain a system whereby it is only the privileged who attend higher education, and the poor will continue to be excluded, so we must not impose tax burdens upon the poor. However, the whole point of the tuition-fee funded system is allegedly to ensure that 'the poor you shall *not* always have with you', so to speak. If we genuinely wish to address issues of social inequality, then we must begin with a drive that leads towards establishing the basic principle that knowledge is available to all, and that it is not tied to wealth at all but rather tied to the general goal of establishing the good society. Justice, like knowledge, should not be subject to mercantile deals.

Finally, a tax-funded system is designed not just as a mode of equalizing our commitments to the shared good society, but also as a mode whereby we protect the relations between generations – between past and future – from the conflicts and wars associated with falling into a Hobbesian state of nature or war of all atomized individuals against all other atomized individuals. When atoms collide, people die; and, in any case, Shakespeare showed us where intergenerational conflict ends up: divided societies, wars, the needless death of the young (Cordelia), and the too-late realization of failures by the fathers (Lear himself). If Shakespeare's *King Lear* is good enough to be a constituent element of a University English literature degree, then it is good enough to offer us all that general lesson.

I explained earlier that it is from theology that we derive the idea that knowledge itself is dangerous, because it diverts us from our alleged 'original state of nature', taking us into the supposed subversiveness of the unnatural. The 'fallen' condition is regarded as unnatural because, once fallen, we can and must extend our autonomy and accept our human responsibility to extend our freedom. The extension of such freedom is nothing other than the exploration of a greater range of human possibilities, possibilities that will allow us to sustain ourselves and to avoid being simply enslaved to a natural condition about which we can do nothing. Knowledge itself – once set into a tight relation with a 'natural order' of the world – is construed ideologically and theologically as something that drives us away from an Eden or Utopia of nature, a natural condition where we are characterized as being at one and at peace.

This has a persistent effect upon our institutions, and above all on the institution through which we determinedly and by definition should commit to extending knowledge, the University. In this account, knowledge (along with the University) is construed as at once desirable, tempting, and seductive, but also as Satanic and evil. It is intrinsically suspect, and seen as a threat to a more 'natural' state of being. This is especially so given that the University is not regarded as compulsory: it is, as in Lear's sense, a kind of 'necessary excess' to nature.

It follows from this that the conservative appeal to nature and a natural order will tacitly presuppose the intrinsic goodness of a natural and 'original' order of things; but in doing so, as here, that appeal again stigmatizes knowledge, and thus reveals a conservative innate dislike for the potentially critical and serious – even disruptive and disordering – fact and purpose of knowledge. That fear is actually a fear of real, substantial, and material change: a change to the 'natural' order of things. It places the security of a nostalgic appeal to an 'original order' against the possibility of a utopian change through 'original' thinking. The contemporary University – and, indeed the whole of education in the advanced economies – regards such change as intrinsically terrifying. As I will show here, it goes so far as to align such a mere possibility of radical change with political terror itself.

If – as a neoliberal ideology wants to insist – our 'natural' condition is determined by the market and by commercial activity, then it follows that anything that criticizes the fundamentals of contemporary capital must be 'evil'. Yet what if contemporary capital is leading to grave social problems, and to problems that threaten our survival? What should the University do when we know that the conditions of contemporary capital are such that they lead not only to the now well-understood conditions and problems of massive inequalities, but also to massive social and political divisions that threaten the very sustainability of societies? What if the University itself is complicit in a drift towards violence and away from political democracy as a means of resolving differences and sustaining the possibility of our joint survival?

In *This Changes Everything*, Naomi Klein details several instances of how capital and ecological survival are at odds with each other. In particular, she traces the way in which nation states have used World Trade Organization (WTO) rules to challenge local attempts to extend green energy activities. She cites a paradigmatic example from her own backyard, in Toronto, where Paulo Maccario set up Silfab to develop and sell solar energy. Ontario was committed to playing its part in reducing CO_2 emissions and in committing itself to renewables. To encourage this, the provincial government put some conditions in place. It wanted to make sure that the scheme was not taken over by big multinationals, but instead that it helped to restructure and re-develop the local economy and conditions of employment. Silfab was required to make use in the first instance of 'local content' to this end. At this point, however, Japan and the European Union intervened, and appealed to WTO rules that describe such 'buy local, hire local' decisions as running contrary to free-market ideals and norms.[22]

This is but one paradigmatic example of how 'trade trumps climate', in Klein's words. The paradox is that individual nation states that have themselves signed up to the Kyoto accords can derail the goals of those accords in the interests of maintaining the kind of free trade regulations that protect neoliberal capitalism, a mode of capitalism that knows no affiliations other than an affiliation with inequalities of wealth.

As Klein describes this, 'three policy pillars of the neoliberal age' are at odds with what we know we must do to ensure the sustainability of life on the planet. Those three pillars include, first, 'the lowering of income and corporate taxes, paid for with cuts to public spending': this is realized in the University sector by the systematic starving of higher education of public funding, and the reversion to private debt as a means of paying for the University. Next, we have 'deregulation of the corporate sector', through which corporate managers have been enabled to circumvent the public duties of their companies in the interests of enriching themselves and their associates. In relation to this, witness the occasional scandals around the establishment of quasi-cartels that raise VCs' salaries.[23] Finally – but above all, as far as the present argument is concerned – we have 'privatization of the

---

[22] Naomi Klein, *This Changes Everything* (Allen Lane, London, 2014), 65–9.
[23] VCs will always refer you to 'independent remuneration committees' that set their pay. They don't often add that those committees typically comprise three people, one of them being the VC, who will vacate the room when her or his own salary is reviewed. They also ignore the fact that VCs will 'benchmark' their salaries against sector averages; but one moment of mathematical thought shows that this is intrinsically and of necessity inflationary.

public sphere'. In the case of the University, this is realized precisely by the structural privatization of knowledge, as I have been describing this throughout.[24]

Interestingly, Klein dates the sudden rise to prominence of the climate agenda to 1989 and the fall of the Berlin Wall, a date that I have argued to be extremely significant for the purposes of my own arguments throughout this study. Of course, as Klein acknowledges, there have been scientific concerns about the climate and global warming at least since the nineteenth century; but it became a part of everyday political discourse when the Cold War appeared to end. *Time* magazine's annual 'man of the year' at the close of 1988 was 'Planet of the Year: Endangered Earth'; and Klein quotes approvingly from the lead essay in the magazine, written by Thomas Sancton and published in the edition of 2 January 1989. Sancton traced a hugely significant shift in how humanity has regarded the earth, indicating that it is only in the emergence of the Judaeo-Christian tradition that we stop thinking of the earth as being 'endowed with divinity', and becoming instead the 'dominion' of the human. In the biblical instruction to 'Be fruitful and multiply, and replenish the earth and subdue it', Sancton pointed out that humanity is given the 'invitation to use nature as a convenience'.[25]

Several months after the appearance of the *Time* front cover, the Berlin Wall fell. Although the initial draft of his essay 'The End of History', published in the summer issue of *The National Interest* in 1989, actually predates the fall of the Berlin Wall on 9 November 1989, Francis Fukuyama's argument – in this first essayistic testing of his thesis – is that we witnessed through the 1980s the 'unabashed victory of economic and political liberalism' that signalled 'the triumph of the West, of the Western *idea*'.[26] For Klein, Fukuyama is among a group of 'right-wing ideologues' who 'seized on this moment of global flux

---

[24] Cited passages here are from Klein, *This Changes Everything*, 72. In my argument, I have reversed the order in which Klein describes the three pillars of the neoliberal age. In both her argument and mine, however, I think it is true to say that it is the privatization agenda that underpins every other element here.

[25] Thomas Sancton, as cited by Klein, *This Changes Everything*, 74.

[26] Francis Fukuyama, 'The end of history', available at: https://www.embl.de/aboutus/science_society/discussion/discussion_2006/ref1-22june06.pdf (accessed 12 January 2018).

to crush all political competition' and who 'waged a frontal attack on political experimentation, on the idea that there might be viable ways of organizing societies other than deregulated capitalism'.[27]

It is worth pointing out that *The National Interest* is itself a neocon-servative journal, founded by Irving Kristol and funded by (among others) neoconservative think-tanks such as the Lynde and Harry Bradley Foundation. It was Allan Bloom, Fukuyama's former teacher, who sponsored him when he addressed his thesis to students and colleagues in Chicago. Earlier, Fukuyama had dabbled in the work of Derrida and of Barthes (even attending their seminars), but had rejected their thinking on the same ill-founded grounds as Bloom would also do. The key element of all this is that we can see the ideology of the 1980s as one whereby neoliberalism not only sought to advance its ideology, but also to present it as utterly inevitable. The idea was to crush any opposition, a tactic closer to the very totalitarianism that it claimed to counter. Further, as Clausewitz would have noted in regard to this, 'war is never an isolated act', it 'does not consist of a single instantaneous blow', and its aim is to render opponents 'incapable of further resistance'.[28]

By presenting neoliberalism as 'the end of history' – admittedly now a position that Fukuyama himself has substantially revised (he has had to, given economic facts) – and thus as a kind of second coming of nature in its primal state, thinkers and agents such as Fukuyama and the neoconservatives around him essentially tried to suggest that, finally, history itself had given way to nature and its unchanging conditions. By contrast, Barthes – in whose seminars Fukuyama once sat – famously announced his own great project in *Mythologies* of 1957 as the mission to reveal the operations of history within all that proposes itself as nature. In the context of myth-making, both ancient and modern, Barthes explains that 'myth has the task of giving an historical intention a natural justification, and making contingency appear eternal'.[29]

The problem, of course, is that we have certainly not arrived at the eternity that stands at 'the end of history', because the structures of a neoliberal economy have been shown to cause disaster on a global

---

[27] Klein, *This Changes Everything*, 75.
[28] Clausewitz, *On War*, 106, 101.
[29] Roland Barthes, *Mythologies*, trans. Annette Lavers (Granada, London, 1983), 142.

scale, certainly after the crash of 2007–08 if not already before that date. Yet the University in our time persists in operating as if that crash had not happened. On the contrary, it sees its mission as being one that serves the continuation of neoliberal market fundamentalism. It proclaims its task as being one of a business-like 'provision of services', 'delivery of teaching', and a basic 'production', in which we do not produce 'graduates' but 'leaders'. Paradoxically, these 'leaders' do not appear to offer any new direction for the society to follow; rather, they slavishly follow the conservative agenda set by the presiding economic structures. By 'leaders', most University managers – VCs and Presidents – simply mean 'people who will be in charge of our existing businesses' and who will therefore accrue the privileges that come from such elevated positions.

Quite simply, the task is to produce people who will become individually rich by conforming to the norms of liberal market-fundamentalist capital; and meanwhile, those who do not attend our Universities and do not get 'the student experience', can continue to go poor and disenfranchised. They can become a contemporary version of 'the wretched of the earth'. That task – producing and legitimizing inequality – might once have been unspeakable, given what it logically implies. However, in our time, it can be expressed quite brazenly. We see it whenever we hear VCs or Presidents resisting any anti-immigration policies, for example. Their concern is not at all for the disenfranchised *countries* from which people might migrate or flee, or for the political conditions that might make individuals want to leave their own jurisdictions; rather, their concern is that they want to continue to seek out 'the brightest and best' from around the world. Once they have secured those already privileged brightest and best, their task is to serve them as individuals. Any concern for those who are not of this elite and select group simply disappears.

Yet the kinds of division and inequality that follow from this does not simply give the earth over to a select few who can now colonize it entirely and ecologically. As Frantz Fanon knew, those damned in such a structure may well turn to violence to re-assert their claims upon the earth itself. While the University produces the next John Browne, to lead a fossil fuel industry that at times shows scant concern either for the environment or for human safety, the wretched of the earth will eventually rise, quite possibly in violence (and, for Fanon, justifiably so). It is not just the survival of the institution that is then at stake; rather, it is the survival of individual human beings and of the ecosystem with which we must work.

One thing that King Lear does learn is that an austerity economy, in which every penny is weighed and is found wanting, serves no one well. And when he eschews an immediate revenge and terror, he turns instead to nature. Out on the heath, solitary and stripped back to a bare life, a 'poor bare fork'd animal', he becomes the victim of nature. He who was wealthy and who lived his life according to a strict economy in which value can be quantified as number discovers instead that value lies elsewhere than in number. He loses reason in this place: 'My wits begin to turn', he says; and yet it is at this point, when he no longer 'reasons the need' himself, that he can turn to grace, generosity, and a concern for those less advantaged than even himself, and can express his concern for those less fortunate others, turning to his Fool and asking, 'Come on, my boy; how dost, my boy? Art cold?'

It would be a good thing for all if our University could itself discover this possibility of grace. We might usually simply call it something like 'acting in the service of the common and public good'. This is the genuine alternative to the prevailing market-fundamentalist model of our University today. Fundamentalism, like totalitarianisms of all kinds, contains within itself the necessity of its own self-destruction. It is time to acknowledge this, and to make the University for tomorrow, to allow the polity and our environment to survive.

7

Preliminary hypotheses towards a manifesto

1

The 'social mobility' agenda permits a society to circumvent the failings that are consequent on its hierarchical class structure. It exists to protect existing unearned privilege and authority, while permitting occasional individuals to be 'admitted' to those class privileges. The entire agenda should be scrapped, and the University should dedicate itself instead to a concern for 'social justice'.

2

Our contemporary societies pretend to honour merit. We are encouraged to believe that those who fail to rise through the social mobility agenda fail because they 'lack aspiration'. This kind of meritocracy permits us to blame the poor for their own lack of advantage and for their own poverty. All talk of 'aspiration' in this manner becomes complicit with a politics that allows the successful to believe that they have always earned their position, and that neither luck nor pre-existing circumstances have played any part in their 'achievements'. It would be better if we were to honour and to validate activities that arise not from aspiration but instead from 'curiosity'. Curiosity intrinsically drives all individuals to extend themselves, to reach beyond the existing range of their individual possibilities and freedom.

3

The 'widening participation' agenda, like 'social mobility', is a palliative designed to cover and excuse the exclusion of individuals from the concerns of intellectual activity itself. It is complicit with an idea of knowledge as the exclusive preserve of particular institutions, to which only selected individuals have access. Knowledge thus becomes intrinsically privatized, as a matter of interest and relevance only for those 'inside' the institution. It would be better to abandon this, in favour of encouraging a much wider engagement of the University with all aspects of social, cultural, and political life.

4

Our Universities increasingly focus attention on 'the student experience'. This is not only consumerist in ideology, but also introspective; and it diverts the student from attending to the experiences of people considered more generally. The student might better become a pivotal representative, requiring the University to attend to extending the range of human possibilities and experiences for all, including those who, for whatever reasons, do not attend our institutions.

5

The language of 'excellence' has excelled itself, such that institutions now routinely describe themselves as being 'world-leading'. If this is to have any authentic reality, it must mean that the University will take a primary interest in the existence and experience of the world, and by extension in securing the sustainability of the planet.

6

Why 'competition' when we can have genuine collaboration shaped by generosity and openness?

7

Never 'appoint' a VC or President. Begin the process of the democratization of intellectual work by having leaders of institutions elected
from within their own ranks. Candidates for such positions should each
present a manifesto for election; and election should be for a limited
period, with a maximum of five years. The same should apply to Deans
of Faculty, and to Heads of Department. Under no circumstances
appoint an 'external' candidate to such a position.

8

Establish a rule barring any VC or President from nomination for
State honours of any kind (such as knighthoods, damehoods, and the
like). This should help ensure that the institution does not subjugate
its proper tasks to those that would make it complicit with any specific
Statist ideology.

9

Dissolve all University 'mission groups', starting with the Russell
Group. These are not reflective of diversity, but are instead organizations that perpetuate class divisiveness. The Russell Group, in particular, exists in order to legitimize and extend all forms of inequality. It has
no institutional or social legitimacy, and should be accorded no special
status, especially given that it seeks to preserve and protect existing
privilege and advantage, to the necessary detriment of others.

10

We should acknowledge that many students worldwide perform their
studies in a second language. In the interests of curiosity and widening
the intellectual relation to communication, the acquisition of a second
language should become compulsory for all 'domestic' students.

11

Re-establish State funding for all education, including University and other forms of higher education. This will ensure that our structures of general taxation reflect the commitment of individuals not just to the present society as a whole, but also to an intergenerational bond that respects the past while acknowledging the demands of the future. It may not suggest that higher education is a 'right', but it does acknowledge that there is a 'duty' or debt to be shared between the intellectual and her or his material and historical conditions of life.

Index